Policy Routing Using Linux

Matthew G. Marsh

Policy Routing Using Linux

Copyright © 2001 by Sams Publishing

International Standard Book Number: 0-672-32052-5

Library of Congress Catalog Card Number: 00-106882

Printed in the United States of America

First Printing: February 2001

04   03   02   01   4   3   2   1

Trademarks

Warning and Disclaimer

ASSOCIATE PUBLISHER
Jeff Koch

ACQUISITIONS EDITOR
William E. Brown

DEVELOPMENT EDITOR
Heather Goodell

MANAGING EDITOR
Matt Purcell

PROJECT EDITOR
George E. Nedeff

COPY EDITOR
Kim Cofer

INDEXER
Erika Millen

PROOFREADER
Candice Hightower

TECHNICAL EDITORS
Thomas Schenk
Michelle Truman

TEAM COORDINATOR
Vicki Harding

MEDIA DEVELOPER
Dan Scherf

INTERIOR DESIGNER
Karen Ruggles

COVER DESIGNER
Aren Howell

PRODUCTION
Ayanna Lacey
Heather Hiatt Miller
Stacey Richwine-DeRome

Overview

Contents

About the Author

Matthew G. Marsh, CISSP, MCNE, PRE, is founder and president of Paktronix Systems LLC. and has been working in network architecture for the last 18 years, and with Linux specifically since 1993. He fondly remembers getting "into" his first DEC box back in 1976 in order to print out the source code to the Star Trek game. After spending some time wandering around the U.S. running sound for various bands, he settled into computers as a less hazardous hobby. Working with the leading router company at the time, Proteon, permanently hooked him on routing and massive networks. He has held many certifications at one time or another and has the dubious honor of being a published authority on the Biological Effects of Stun Guns as applied to Skin (http://www.paktronix.com/library/physics.php) for the IEEE.

Along with running Paktronix, he currently is the Chief Scientist of the NebraskaCERT (http://www.nebraskacert.org) working with CERT/CC, IBM, the U.S. Strategic Command, the FBI, and other groups on network security structures and hosting the annual International CERT Security Conference(http://www.certconf.org). He is the creator of PakSecured Linux, an IPv4 and IPv6 secure Policy Routing distribution for Linux available under the GPL, and an IPSec VPN solution using Policy Routing structures under Linux. Currently he is actively researching Linux security on the IBM S/390 as well as implementation of IPv6 security and Policy Routing on PakSecured/390.

He can be reached through any of his known aliases. But to more easily find him, just check out the links on http://www.policyrouting.org.

Dedication

To Alexey N. Kuznetsov, Lord of Layer 3, Sultan of SoftNet, Tsar of TC

Acknowledgments

My wife Doctor Andrea and my children, Peter Paul and Merrie Melody, for allowing me to just type. Paul Greunke for putting together the test network, the PakSecured distribution, and running interference from our clients. Heather Goodell for her sense of humor and non-impairment of most of mine. William Brown for patching the fence and taking a chance that my procrastination would end. And the rest of the staff at Sams/Pearson/et al. for assisting in the creation of this missive. Last but not least, Linus and the gang for an absolutely awe-inspiring operating system...

Tell Us What You Think!

As the reader of this book, *you* are our most important critic and commentator. We value your opinion and want to know what we're doing right, what we could do better, what areas you'd like to see us publish in, and any other words of wisdom you're willing to pass our way.

As an Associate Publisher for Sams Publishing, I welcome your comments. You can fax or write me directly to let me know what you did or didn't like about this book—as well as what we can do to make our books stronger.

Please note that I cannot help you with technical problems related to the topic of this book, and that due to the high volume of mail I receive, I might not be able to reply to every message.

When you write, please be sure to include this book's title and author as well as your name and phone or fax number. I will carefully review your comments and share them with the author and editors who worked on the book.

Fax: 317-581-4770
Mail: Jeff Koch
          Sams Publishing
          201 West 103rd Street
          Indianapolis, IN 46290 USA
E-mail: feedback@samspublishing.com

Introduction

This book attempts the Herculean task of defining and exemplifying Policy Routing. Policy Routing is the ultimate stage of evolution in the consideration of IPv4 networking structures. Often referred to as advanced routing or similar nomenclature, Policy Routing provides a framework for understanding all networking interconnections under IPv4 and beyond.

Any discussion of how Policy Routing works must draw upon the essential nature of the original Unix TCP/IP networking. Basic IPv4 routing refers to the process of getting a data packet from one TCP/IP network to another. This always involves a machine of some type that is connected to both networks. This machine is referred to as a router whenever it is the mechanism by which a packet is passed from one network to another.

In the book there are several assumptions made about the level of knowledge you possess. These assumptions are spelled out for you now along with some references for more information. This book is not concerned with the actual software or operating system source code needed to perform the routing functions. This book speaks from a network administration standpoint as opposed to a network programmer's viewpoint. In short, you should have working knowledge of the following:

- ISO/OSI 7 Layer Model
- TCP/IP IPv4 Specifications:
  - Addressing
  - Protocols
  - Ports
- CIDR—Classless InterDomain Routing notation
- Configuring IPv4 networking on some platform
- Configuring Basic IPv4 routing on some platform
- Security structures, such as ACLs, Packet Filters, and so on

For the first three items you can refer to *TCP/IP Illustrated Volume 1*, by W. Richard Stevens. For the configuring issues I recommend you refer to the manual configuration such as you would perform on a Cisco router or on most Unix platforms or even as on a Novell NetWare 3.x system. Keep in mind the stress on performing the manual configuration. GUI configuration systems leave you with little or no knowledge of what actual steps and actions are taken with respect to the implementation within the parameters of the operating system. For the security parts I recommend a good network security reference that includes the Cisco and IBM IP security books.

You must be comfortable with the command line as a basic necessity. All of the examples and most of the references herein will assume that you are typing the commands either into the command line or into some text-based configuration file. Knowledge of an editor is recommended but not required as the examples are primarily designed to be entered interactively.

Accompanying this book is a CD-ROM containing a copy of the PakSecured Linux distribution. This distribution is the platform that all of the examples and scripts were developed upon. See Appendix B, "Source Code Listings and Locations," for details on installing it if you want to use it for the examples.

Enjoy the power!

Conventions Used in This Book

The following typographic conventions are used in this book:

- Code lines, commands, parameters, and any text you would see onscreen appear in a `computer` typeface.
- Any text you need to type appears in **`bold computer typeface`**.
- Placeholders in syntax descriptions appear in an *`italic computer`* typeface. Replace the placeholder with the actual filename, parameter, or whatever element it represents.

PART I

Theory, Usage, and Utilities

CHAPTER 1

Basic IPv4 Routing

All of the operations considered in this book are operations upon a router, whether that router is a Linux box, Cisco dedicated hardware, or some other type of machine. In this chapter I consider the traditional methods of IPv4 routing as using static configurations that are manually input by the network administrator.

Traditional IPv4 Routing

In the simplest IPv4 routing case you would have a router and you would only need to consider how to allow two networks to talk between themselves. For this case you would only need to have an appropriate IP address assigned for each of these networks. Since this simple case does not concern any networks other than the two that are directly connected, you need only define the address and mask for each network and dictate the appropriate interface for forwarding packets to that network.

In reality, however, you often need to consider other networks beyond the scope of two connections. In these cases you must have a way to talk to the other networks. This is done by having routes that point to other routers that are responsible for those networks. In the simpler case you will have one of the connected networks that only needs to talk with the rest of the network structure and is routed with only a single default route. A default route is traditionally coded as a route to the 0.0.0.0/0 destination. However, it may be that you are within a structured network with a given finite range or that you want to implement better security, in which case your default route may only cover your network scope. The point is that a default route is really defined as the "route of last resort," which is used if no other route covers the packet destination.

These considerations illustrate the fundamental thought behind traditional IPv4 routing:

All routing is a destination-driven process.

Every packet that enters a router is inspected to determine the destination IP address. Based on that destination address the router then consults the routing table to determine where to send the packet. The only item of interest to the router is the destination address. Nothing else matters.

UNIX Configuration Commands

You should now understand the fundamental thought behind traditional IPv4 routing. However, at this point, you need to step back and look into the methods of implementation. First consider UNIX commands. These commands are traditional both in function and in age. Once you have learned how to use them under one UNIX, including Linux, you will know essentially how to use them in any UNIX. This section details how to use these commands under Linux to configure a basic two-network router with a single default route. You will also add additional specific routes to illustrate the meaning behind the fundamental thought of traditional routing.

The two primary utilities used in configuring IPv4 routing under UNIX are `ifconfig` and `route`. You will step through the use of both of these utilities to configure a simple dual connected router under Linux.

`ifconfig` Utility

The `ifconfig` utility has been used with UNIX systems for quite some time and is the original utility for configuring network interfaces under UNIX. The utility is appropriately named InterFace CONFIGuration, or `ifconfig`. On many UNIXes as well as Linux, `ifconfig` supports multiple protocol suites, or *address families*. The complete syntax and supported address families can be found in the man pages. This book is only concerned with the *inet* family, which is the address family for IPv4. There is also an *inet6* family for IPv6 but we will not cover that usage in this book. In Chapter 9, "IPv6," you will learn how the `ip` utility is used for Policy Routing in IPv6.

The basic `ifconfig` syntax for an IPv4 interface under Linux is as follows:

```
ifconfig interface IP-address netmask netmask broadcast broadcast
```

The italicized words will be replaced with the relevant information to configure the interface.

On most UNIXes you can find out the names of the available interfaces through `ifconfig` by asking it to list all of the interfaces it knows about. Type **`ifconfig -a`** and you will see a list of all the interfaces on the system, regardless of whether they are configured. You can also call `ifconfig` with the name of a single interface to obtain information about that interface only. This feature helps when you are on a strange system and need some quick information.

In UNIX there is an IP interface that should be present whenever the system is enabled for TCP/IP communication. This is the *loopback* interface, usually specified by the name lo or lo0. By conventional standard this interface has the IPv4 address 127.0.0.1/8 assigned to it. This interface is very important to the correct operation of the TCP/IP networking subsystems. In Chapters 2–8, as the details of the Linux Policy Routing structures are illustrated and then exemplified, you will see that this interface has a myriad of uses.

The other interfaces that may be on the system will have names that vary according to the UNIX flavor. I will use the Linux conventions herein and refer primarily to using Ethernet (eth*xx*) and Token Ring (tr*xx*) interfaces.

Consider a router that has one Ethernet interface, eth0, and one Token Ring interface, tr0. The appropriate information is as follows:

```
eth0 - 192.168.1.254/24
tr0 - 10.1.1.254/24
Default Gateway - 10.1.1.1/24
```

Two networks are represented here, and from the default gateway address you can deduce that the Ethernet network is a stub network off of the main network. The Token Ring could be considered the backbone network if you prefer that terminology because it contains the default gateway.

To set up the interfaces using ifconfig on a typical Linux system, do the following from the command line:

```
ifconfig eth0 192.168.1.254 netmask 255.255.255.0 broadcast 192.168.1.255
ifconfig tr0 10.1.1.254 netmask 255.255.255.0 broadcast 10.1.1.255
```

You could then list the interfaces and get information about them using the straight ifconfig command by itself.

route Utility

Now you have a router with three IPv4 configured interfaces. Do not forget about the loopback interface when counting the interfaces! You should now set up your router to actually be able to route between the locally connected networks. In order for the router to do this it needs to have all three of the locally connected networks in the routing table. Here you call upon the route command to populate the routing table.

In general usage the route command is called as follows:

```
route add -net|host IPv4 Address netmask netmask gw gateway dev interface
```

Note that there are many other options that can be specified to the route command. Many of the options are UNIX flavor specific. The preceding options are fairly general and should work on most UNIXes. Also the route command, when issued by itself on the command line, will give different outputs depending on the UNIX flavor. In Linux, issuing a route command by itself will dump the main kernel routing table. However, on most UNIXes you will need to use the netstat -r command in order to dump the routing table.

LINUX 2.0 VERSUS LINUX 2.2 ROUTING CHANGES

In Linux there are some fundamental differences in the IPv4 configuration process between the 2.0 series of kernels and the 2.1 and newer kernels. When configuring an interface for IPv4 using `ifconfig` under a 2.0 series kernel, only the interface is configured. But the kernel does not know how to get to this address or to the network it defines. You have to add a network route manually in order for the kernel to see where to send the packet.

In kernel 2.1 and newer, the situation is different. When Alexey Kuznetsov rewrote the network routing code for Linux during the 2.1 development kernel series, he added automatic route creation for directly connected networks. Thus, if you run the same `ifconfig` configuration command on a 2.1 or higher series kernel, you will be able to connect immediately to the network defined by the interface.

Having the route automatically added by the kernel helps users unfamiliar with networking immensely in normal operation of a Linux network. If you want to configure an interface, the kernel will automatically create a connection to the interface address and network. Thus, as soon as you are done configuring the interface, you are ready to use it. However, for advanced usage this can become a nuisance.

For advanced usage you can override this behavior by explicitly configuring the interface with the true host address, which is a netmask of all ones. If you want to have the same behavior in 2.1 and higher that you had in 2.0 for `ifconfig`, use `ifconfig` *interface IPv4 Address* `netmask 255.255.255.255 broadcast` *broadcast*, and the automatic route will not be created.

Now that you have seen the syntax for basic routing configuration, it's time to apply it to the router configured in the `ifconfig` section.

```
route add -net 127.0.0.0 netmask 255.0.0.0 dev lo
route add -net 192.168.1.0 netmask 255.255.255.0 dev eth0
route add -net 10.1.1.0 netmask 255.255.255.0 dev tr0
```

Note that the loopback interface route is explicitly included here for completeness. You did not see the actual `ifconfig` statement in the previous section; it is left as an exercise for the reader to determine what command was needed. Note that in all cases where you would want to ensure that your system is correctly configured, you will want to configure all the interfaces, including the loopback interface, manually or through your own set of scripts. Under Linux, and in UNIX in general, any system interface including loopback is not automatically configured.

The router at this point is ready to route all traffic between the 192.168.1.0/24 network and the 10.1.1.0/24 network. But if there is any traffic from either of those networks with a destination address that does not belong to either 192.168.1.0/24 or 10.1.1.0/24, the router will return an error. This is because it has no default route at this point in time.

The subject of default routes contains an explicit security concern. Essentially, a default route enables a router to trust all traffic to another router. In many cases this may not be a necessary or wise decision. For example, in the network structure considered here there may only be one or two other networks of interest. Alternatively, you may not want the systems on 192.168.1.0/24 to see any other networks. The route setup at this point would ensure, in the absence of source-routing capabilities, that the systems on 192.168.1.0/24 would only be able to talk externally to systems on 10.1.1.0/24. When we consider the theory of Policy Routing in Chapters 2 and 3 and the actual implementation usage in Chapters 5–8, you will see various methods of considering this fundamental security problem.

But to consider standard and traditional usage you should install a default route into your router. This default route provides your router with a router to which all unknown destination addressed traffic should be forwarded. In this case you have a gateway that has been specified for this route. You can then add it in with the following command:

```
route add -net 0.0.0.0 netmask 0.0.0.0 gw 10.1.1.1
```

Note that under Linux and under many other UNIXes this command can also be expressed as `route add default gw 10.1.1.1`, where the `default` keyword stands for the `-net 0.0.0.0 netmask 0.0.0.0` parts of the given example.

You now have a router that will route traffic between the 192.168.1.0/24 and 10.1.1.0/24 networks and will also provide connectivity to any other network destination from the 192.168.1.0/24 network. Of course that does not mean that those networks can get back to the 192.168.1.0/24 network, but that is a different problem.

Cisco IOS Configuration Commands

Now that you have seen how to use the standard UNIX tools to configure a simple router, consider configuring a generic Cisco router to perform the same task. Even if you have no interest in using Cisco for this purpose, please read on as you will see a marked similarity between the command sets shown here and the Linux Policy Routing toolset. If you are already familiar with Cisco IOS (Internetwork Operating System) command sets, feel free to skip this section.

This section will assume that no special configuration tasks are needed for the Cisco router. I will only show how to set it up to perform the exact same task and configuration as you have just seen with the Linux router.

The Cisco IOS configuration commands are entered at a terminal session with the router directly into the configuration. This session is either directly connected through the management port or a telnet session. Alternatively, you can enter in all the commands to a file, which is then either uploaded into the router or the router can boot off of a TFTP server and load the configuration file. If you want to learn how to do these various things, please refer to the Cisco IOS documentation. This section assumes that you already have this knowledge.

The core command used in most of this section is the `ip` command. This command is then followed by the action to take. For example, you have the `ip address` command for adding and deleting TCP/IP addresses, and the `ip route` command for adding and deleting TCP/IP routes. Other subcommands are covered as you read through this book. For more information refer to the Cisco IOS documentation.

ip address

The `ip address` form of the command will let you configure your interfaces with IPv4 addresses. On the router you would then have the following configuration command file sections:

```
interface FastEthernet0
 ip address 192.168.1.254 255.255.255.0
!

interface TokenRing0
 ip address 10.1.1.254 255.255.255.0
```

Note that unlike UNIX, the interface to operate upon is specified by a different command, `interface`. Thus in IOS a group of commands can be specified to operate upon an interface by including them under the appropriate interface section.

In IOS, as in Linux 2.1 and higher, assigning an IP address to an interface automatically places the appropriate network route into the routing table. Thus the preceding configuration file snippet has already defined the directly connected network routes for 192.168.1.0/24 and 10.1.1.0/24.

ip route

In order to complete your configuration you need to specify the default route. This is done through the `ip route` subcommand. You need to add the full default route specification:

```
ip route 0.0.0.0 0.0.0.0 10.1.1.1
```

This will add the default route to all other destinations. This Cisco router is now in the same state as your Linux router from the previous section. Of course there are other commands that need to be in the Cisco configuration file in order for this router to work, but this section is only considering what you need to input to enable the same behavior you saw with the UNIX router system.

IPv4 Dynamic Routing

Now that you have seen how to configure simple routing on both the Linux and Cisco platforms, consider how to automate some of the routing structure itself.

In most networks today, especially corporate and ISP internal networks, there are more than a few physical and logical networks. These networks also tend to change both through additions and deletions as well as simple reconfiguration. Tracking and updating all of the routers within such a network is painful enough when you consider just a handful of networks and routers, but it becomes an absolutely daunting task when the networks and routers exceed the fingers on one hand, especially when the network spans locations and topologies.

Another problem often seen in larger routed networks is maintaining a list of networks that are non-operational. In such a case, the reachability of the network becomes a prime concern. When a network is unreachable, packets sent to it are just discarded and the emphasis is placed on the ICMP error messages providing the routers with this information. In an automated, or dynamic, routing environment the routing protocol itself can often fulfill this notification function in a more consistent manner.

The early answer to this was the original Routing Information Protocol, RIP. Version 1 of this protocol, as defined in RFC-1058, under IPv4 provided an automated means for routers and systems to transfer knowledge of the routing structure of the network between the devices. For serious study and details, see Stevens and RFC-1058. Note that RIPv1 has been declared historic (see RFC-1923), which means that it is good for study only. This is due to its classfull nature. Because the RFCs define in many cases the actual protocol specifications and implementations for many facets of networking, you might want to know where to obtain and read them. A good place to start is the official core repository located at http://www.rfc-editor.org.

RIP/Distance Vector

RIPv1, and the next generation RIPv2 as defined in RFCs 1387–1389 (which I will generally refer to simply as RIP), is the primary dynamic routing protocol considered on IPv4 networks. RIP is based on the Bellman-Ford (or distance vector) algorithm. The Bellman-Ford algorithm has been used for routing computations in computer networks since the early days of the ARPAnet. RIP is most useful as, and is usually seen as, an "interior gateway protocol." This concept refers to the dynamic routing methods used within a single network structure such as a corporate network.

Under RIP the concept of passing a packet through a router is considered as a discrete action. This action is referred to as a *hop*, and the number of times a packet passes through routers from source to destination is the *hop count*. Routers that participate in the RIP routing structure will pass information to each of the local directly connected networks about all of the routes it has and the associated hop count for each route listed. This information is presented on the directly connected network using a broadcast. Usually there is one router that has a defined default route that it also provides through RIP.

By configuring RIP on a router you can remove the need to define static default and additional routes on each system. You need only ensure that the router knows about its own directly connected networks and how to talk with other RIP-enabled routers. Then the various routers talk among themselves and provide routing information to each other.

One of the few drawbacks to RIP is that routes with a hop count greater than the network defined radius of 15 will be ignored by the receiving router. Also, RIP does not provide a method of having more than one route between any two networks. These and other limitations are discussed in Chapter 2, "Policy Routing Theory" and Chapter 7, "Dynamic Routing Interactions."

The basic problem with using RIP in a large-scale network lies in the core algorithm. The Bellman-Ford distance vector concept refers to a partial routing state within the scope of the locally connected networks. In other words, none of the routers participating in RIP can know the full extent and state of the network. All they know is the local routers within their directly connected networks and the routes that are known to those routers. This is often referred to as "routing by rumor." Since the routers cannot know the full routing state of the network, all they know is what they obtain by gossiping with their neighbors.

OSPF/Link State

This gossiping limitation leads into the higher stage of interior gateway protocols, where each router has full knowledge of the entire network scope. This type of dynamic routing protocol refers to the link-state of the network. A *link-state* encompasses the current status of an individual connection between two routers on a common network. This includes allowing for the relative speeds, types, and uses of the intermediary network and routers. Since each router participating in a link-state routing structure has knowledge of all other connections within the network scope, you can have multiple connections between networks and multiple definitions of the logical networks themselves.

The defining protocol for link-state is Open Shortest Path First, referred to as OSPF. The OSPF protocol was first defined in RFC-1131 and has been updated to version 2 and a forthcoming version 3 also known as OSPF for IPv6. OSPFv2 is the preferred protocol for use within a single structure network due to the ability to correctly handle large IP-based networks with multiple connections.

As detailed in RFC-1245, OSPF routers exchange link-states through link-state advertisements (LSAs) that describe pieces of the OSPF routing domain. These LSAs are flooded throughout the routing domain, with each router aggregating these LSAs to form the link-state database. Thus each router has an identical link-state database. Synchronization of link-state databases is maintained via a reliable flooding algorithm, which is based on multicast capabilities with fallback to directed broadcast or single programmed connections. From this link-state database, each router builds a routing table by calculating a shortest-path tree, with the root of the tree being the calculating router itself. This calculation is commonly referred to as the Dijkstra procedure.

OSPF brings several levels of security and robustness to the dynamic routing structure. For more details please see RFC-1245 (http://www.ietf.org/rfc/rfc1245.txt), which discusses the OSPFv2 protocol technical details. For this book's purposes I will treat OSPF as the preferred dynamic routing structure and will detail how it can interoperate with the Policy Routing structures in Chapter 7.

Dynamic Routing Tradition

At this stage you are probably wondering why I am talking about all of these routing protocols. They sound as if they take care of a lot of problems with an IP-routed network. They do. But they still adhere to and promote the fundamental thought of traditional IPv4 routing: All routing is a destination-driven process. Dynamic routing protocols merely make it easier to spread the destination-driven routing information around the network. When you begin to consider Policy Routing structures and the needs that drove their creation (discussed in Chapter 2), this dissemination of information becomes a hindrance. Chapter 7 will take up the question of how to strike the best balance between the ease of dissemination provided by dynamic routing and the needs for structure in the Policy Routing world.

UNIX routed and Cisco RIP Configurations

In order to ensure complete coverage of traditional IPv4 routing setups, I will show you how to configure and use the RIP protocol within your router. I will illustrate both the UNIX and Cisco viewpoints. While I will assume only that you are going to be running the RIP or RIPv2 protocols, much of what I say will be valid for running other dynamic routing protocols. In Chapter 7 I will cover the link-state, inter-AS, and distance-vector dynamic routing protocols as they work within the framework of a fully policy-routed network.

To this end, recall where I left off at the end of the section "UNIX Configuration Commands." You had a fully functional Linux router running a static routing configuration. This router was capable of routing between the 10.1.1.0/24 and the 192.168.1.0/24 IPv4 networks. It also possessed a default route pointing to a previously known router, 10.1.1.1. It's time to add to that router the ability to participate in a dynamic routed IPv4 network through the use of RIP.

routed

In general, UNIX usage and Linux in particular offer many extra functions through the use of daemons. In the case of dynamic IPv4 routing, this is particularly true. Indeed, the very RFCs that define the original RIP protocol refer to the protocol as the description of the operation of the routed daemon. This is because the routed daemon came along before the RIP protocol was ever formally defined. Thus the very definition of the RIP structure came from the mechanism and workings of the routed daemon functions. So to configure RIP on a Linux system you merely have to run the routed daemon.

The routed daemon may be run from the command line but is usually started in the networking initialization script for the system. In normal operation, routed listens on UDP port 520 for routing information packets from other systems. If the system is considered a router, it also periodically broadcasts copies of its routing tables to all directly connected networks.

When `routed` is first started it finds all directly connected interfaces configured and running on the system ignoring the loopback interface. If multiple interfaces are found, the system is defined as a router for the purpose of sending out broadcasts. After determining the interface(s) to which it will bind, `routed` transmits a request packet on each interface and loops listening for request and response packets from other routers.

Upon receiving a request packet `routed` replies using the information maintained in the system routing table. The response packet generated contains a list of routes marked with a hop count metric. The metric associated with each route provides a rough distance as relative to the originating router.

Response packets received by `routed` may update the routing tables if any of the following conditions are satisfied:

1. No routing table entry exists for the destination network or host, and the metric indicates the destination is reachable (hop count < 16).
2. The source of the packet is the same as the router in the existing routing table entry. That is, updated information is being received from the router through which packets for the destination are being routed.
3. The existing entry in the routing table has not been updated for some time (standard definition of 90 seconds) and the route is of the same or lesser hop count as the current route.
4. The new route describes a shorter route to the destination than the one currently stored in the routing tables; the metric of the new route is compared against the one stored in the table to decide this.

In addition to processing incoming response and request packets, `routed` also periodically checks the routing table entries. If an entry has not been updated for 3 minutes, the hop count is set to 16 and marked for deletion. Before actually deleting the route from the table, `routed` will wait an extra 60 seconds to ensure that the deleted route will propagate correctly.

`routed` will periodically broadcast the routing tables every 30 seconds to all directly connected networks. This timeout can be adjusted but since it is part of the standard setup, you will want to leave it alone for most networks.

`routed` also supports the notion of distant passive and active routers. When `routed` starts up it looks for the optional configuration file `/etc/gateways`, and if it exists it reads the file to find routers that may not be located by other means. Routers marked passive in the file do not exchange routing information but may be referred to, while routers marked active will exchange routing information. Routes through passive routers are specified using manual static routes that refer to those routers, but those static routes are not included in any routing information transmitted. Routers marked external are also passive, but are not placed in the kernel routing table or included in routing updates. The function of external entries is to inform `routed` that another routing process, such as `gated`, will install a route using that router so `routed` will not override that route. Such entries are only required when both routers may learn of routes to the same destination. You will see in Chapter 7 that there are many complexities to this when combined with Policy Routing.

Run routed from the command line to illustrate how to turn on RIP routing:

routed

Difficult—no? Actually there are several options to routed that you can specify. These include forcing routed to consider the system a router and also allowing routed to only listen for packets but not send any.

Cisco IOS RIP Configuration

Now that you have seen how easy it is to configure and run routed on a Linux system, it's time to set up the same level of functionality on a Cisco router.

Since we are considering RIP you can see that just as in Linux the actual initiation of the protocol is to simply turn it on. In Cisco IOS there is no concept of active interfaces, so you must manually specify all networks for which you want the RIP protocol to be included in the active broadcasts. Thus where Linux routed will listen to and accept RIP information about any network from a connected router, Cisco will passively listen to RIP broadcasts from any router but will only broadcast information about networks it has been told to advertise. Following is a simple example of turning on RIP for our Cisco router.

```
router rip
  network 10.1.1.0
  network 192.168.1.0
```

This told the Cisco router to turn on and start using the RIP protocol on all interfaces connected to networks 10.1.1.0/24 and 192.168.1.0/24. The zeros in the network command above refer to full class-based networks.

There are many options in Cisco RIP that you can specify and use. You can specify the type of RIP, as in version 1 or version 2, which is important in that RIPv2 allows for authentication, CIDR, and multivalued netmasks. With routed you must use a version of routed that understands RIPv2, but you would usually in that case use gated or zebra, as you will see in Chapter 7. Also, you can specify changing the various timeouts, apply passive interface rules, and specify active and passive routers as in the /etc/gateways file. See the Cisco IOS documentation for all of the details.

Essentially you now have a fully functioning RIP router participating in the dynamic routing structure of your network.

Sample Linux Router Setup

Keeping in mind all you have seen, consider a quick overview of a Linux router setup. I will show you a script that takes the setup illustrated in the beginning and turns on all the IPv4 traditional networking functions needed to perform traditional dynamic routing as you would see in countless small network connections.

So consider again the scenario. You have two networks, an Ethernet with IPv4 scope 192.168.1.0/24 and a Token Ring with IPv4 scope 10.1.1.0/24. The default router for the world as you know it is 10.1.1.1 on the Token Ring. You are running RIPv1 and want to participate in the dynamic routing scheme. You need to create one single script that will take your Linux system and turn on IP routing, configure the system, and enable dynamic routing. Here it is:

```
#!/bin/bash

# Turn on IPv4 packet forwarding

echo "1" > /proc/sys/net/ipv4/ip_forward

# We know our interfaces ...

/sbin/ifconfig eth0 192.168.1.254 netmask 255.255.255.0 broadcast 192.168.1.255
/sbin/ifconfig tr0 10.1.1.254 netmask 255.255.255.0 broadcast 10.1.1.255

# the above ifconfigs defined the routes also (2.2 kernel) so...

# default route

/sbin/route add default gw 10.1.1.1

# and enable RIP

/sbin/routed

exit 0

# Thats all folks....
```

Now this seems like a sneaky end to the chapter, but bear in mind the fundamental thought behind traditional IPv4 routing:

All routing is a destination-driven process.

The rest of the chapter showed you how IPv4 is configured in the traditional manner and was intended as a quick refresher or overview. The rest of the book is concerned with the limitations of the traditional routing thought and the ways of Policy Routing.

CHAPTER 2

Policy Routing Theory

Traditional IPv4 routing is summarized as "All routing is a destination-driven process." When a router looks at an IPv4 packet it cares only about the destination address in the header of the packet. It uses this destination address to make a decision on where to forward the packet. This scenario works fine for simple networks where all of the machines in the network only need to get out to some place. Think of a standard driveway on a house. It starts at the house and goes to the road. When you get to the road you have two choices: turn right or turn left. The choice you make depends on where you want to go. Thus you make a destination-based routing choice. In the simplest case your driveway connects to a dead-end road and you will always turn the same way. This would be the single default route scenario.

But to somewhat extend the analogy, what if your driveway opened onto a 6-way intersection? And to complicate the picture further, one of the intersecting roads is a highway on-ramp that only permits sedans, one of the other roads is a gravel road only usable by tractors, and so on. In these cases you need to make a decision based on what you are driving as well as where you are going. These are the types of network setups where you route packets differently, depending not only on the destination addresses but also on other packet fields such as source address, IP protocol, transport protocol ports, or even packet payload. This type of routing is called *Policy Routing*.

Defining "Policy" in Policy Routing

The standard dictionary definition of policy is

1. A definite course of action adopted for sake of facilitation.
2. A course of action pursued by a government or organization.

Both of these definitions imply that a policy is a describing or proscribing set of rules and actions that encompasses an ideal goal. And that implication fits in well with the scope of Policy Routing.

The policy in Policy Routing is to provide routing capability based on any or all facets of a packet. This includes not only the header information, but also the data contained within the packet itself. As you will learn in Chapter 3, "Linux Policy Routing Structures," there are some concrete limitations in implementing the entire functionality of ideal Policy Routing. In Chapters 5 through 8 you will implement and manipulate some very intricate networks. For now I will talk about the ideal nature of policy.

Even in the early days of networks, back in the early '70s, there were discussions on what constituted the minimum set of information needed to route a packet. These discussions mostly covered the reality of the ARPAnet design, namely how to survive a nuclear holocaust and still provide network services. Within this scenario the destination-based routing made more sense because you did not care how your packet was treated but were only concerned with getting your packet to the final destination. Many of the problems with the destination-only treatment, such as long delays or retransmissions, were not as critical. The applications of that time, such as FTP or email, were much more forgiving. In the '80s and through the explosion of the '90s, the essential nature of the ARPAnet changed to become today's Internet. Now the need is to grease the wheels of business and not to care about the nuclear winter.

With the imperatives of business comes the need for security and flexibility. You need to protect the business assets while making it easy for customers and associates to access and use those assets. Now you do not have just a network, you have an intranet, connected to the Internet and to your supplier's, vendor's, partner's, and customer's intranets. The complexity of the network connectivity may be dealt with through standard dynamic routing, but what about the service and security?

Service is a key to success in any business environment. To provide a good impression of your business you coach and train your telephone and counter people to show competence and give good service. But how do you present a good image through your network? This question is becoming a prime concern for many companies as they struggle to differentiate themselves online. The answer lies in technology that was beginning to be discussed and considered back when the current Internet Protocol, IPv4, was making its debut.

As you probably have guessed from the terminology I have chosen, the not-so-secret technology is Quality of Service (QoS), also known as Differentiated Services (DiffServ) or Integrated Services (IntServ). While purists of the IP protocol will castigate me for doing so, as a network engineer I coalesce these services into a single thought. All of the various types of QoS exist to solve the same problem, namely how to provide different treatment for different data streams. And now the circle begins to close, as the earliest implementations of Policy Routing were primarily implementations of various QoS concepts.

So when I speak about the "policy" in Policy Routing I refer to the set of describing and proscribing rules that implement the routing structure of a network or assortment of networks. This policy constitutes the ideal uses and services of the network. While the actual implementation of this policy may differ by device, by type, or by the nature of the data streams themselves, the overall effect implements the business imperative of the network. As you will see throughout this book, the policy can range from a simple concern for resources to a global scale definition of data stream priorities.

Common IPv4 Routing Problems and Solutions

As I implied earlier in the chapter, Policy Routing grew out of several different needs within IPv4 networks. One of the more recent and prominent discussions was the entire topic of QoS. But there have been many problems with the destination-based routing structures. Some of you may remember that it was only recently, in the early '90s, that the Internet was allowed to carry any commercial traffic. Indeed there existed for some time parallel networks where one carried commercial traffic and the other carried Internet traffic. While this was a somewhat extreme and short-lived situation, there was call for and discussions about methods of differentially treating the routing based on the source of the packet as well as the destination. Consider, for example, an educational institution that carried on correspondence with both a commercial entity and a governmental entity on the same project. Under the parallel networks the educational institution would have to send out two copies of all work and provide two different connections to the internal networks. They would need to use two completely different sets of internal routing tables to allow data from perhaps one experimental computer to be sent through a "commercial" connection and through a "research" connection. If the connections were indeed physically separate, then destination routing could still be used. But if the connections were intermingled (as was usually the case), at some point in time it would be necessary to artificially separate the data streams and route one of them through a defined path and the other through an alternate path. These decisions would be based on the source address as well as the destination address of the packet. This is Policy Routing.

Aside from this extreme example, you can see that even in the networks that were being developed internally by many corporations and other large entities there was a need to route packets based on the properties of the packet besides just the destination. An actual case I was involved in illustrates the vagaries of the routing needed under destination-based systems.

In this instance there was an accounting network that contained the user desktops for the auditing staff. All of the work these auditors did was on servers that resided on the main accounting network located in a different building on the corporate campus. Getting the traffic through to the accounting network from the auditor network required connecting to the main corporate campus backbone.

The problem resided in the fact that some other employees of the company had been recently reprimanded for attempting to access the accounting systems. These actions were caught by the auditing staff. After these incidents the accounting network itself was locked down physically and through other various network security measures. However, there remained the problem that any and all traffic from the auditing division could be seen and potentially used to access the accounting network. The corporate campus backbone was connected to many other buildings and in some cases all of the traffic on the backbone actually traversed several corporate campus buildings.

The company brought in my team to find a way to route the auditor traffic so that it passed through the backbone in such a path as to not allow any of the traffic to traverse these other buildings. For security reasons since the network is still operational I will not go into detail as to the exact setup of the network involved. Generally speaking, the backbone network consisted of several multiply-connected network segments bridged together. The majority of the routing tables were set up to route all traffic through the backbone even if there was more than one connection. Due to the bridging structure you could not access the backbone router connections directly. We ended up defining new IP networks for many of the routers and setting up a ring of static routes, which would force traffic within those address scopes only through a different network path.

Suffice it to say that what would have been a simple Policy Routing decision within the auditing and backbone routers ended up requiring us to set up multiple IP network scopes with different destination route tables. If we could have specified routing based on IP source address we would not have had any problem setting up the route structure. While we did try using a strict source routing packet header structure, the only method that worked was to use a completely different set of IP network addresses and set them up statically to force the route flow. And with such a static forced route structure there were problems when machines were added to or removed from the secured networks.

This was one of the scenarios that started me down the path to Policy Routing. It was obvious even then that if we could have specified the source IP address or network as a routing factor, we could have solved the problem quickly and easily. The need for redundancy, which drove the original destination-based routing, was rapidly coming into conflict with the security and structure of the network. Ideally, we should be able to have our redundancy and security too.

The Quality of Service Explosion

Fast forward to the mid '90s to the explosion of the other, and considered by many the primary, driving force for Policy Routing structures, QoS. The commercialization of the Internet has driven the entire assumption base for the IPv4 protocol family into intense scrutiny. The traditional packet delivery basis for IPv4 has been described as "best-effort." This summarizes the entire process quite aptly. The underlying reason for the split between UDP (User Datagram Protocol) and TCP (Transmission Control Protocol) is related to the fact that IP (Internet Protocol) is a best-effort delivery service. In this split UDP packets get there if they can, when they can, and that is fine. TCP packets are checked on through all sorts of mechanisms to ensure that the packets get there at all. In either case, the routing is left to the routers and is decided based on where the packet is going.

Now as a corporate or other entity, what if I am willing to pay for better, faster, or available packet delivery? Enter the entire rationale for QoS. QoS, as a basic premise, means that I as a service provider of networking connectivity will guarantee you some level of service that you pay a premium for using. Under IPv4 networks, this mechanism depends on the routing and queueing of network packets depending on the TOS (Type of Service) tag associated with the QoS service provided.

There are a few standards for TOS tags and many of the actual drawbacks of the system are related to the definition of what is provided for a particular TOS tag. But that also is the bulk of the discussion and work relating to the various QoS systems today. For example, you can look at the various specifications and definitions for Differentiated Service (DiffServ) which specify the TOS values related to various types of queueing disciplines. The assumption of course is that the queueing structure, by providing mediated preferential access to the existing finite bandwidth connection, allows for better service of your packet stream. This begs the question of what additional structures are possible with QoS.

Routing structures that take advantage of the tagging of QoS are the natural extension. By providing a route that depends on the TOS tag in the packet, it is possible to now provide certain guarantees of packet delivery. Under queueing alone, about all you can guarantee is that the tagged data stream will get a defined percentage of the available bandwidth. With Policy Routing, based on the TOS tag you can add in methods of congestion avoidance and preferential packet paths.

Consider a setup as illustrated in Figure 2.1 where you have two potential data paths. Each data path is a private connection to a different network. Each of these networks is then connected to a final destination. As a peer to these external networks your router is knowledgeable about the availability, load, and capacity of these networks. My agreement with you is to provide a certain bandwidth to my packets with a clause specifying an additional payment for low latency connections. You would like to maximize your income from my contract so you will set up the policy in your routers to always send my packets by whatever path offers the lowest latency. Since your router knows the latency at points TRN1, TRN2, RET1, and RET2, you can calculate the latency of First Path versus Second Path. Thus you can provide both a queueing guarantee to me and you can then route my packets for lowest current latency. This would work by having your router make a per packet or per queue decision based on the current calculations of Latency(TRN1 + RET1) versus Latency(TRN2 + RET2) and then routing the packet based on that decision. This packet selection can use the same TOS tag you use to queue on for the bandwidth guarantee.

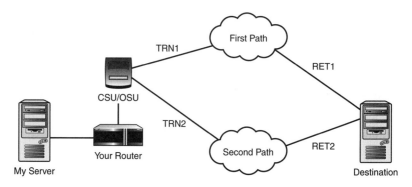

Figure 2.1

Dual path cost structure.

Policy Routing Structure

This brings up the notion of the structure of a policy routed network. As you can surmise from this chapter, such networks comprise not only the actual routing structure itself but also the intelligence of the devices participating in the network. This is the reason that Policy Routing was often and still is often referred to as "intelligent routing." I prefer the Policy Routing term because "intelligent routing" could refer to anything better than simple single static default routes.

The structure of a Policy Routing network encompasses participatory elements of the network. This ranges from the core routers through to the user endstations. Any device that participates in the infrastructure of the network may also participate in the policy. Conversely, just because a device participates in the network infrastructure does not mean it participates in the network policy.

The primary source of the policy for the routing structure is usually found in the core routers. As the source for the majority of the routing decisions it is natural to expect them to provide the majority of the policy structure. As you will see later in this chapter, this is not always the case, especially in high security networks where the routing devices tend to be very limited in their capabilities.

A core router is usually designated as such because of the functions it provides to the network. Often this is the central router in a hub-and-spoke routed network. However, the core router with regard to policy is often the router or other security device that provides the main interconnectivity between the internal corporate network and external allied networks. A central router in a hub-and-spoke system historically needed only to perform traditional routing to service the corporate network needs.

The recent trends within corporate networks have been to incorporate more advanced services for use. As services such as streaming audio and video are introduced to corporate networks, there is a greater need to allocate and economize the resources within the network. As these services are added the central routers become strained trying to handle all of the traffic being generated. The standard solution is to throw more money at the problem and purchase larger routers and higher-speed networks. The reality in almost every case is that redesigning and optimizing the network traffic using Policy Routing often returns a far higher cost savings through greater efficiency. But it is not glamorous to management and not highly profitable for VARs (Value Added Resellers).

As in network security, policy and the resultant structures promulgated from implementing the policy must be balanced between the need to provide a specific set of functions and the need to reduce the cost associated with providing such structures. These costs are not only material but also highly intangible with respect to the human factors. If it is easier to bypass the policy when using the network or the policy in place renders usage of the network difficult, the policy hinders rather than helps. The analogy to network security policy structures is very precise and deeply intertwined.

A carefully crafted and implemented Policy Routing structure can assist on many fronts. As a concrete example, consider a Policy Routing structure that defines that all Internet traffic from the outbound call center be administratively denied. This serves to implement a security policy for Internet access, a network policy reducing extraneous traffic, and a business policy for divisional workflow. This multiplicity of usage points out the fundamental shift in today's corporate networks: The network defines and drives fundamental productivity in much the same way as the telephone before it. And as business grew from single telephones to PBX systems and call centers, so too has computing grown to networks and NOCs (Network Operation Centers). As with the telephone usage policies earlier, network and security policies now concern themselves with the usage of the corporate network resources. And these policies are implemented through a Policy Routing structure.

Implementation Considerations for Policy Routing

Implementing a Policy Routing structure requires that all extant policies for network usage be considered along with the actual logical/physical configuration of the network. In many cases, the logical and physical configuration of the network may be changed to facilitate the implementation. The best place to start when considering a Policy Routing structure is to map the logical structure of the network. This logical map will show the network intermesh. The logical intermesh is important as most networks today still incorporate the single connection philosophy. The single connection philosophy defines that any two networks should be connected only at a single point.

In traditional routing, especially under RIP dynamics, you should not have two routes to any network. If you did, then only one of the routes would be used. This style of network design led to the two popular network topologies, the hub and spoke and the backbone. In a backbone system there is a central network with many routers attached to this backbone network. These attached routers connect the leaf or branch networks to the backbone network. Any conversations between leaf networks require traversing the backbone. A backbone system works well for distributed computing where the majority of each leaf network's traffic is within the leaf network. A hub-and-spoke system usually has a single large router that is connected to all of the leaf networks directly. Thus a hub and spoke is often referred to as a collapsed backbone system.

In either of these types of network, the implementation of a Policy Routing structure requires a careful analysis of the objectives and a clear understanding of the actual logical structure. Implementing Policy Routing on a leaf router when the traffic does not pass through that router not only wastes resources but can actively deteriorate network traffic flow. Worse still, implementing a Policy Routing structure without understanding the packet traversal paths and the oddities of the desktop operating systems connected to the networks can crash your network.

To illustrate, consider a backbone network where several of the stub networks contain traffic destined for the Internet as illustrated in Figure 2.2. The connection to the Internet is through a router, Inter1, connected to the backbone and to an external network. Originally all the stub networks sent their traffic to Inter1 as the default gateway. Then Inter1 would send on all the traffic to the Internet. A firewall placed between Inter1 and the Internet connection was responsible for blocking the traffic from those stub networks not allowed to the Internet.

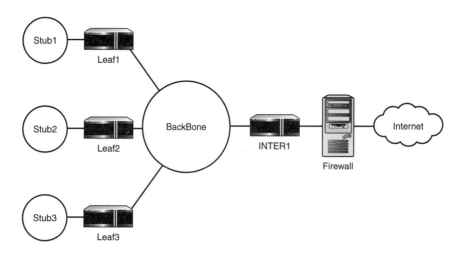

Figure 2.2

Multinetwork policy structures.

The backbone network was upgraded twice to faster speeds due to the increasing level of traffic, and there were attempts to use static routes to contain the internal traffic. With the backbone now saturated again, the decision was made to try to tune the network. The first attempt implemented Policy Routing on Inter1. The Policy Routing structure on Inter1 mediated access to the Internet based on source IP address. The backbone network collapsed on the first full business day after the implementation.

A packet dump of the backbone showed that the packets destined for the Internet from the stub networks arrived at Inter1 and that Inter1 then sent back an administratively denied response packet. The desktop OS in use ignored these packets and resent the request. Thus the traffic on the backbone due to these requests at least tripled in volume. Under the old method, the firewall between Inter1 and the Internet had simply dropped the packets so there was no further response and the original request timed out. Under this first attempt the original goal—reduction of the backbone traffic—was reversed.

The successful second attempt implemented a Policy Routing structure on the leaf routers as well as Inter1. The leaf routers were instructed to simply drop, or "black-hole," the packets that were denied access to the Internet based on the source address incoming from the Stub network. Packets from addresses that were allowed out onto the Internet were additionally tagged with a TOS field id that defined the Stub that the packet came from and additionally the protocol used such as http. Then Inter1 was configured to queue these packets according to the network policy allowed rates for those services. Later on the leaf routers were configured to TOS tag and differentially route various internal network data flows, thus maximizing the available backbone bandwidth and making the network seem much faster than ever before to the end users.

Summary

Defining and deciding what constitutes a Policy Routing structure is harder than implementing one. Most importantly you should understand that routing policy is NOT Policy Routing. Policy Routing refers to the network-centric structure that performs the routing. Routing policy is an administrative or otherwise externally imposed requirement on the network. While they are very closely intertwined, they need to be understood separately. That is why in this chapter I spoke of using Policy Routing structures to implement security, network, and routing policies.

When considering the implementation of a Policy Routing structure you must understand your entire network and the scope of the network operations. Understanding both the uses of your network and the operations of the protocols traversing your network is critical to designing a good Policy Routing structure. In short, if you do not know how a simple TCP transaction differs from a UDP transaction at the packet level, you will burn yourself on the flame of Policy Routing. Like any good tool it requires skill, knowledge, and a good idea of what you want before you will get usable results.

CHAPTER 3

Linux Policy Routing Structures

The case for implementing Policy Routing and the related structures is easy to see. What is harder to grasp is the scope and the impact on the packet-passing paths within a TCP/IP network. The question of where and how the packets are passed from and through a network-connected device can deeply affect the points of application of Policy Routing structures.

This chapter will explore the structure that allows packets to pass through a system. Most of this discussion will center on understanding the logic of the packet traversal. At times you may need to delve into the actual operation of the system innards.

The overall structure of this chapter is written with an eye to generalize as much as possible to ease understanding across disparate systems. The implementation structure will be drawn from the posits and foundations of the need for Policy Routing as espoused to a large extent in Chapter 2, "Policy Routing Theory." Where possible the examples of usage for Policy Routing as arisen from the limitations of traditional routing will be referenced to clarify why particular Policy Routing structures exist.

The Triad Elements—Address, Route, Rule

The core of Policy Routing rests on the use of three elements. These are the traditional elements of Address and Route as extended by Policy Routing, and the additional Policy Routing element: Rule. The *address* refers to the assigned network address under the protocol in use. The *route* is the corresponding directional element for the address. And the *rule* implements the additional information provisions demanded by Policy Routing.

These three elements comprise the structure around which the implementation of Policy Routing is built. All three play unique roles that can act singularly, but they are most effective when combined. The interactions between these elements provide the flexibility, and the complexity, seen in Policy Routing.

The order in which you look at these elements determines the output you derive from the system. Because each element is totally independent of the others, you can consider the effects of each on the system. The interactions then add the extra dimension to complete the scope. In Chapter 5, "Simple Network Examples," and Chapter 6, "Complex Network Examples," you will actually implement some real examples using these elements individually and then in concert. To understand the implementation details you need to understand first the background of each element.

Address

The first element of the triad is address. This element refers to the actual identification of a set of services. The address specifies the object that is acting or is acted upon. This sounds very general, but you must step back and consider how any service is provided on a network.

For example, consider how you access a Web server on the current IPv4 Internet. The first step is usually to try to connect to the system. You type the protocol and address into your browser, such as http://www.policyrouting.org. Then your browser asks your DNS server to resolve the name. Resolving the name means that the browser is asking for the IP address associated with that name; that is, you are requesting the http service from that IP address.

Now that IP address may not have anything to do with any physical machine. In Chapter 5 you will actually run through examples of this type of behavior. But for the moment consider what use you are making of this address. To your browser it serves as a marker that defines where the browser should go to look for the information it is seeking. It defines to your browser the location of that service.

Up to this point you have looked at the destination address. This is one of two core parts of the traditional routing. As you saw in Chapter 1, "Basic IPv4 Routing," traditional routing is destination based. And in traditional routing, the destination implicitly and explicitly referred to is the destination IP address within the packet header.

To see the depth of this statement, suppose that you have decided to implement a new packet header for your new "SuperTrad" traditional IPv4 router. This header will be added as a wrapper when the packet traverses a "SuperTrad"-only network. Don't laugh unless you too remember systems such as ProNet, the fight between NetBEUI and NetBIOS, or have tried to import an EIGRP-only network into a gated environment. In your new header you decide that all you need is the destination IP address and checksum of the whole packet. After all, nothing else matters to the routing. This packet would function fine in almost all of the routing cases in IPv4 for the last twenty years.

Now you come to Policy Routing. In Policy Routing, as it should have been in traditional routing, both of the addresses within the IPv4 packet header are important. Indeed, the entire packet header can be used to define a route. This elevates the source IP address to the same intense scrutiny as the destination. If you think about it, if the source address had been as important in traditional routing as the destination address you would not see any spoofed addresses. After all, when a router is paying attention to the source address and it is looking for a specific set of source addresses, using a faked source address (spoofing) is limited to a small set of internal source addresses. That legal set could be shrunk to one address, which makes spoofing impossible.

Both of the addresses provided in an IPv4 and IPv6 packet are important in Policy Routing. And the importance is not limited to the actual single address itself. There is a whole method for specifying groups of addresses similar to the way you specify networks. The notation used is the same—CIDR (Classless InterDomain Routing).

The result of applying a CIDR scope to an address is used to associate the address with the network as it needs to be defined for the purpose of implementing the Policy Routing structure. It should not be confused with the definition of the network by a CIDR mask. In Chapter 5 there is a set of examples you can work through to see exactly how this works.

In brief, consider that the address CIDR mask has nothing to do with the network CIDR mask. If I have a network that is 192.168.1.0/24 and I decide to use the address 192.168.1.1/25, I can. I can even use the address 192.168.1.1/16. The network does not and should not care what my address scope is so long as I obey the routing rules of the network and provide the machine with the correct local network broadcast address which may differ from the address scope. For the moment, you should just remember that the scope of an address does not necessarily have anything to do with the definition of the network.

The scope of both addresses within the packet header is either explicitly stated when dealing with the address or it defaults to the network scope. In both cases, once the scope is given it associates the address with some grouping, which then defines the relevant route used. This brings you to the second core element of the Policy Routing triad—routes.

Route

Essentially, routes are little changed from the traditional variety. They code the forward method for getting to the destination address. And when you consider the larger viewpoint this makes sense. Most of the routing that is done is straightforward. You have a destination in mind and you want to get there by the best means possible.

All of the discussion in Chapter 2 merely adds to this point. When you look into Policy Routing, what you notice is that it helps you make a decision on where to route a packet based on alternate criteria. The method of actually selecting a route is changed, but the method of using the route once obtained is the same.

What is different when contrasting the Policy Routing route element with the traditional method is more versatility and flexibility in specification and destination options. The traditional route command allows you to specify a gateway and some options on the path to that gateway for a network or host destination address. Additionally, most route command implementations allow you to specify a "reject" or "denied" route option. This is essentially the same as a route lookup failure and returns an ICMP Type 3 Code 0 "network unreachable" error.

Besides the standard gateway object, in the Policy Routing schema a route may provide reference to an outgoing source address, interface, or specify an error destination. The errors returned may exist in the ICMP codes or the packet may be simply dropped or changed. When the packet is changed, the action becomes a NAT (Network Address Translation) function, which you will see in Chapter 8, "NAT Functions." The additional destinations are not required but are specified on an implementation basis. Within Linux you will see that the Policy Routing subcommand has a range of additional targets for the route object. Some of these targets refer to types of network structure such as broadcast or multicast. Others provide alternate destination targets for control such as prohibit or blackhole. You will use these features in Chapters 5 and 6 when you start to see how to implement Policy Routing structures.

For now you want to consider the route element of the Policy Routing triad as an advanced version of the traditional route structure. Indeed, for simple networks where you are providing standard routing functions the Policy Routing implementation reduces to the traditional specification. But the greater functionality is always there for use.

Rule

So if the route element is not all that different, how do you select a route using all of the advanced methods discussed in Chapter 2? Where are the route by source address, route by packet header data, and other selection mechanisms?

This is where the rule element comes into play. Think of the rule as a method for implementing ACLs (Access Control Lists) for routes. The rule allows you to specify the filters that match packets, and which route structure to select when the filter does match. Because the filter is part of the rule selection mechanism, you can also use rules to specify other advanced options such as destination targets and NAT functions.

Using a rule you can perform the most common Policy Routing function, route by source address. The rule can specify to select a packet based on whether or not the source address of the packet falls into a designated address scope. If it does match, the rule states which route structure to use or other destination to choose. But if you stop to think about this for a moment, you realize that on a system where you only have one routing table a rule set is usable only under limited conditions.

Multiple Routing Tables

In a single routing table system, such as current network router devices, or most operating systems, all of the routes specified are in a single group called a table. This table is then read through (in network speak the route is "looked up") sequentially and the longest match of the packet destination is made. This longest match then returns the gateway to which to forward the packet.

Suppose you have three routers to the same network. Each router has a different speed connection to your network core. Which one should you use in your routing table? Even under OSPF this type of routing structure still results in a single "best" route for the condition of use.

Consider this conundrum in a different light. Most of your network clients only need limited access to a particular network. They would be fine on a slow link. A select group of your network clients needs a higher rate access to this network. If you have only one routing table, you can only put in one route to this destination network. Which one do you use? In this case even if you use rules to select the traffic, where are you going to end up sending them? To the routing table.

Thus the implementation of the rule in Policy Routing implies that for true global structure you must also implement multiple routing tables. A complete Policy Routing structure is found in the Linux kernel, version 2.1 and higher. It provides full use of Address, Multiple Independent Route Tables, and a Rule selection mechanism that can interact bidirectionally with the route tables. Additionally, there are the policy actions that are contained within Cisco IOS 11.2 and above. If you are curious about this check out the Cisco documentation on the Web (http://www.cisco.com/warp/public/732/jump.shtml).

RPDB—The Linux Policy Routing Implementation

Under Linux, the implementation of Policy Routing structure is carried out through the mechanism of the Routing Policy DataBase (RPDB). The RPDB is the cohesive set of routes, route tables, and rules. Since addressing is a direct function of these elements, it also is part of the system. What the RPDB primarily does is provide the internal structure and mechanism for implementing the rule element of Policy Routing. It also provides the multiple routing tables available under Linux.

Linux with the RPDB and the complete rewrite of the IP addressing and routing structures in kernel 2.1 and higher sustains 255 routing tables, and 2^32 rules. That is one rule per IP address under IPv4. In other words, you can specify a rule to govern every single address available in the entire IPv4 address space. That works out to over 4 billion rules.

The RPDB itself operates upon the rule and route elements of the triad. In the operation of RPDB, the first element considered is the operation of the rule. The rule, as you saw, may be considered as the filter or selection agent for applying Policy Routing.

The following text about the RPDB and the definition of Policy Routing is adapted from Alexey Kuznetsov's documentation for the IPROUTE2 utility suite, with Alexey's permission. I have rewritten parts of the text to clarify some points. Any errors or omissions should be directed to me.

Classic routing algorithms used on the Internet make routing decisions based only on the destination address of packets and, in theory but not in practice, on the TOS field. In some circumstances you may want to route packets differently, depending not only on the destination addresses but also on other packet fields such as source address, IP protocol, transport protocol ports, or even packet payload. This task is called *Policy Routing*.

To solve this task, the conventional destination-based routing table, ordered according to the longest match rule, is replaced with the RPDB, which selects the appropriate route through execution of rules. These rules may have many keys of different natures, and therefore they have no natural order except that which is imposed by the network administrator. In Linux the RPDB is a linear list of rules ordered by a numeric priority value. The RPDB explicitly allows matching packet source address, packet destination address, TOS, incoming interface (which is packet meta data, rather than a packet field), and using fwmark values for matching IP protocols and transport ports. Fwmark is the packet filtering tag that you will use in Chapter 6 and is explained later on in this chapter in the section "System Packet Paths—IPChains/NetFilter."

Each routing policy rule consists of a selector and an action predicate. The RPDB is scanned in the order of increasing priority, with the selector of each rule applied to the source address, destination address, incoming interface, TOS, and fwmark. If the selector matches the packet, the action is performed. The action predicate may return success, in which case the rule output provides either a route or a failure indication, and RPDB lookup is then terminated. Otherwise, the RPDB program continues on to the next rule.

What is the action semantically? The natural action is to select the nexthop and the output device. This is the way a packet path route is selected by Cisco IOS; let us call it "match & set." In Linux the approach is more flexible because the action includes lookups in destination-based routing tables and selecting a route from these tables according to the classic longest match algorithm. The "match & set" approach then becomes the simplest case of Linux route selection, realized when the second level routing table contains a single default route. Remember that Linux supports multiple routing tables managed with the ip route command.

At startup, the kernel configures a default RPDB consisting of three rules:

1. Priority 0: Selector = match anything
    Action = lookup routing local table (ID 255)
    The local table is the special routing table containing high priority control routes for local and broadcast addresses.
    Rule 0 is special; it cannot be deleted or overridden.
2. Priority 32766: Selector = match anything
    Action = lookup routing main table (ID 254)
    The main table is the normal routing table containing all non-policy routes.
    This rule may be deleted or overridden with other rules.
3. Priority 32767: Selector = match anything

Action = lookup routing table `default` (ID 253)

The table `default` is empty and reserved for post-processing if previous default rules did not select the packet. This rule also may be deleted.

Do not mix routing tables and rules. Rules point to routing tables, several rules may refer to one routing table, and some routing tables may have no rules pointing to them. If you delete all the rules referring to a table, then the table is not used but still exists. A routing table will disappear only after all the routes contained within it are deleted.

Each RPDB entry has additional attributes attached. Each rule has a pointer to some routing table. NAT and masquerading rules have the attribute to select a new IP address to translate/masquerade. Additionally, rules have some of the optional attributes that routes have, such as realms. These values do not override those contained in routing tables; they are used only if the route did not select any of those attributes.

The RPDB may contain rules of the following types:

- `unicast`—The rule prescribes returning the route found in the routing table referenced by the rule.
- `blackhole`—The rule prescribes dropping a packet silently.
- `unreachable`—The rule prescribes generating the error `Network is unreachable`.
- `prohibit`—The rule prescribes generating the error `Communication is administratively prohibited`.
- `nat`—The rule prescribes translating the source address of the IP packet to some other value.

You will see how these rule actions operate primarily in Chapters 5 and 6. There you will make hands-on use of the command set and implement several Policy Routing structures.

The RPDB was the first implementation of and first mention within the Linux community of the concept of Policy Routing. When you consider that the `ip` utility was first released in late spring of 1997, and that Alexey's documentation was released in April of 1999 coinciding with the official Linux 2.2 kernel release in May of 1999, then you realize that the Linux Policy Routing structure is already over four years old. In Internet time that is considered almost ancient. But as with most new network subjects, such as IPv6 and Policy Routing, Linux leads the way.

The RPDB itself was an integral part of the rewrite of the networking stack in Linux kernel 2.2. The way in which the Policy Routing extensions are accessed is through a defined set of additional control structures within the Linux kernel. These are the `NETLINK` and `RT_NETLINK` objects and related constructs. If you are curious about the programmatic details you can look through the source to the `ip` utility itself. The call structure and reference to the kernel internals is laid out quite well.

One of the important features that makes the RPDB implementation so special is that it is completely backward-compatible with the standard network utilities. You do not need to use the `ip` utility to perform standard networking tasks on your system. You can use `ifconfig` and `route` and get along quite fine. In fact, you can even compile the kernel without the `NETLINK` family objects and still use standard networking tools. It is only when you need to use the full features of the RPDB that you need to use the appropriate utility.

This backward compatibility is due to the RPDB being a complete replacement of the Linux networking structure, especially as it relates to routing. The addressing modalities for Policy Routing, as discussed in the "Address" section earlier in this chapter (and illustrated in depth in Chapter 5), were also implemented as part of this change. But the main changes, besides the addition of the rule element, were the changes to the route element. Drawing upon Alexey's documentation again I provide the following information on the route element construct.

In the RPDB, each route entry has a key consisting of the protocol prefix, which is the pairing of the network address and network mask length, and optionally the TOS value. An IP packet matches the route if the highest bits of the packet's destination address are equal to the route prefix, at least up to the prefix length, and if the TOS of the route is zero or equal to the TOS of the packet.

If several routes match the packet, the following pruning rules are used to select the best one:

1. The longest matching prefix is selected; all shorter ones are dropped.
2. If the TOS of some route with the longest prefix is equal to the TOS of the packet, routes with different TOSes are dropped.
3. If no exact TOS match is found and routes with TOS=0 exist, the rest of the routes are pruned. Otherwise the route lookup fails.
4. If several routes remain after steps 1–3 have been tried, then routes with the best preference value are selected.
5. If several routes still exist, then the first of them is selected.

Note the ambiguity of action 5. Unfortunately, Linux historically allowed such a bizarre situation. The sense of the word "the first" depends on the literal order in which the routes were added to the routing table, and it is practically impossible to maintain a bundle of such routes in any such order.

For simplicity we will limit ourselves to the case wherein such a situation is impossible, and routes are uniquely identified by the triplet of prefix, TOS, and preference. Using the `ip` command for route creation and manipulation makes it impossible to create non-unique routes.

One useful exception to this rule is the default route on non-forwarding hosts. It is "officially" allowed to have several fallback routes in cases when several routers are present on directly connected networks. In this case, Linux performs "dead gateway detection" as controlled by Neighbour Unreachability Detection (nud) and references from the transport protocols to select the working router. Thus the ordering of the routes is not essential. However, in this specific case it is not recommended that you manually fiddle with default routes but instead use the Router Discovery protocol.

Actually, Linux IPv6 does not even allow user-level applications access to default routes.

Of course, the preceding route selection steps are not performed in exactly this sequence. The routing table in the kernel is kept in a data structure that allows the final result to be achieved with minimal cost. Without depending on any particular routing algorithm implemented in the kernel, we can summarize the sequence as this: Route is identified by the triplet {prefix,tos,preference} key, which uniquely locates the route in the routing table.

Each route key refers to a routing information record. The routing information record contains the data required to deliver IP packets, such as output device and next hop router, and additional optional attributes, such as path MTU (Maximum Transmission Unit) or the preferred source address for communicating to that destination.

It is important that the set of required and optional attributes depends on the route type. The most important route type is a unicast route, which describes real paths to other hosts. As a general rule, common routing tables contain only unicast routes. However, other route types with different semantics do exist. The full list of types understood by the Linux kernel is as follows:

- unicast—The route entry describes real paths to the destinations covered by the route prefix.
- unreachable—These destinations are unreachable; packets are discarded and the ICMP message host unreachable (ICMP Type 3 Code 1) is generated. The local senders get error EHOSTUNREACH.
- blackhole—These destinations are unreachable; packets are silently discarded. The local senders get error EINVAL.
- prohibit—These destinations are unreachable; packets are discarded and the ICMP message communication administratively prohibited (ICMP Type 3 Code 13) is generated. The local senders get error EACCES.
- local—The destinations are assigned to this host, the packets are looped back and delivered locally.
- broadcast—The destinations are broadcast addresses, the packets are sent as link broadcasts.
- throw—Special control route used together with policy rules. If a throw route is selected, then lookup in this particular table is terminated, pretending that no route was found. Without any Policy Routing, it is equivalent to the absence of the route in the routing table, the packets are dropped, and ICMP message net unreachable (ICMP Type 3 Code 0) is generated. The local senders get error ENETUNREACH.
- nat—Special NAT route. Destinations covered by the prefix are considered as dummy (or external) addresses, which require translation to real (or internal) ones before forwarding. The addresses to translate to are selected with the attribute via.
- anycast (not implemented)—The destinations are anycast addresses assigned to this host. They are mainly equivalent to local addresses, with the difference

that such addresses are invalid to be used as the source address of any packet.

- multicast—Special type, used for multicast routing. It is not present in normal routing tables.

Linux can place routes within multiple routing tables identified by a number in the range from 1 to 255 or by a name taken from the file /etc/iproute2/rt_tables. By default all normal routes are inserted to the table main (ID 254), and the kernel uses only this table when calculating routes.

Actually, another routing table always exists that is invisible but even more important. It is the local table (ID 255). This table consists of routes for local and broadcast addresses. The kernel maintains this table automatically, and administrators should not ever modify it and do not even need to look at it in normal operation.

In Policy Routing, the routing table identifier becomes effectively one more parameter added to the key triplet {prefix,tos,preference}. Thus, under Policy Routing the route is obtained by {tableid,key triplet}, identifying the route uniquely. So you can have several identical routes in different tables that will not conflict, as was mentioned earlier in the description of action 5 and "the first" mechanism associated with action 5.

These changes to the route element provide one of the core strengths of the RPDB, multiple independent route tables. As you will see in Chapter 5, the rule element alone can only perform a selection or filter operation. It is still up to the route to indicate where the packet needs to go next. Adding on top of these elements the QoS mechanisms to determine and set the TOS field and the ability to route by the TOS field provides you with the most powerful and flexible routing structure available under IPv4 and IPv6.

In summary, the RPDB is the core facility for implementing Policy Routing under Linux. The RPDB streamlines the mechanism of dealing with rules and multiple route tables. All operations of the rule and route structure are centralized into a single point of access and control. The addition of various alternate actions and destinations for routes and rules through the RPDB allows you to fine-tune the mechanism of Policy Routing without needing to hack sections of the networking code.

System Packet Paths—IPChains/NetFilter

Understanding the RPDB brings up the question of at what point within the system the RPDB operates. To understand this within the context of the system you need to first see the logic of packet traversal within the system. The best way to approach this traversal is to consider how the packet filtering mechanisms treat this flow.

The various packet filtering mechanisms within the Linux kernel structures deal directly with the conceptualization of the packet flow as a means to identify the control points. They do this so that they may apply their security mechanisms at the control points. These control points are also of interest to the Policy Routing structure because these are the same control points that you would think to operate upon with Policy Routing structures.

IPChains—Kernel 2.1/2.2

Start by considering the logical structure of the packet filtering mechanism within the Linux 2.1/2.2 kernel series. This kernel series is also the one within which the RPDB was implemented and the full scope of Policy Routing structures was developed. The relevant mechanism is that of IPChains. As the name implies, the IPChains packet filtering mechanism considers the implementation of logical control through "chains" of commands implemented to operate upon the defined control points.

The conceptual model is taken from the older IPFWADM model that was implemented in the Linux 1.3/2.0 series kernels. The model describes the traversal of a packet within the system by differentiating between two distinct types of packet sourcing. The first type of packet is one that originates externally to the system and then traverses the system. The second type of packet is one that is either originated from within the system or is originated externally but ends within the system.

This differentiation of origination actually suits the consideration of Policy Routing structures very well. There is a difference when a packet is sourced from the internal system as opposed to a transverse packet passing through the system. Suppose, for example, that you want to apply TOS tagging to the packet. The point at which you apply the tagging would be different for an internally generated packet than for one that passes through the system. In both cases, however, you will probably generate the tagging at an interface.

The concept as proposed with the release of IPFWADM and extended by IPChains is that there are three primary locations in the packet path: the INPUT, OUTPUT, and FORWARD chains. These are the locations at which you would want to intercept the packet. A transverse packet that crosses through the system crosses all three chains, whereas a packet that originates from within the system only crosses two.

Considering again the transverse packet, the logic of traversal is as shown in Figure 3.1.

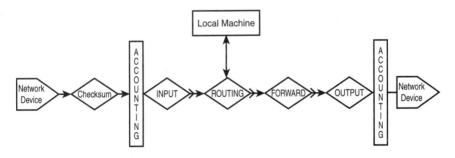

Figure 3.1

Packet paths for IPv4 packet filters in Linux 2.1/2.2.

You can see the three main chains: INPUT, OUTPUT, and FORWARD. Think again of the differentiation of the packet paths. Any packet can take one of three paths through the system:

1. A packet externally sourced that is destined for a service on this machine will enter the system, pass through INPUT, and be routed to the Local Machine.
2. A packet internally sourced that is destined for an external destination will be routed to OUTPUT.
3. A transverse packet will pass through INPUT, FORWARD, and OUTPUT, in that order.

Now a note on the actual logic of the packet paths. In all of these considerations the most important one is the location of the ROUTING diamond. This is the location of the RPDB. A packet filter may act on packets entering the system through the INPUT chain. And it may act on packets exiting the system through the OUTPUT chain. But the FORWARD chain actions are modified by the result of the output from the ROUT-ING. You will go through the examples of how to change the NAT and IP MAS-QUERADE addresses using this logic in Chapter 8. For now, you should note that the actions of the ROUTING control the connectivity to the Local Machine and also the connectivity to the FORWARD chain.

So using the IPChains packet filter you can modify and preselect the packets that are seen by the RPDB. Thus this acts as an extension of the RPDB rules. One of the more powerful features is the allowance in the RPDB rules to act upon a fwmark. A fwmark is a binary code set in the packet header by the packet filter software. Using this fwmark you can implement packet filter routing mechanisms. An even more powerful feature is the use of the u32 classifier for setting the TOS field in the packet. You will use both of these functions in Chapter 6 to perform advanced selection.

All of these types of tagging functions take place at the INPUT or OUTPUT chains. Now the interactions with the RPDB are only within the ROUTING section, but the interactions with Policy Routing are throughout the system. Consider the example of applying TOS tagging to the packet. If the packet is locally sourced, you would apply the TOS tag after the OUTPUT chain because that is where the tc utility operates. Conversely, for traversal packets you can apply the TOS tag either before the INPUT or after the OUTPUT chain. Also the IP MASQUERADE function of IPChains is applied within the FORWARD chain while the related NAT functions of the RPDB are applied within the ROUTING diamond. These concepts will become points of con-tention in Chapter 8.

NetFilter—Kernel 2.3/2.4

This contention of packet path location brings up the latest iteration of packet filtering in Linux. NetFilter is the extension of the traditional IPChains with a complete rewrite of the functionality especially with respect to the NAT and IP MASQUERADING functions. The new concept is to consider pure packet selection mechanisms as defin-ing packet filtering while defining any packet selection mechanisms that change the packet information as packet mangling. This makes sense from many standpoints. It even casts a good light on the traditional split of consideration between routing and TOS/QoS structures as you will see in Chapter 6.

What NetFilter does is make this division of function obvious. Consider the packet paths in Figure 3.2.

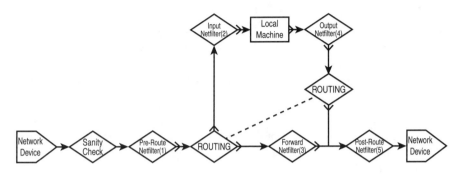

Figure 3.2

Packet paths for IPv4 packet filters in Linux 2.3/2.4.

Note that the dotted line tying together the two routing diamonds indicates that these are the same function, the RPDB. The reason for the split is that the routing function is entered in different places in the packet path.

This is due to another change in the packet path policy within NetFilter. The Input(2) and Output(4) chains now only refer to the Local Machine. When you consider that the primary function of a firewall is to protect machines behind it, and that implies transverse packets, then the packet path for NetFilter is much cleaner. Additionally, by placing the INPUT and OUTPUT chains as operating only upon the Local Machine you can create secured server machines.

Consider the path for a transverse packet. It enters the system and is processed by the entrance packet mangling and tagging stage, Pre-Route(1). This stage is where you would apply packet mangling operations such as fwmark and TOS/QoS tagging. The packet then enters the RPDB to obtain routing. From the RPDB it enters the primary firewall chain, Forward(3). The Forward chain is where the firewalling decisions are made. After the Forward chain it enters the exit packet mangling and tagging stage, Post-Route(5). The Pre-Route and Post-Route locations are where you would also apply NAT and IP MASQUERADING functions. Note that these NAT functions are not the same as the RPDB NAT. Indeed, if you want to really confuse matters you can apply both RPDB NAT and NetFilter NAT. You will try this in Chapter 8.

This transverse packet path, assuming you do not do any packet mangling, only then needs to be inspected by two entities, the RPDB and the Forward firewall chain. This is a great improvement in speed and logic when you start considering the interactions of Policy Routing and firewalling. For the purposes of a secured service machine, things are also more logically handled.

Consider the path for an externally sourced packet destined for an internal service. It enters the system and is processed by the entrance packet mangling and tagging stage, Pre-Route(1). This stage is where you would apply packet mangling operations such as fwmark and TOS/QoS tagging or perhaps the NetFilter NAT. The packet then enters the RPDB to obtain routing and is routed to the Input(2) chain. The Input chain provides the firewalling functions for packets destined to the Local Machine services.

The reverse scenario is the packet path for an internal service sourced packet destined for an external system, such as the reply packet to the one described in the previous paragraph. It exits the Local Machine and enters the Output(4) chains, which provides the firewalling functions. It then enters the RPDB for route processing and exits the system via the exit packet mangling and tagging stage, Post-Route(5).

Note that in all of these packet paths, the packet never crosses through more than one packet filter chain, and that in all cases the packet does get processed by the RPDB. So all of the functions associated with the Policy Routing structures under the RPDB may be applied to the packet.

Summary

You have seen the fundamental triad of Policy Routing and how these elements are implemented within the Linux kernel through the RPDB. You then traced through the logic of the packet paths for the packet filters and the RPDB action locations. Now you understand the logic of the traffic flow for Policy Routing in Linux.

Chapter 4, "IPROUTE2 Utility for Linux," will cover the usage and operation of the `ip` utility from Alexey Kuznetsov. This is the main utility implementing all of Policy Routing with the exception of TOS/QoS. Within the utility suite, however, is the `tc` utility, which performs all of the TOS/QoS functions of Policy Routing. After you have learned about the `ip` utility you will start to delve into hands-on experiences with Policy Routing by implementing a series of increasingly complex examples.

CHAPTER 4

IPROUTE2 Utility for Linux

This chapter covers the tool used in Linux for implementing Policy Routing. Because there are few other sources of information on this utility, this chapter's primary use will be as a reference on the command syntax and usage. As I illustrate the utility I will include examples of usage as well as notations about interactions with other networking utilities within Linux.

The utility used under Linux to implement Policy Routing is named `ip` as in the `ip` command from Cisco IOS. This utility was written by Alexey N. Kuznetsov, who also wrote the IPv6 and IPv4 routing code for Linux kernels starting with the 2.1 series. The `ip` utility can be used to provide all of the standard IPv4 functions discussed in Chapter 1, "Basic IPv4 Routing." As you will see in the rest of this book, I will make exclusive use of this utility for all IPv4 and IPv6 configuration needs.

NOTE

The `ip` utility was specifically written for directly manipulating the Linux network internals through the `netlink` facility. This facility is provided in all Linux kernel series from 2.1 onward. In order to use the `ip` utility or any of the related `netlink` utilities, you must have both `NETLINK` and `RTNETLINK` defined in your kernel configuration. These options appear as "Kernel/User netlink socket" and "Routing messages" in the 2.1 and higher kernel `menuconfig` or `xconfig`. The kernel on the included distribution has all of these and other advanced routing options selected. If you would like you can use the `.config` file from that kernel to see which options are needed.

You first will learn where to obtain and compile the `ip` utility. I then document those uses of the utility covered in this book. These sections draw heavily upon Kuznetsov's own documentation of the command itself, with occasional additional discussion and examples provided. Note that many of the uses of the command are not covered in this book, therefore some of the command documentation is used in order to make the examples and exercises understandable. No man pages currently exist for the `ip` command and Kuznetsov's own current documentation is only available in LaTeX format. With Kuznetsov's permission I have edited and expanded the LaTeX documentation into the sections found here and elsewhere in the book. If there are errors in these sections, they belong to my translation and should be addressed to me first.

Obtaining and Compiling IPROUTE2

The `ip` utility is just one of the utilities in the IPROUTE2 utility package from Alexey Kuznetsov. The primary FTP site is located in Russia at `ftp://ftp.inr.ac.ru/ip-routing/`, and mirrors exist all over the world. You will need to obtain the latest package, usually called `iproute2-current.tar.gz`, symlinked to the latest dated version. The version covered here is the 2000-10-07 version of IPROUTE2. Note that unless you have a custom compiled kernel with all of the advanced routing elements selected, most of the examples here and in the rest of the book will not work. See Appendix B, "Source Code Listings and Locations," for the options you will need in your kernel.

Once you have the utility, you need to unpack it into whatever directory you use for compiling source code. The default is to use `/usr/src`. When you have the package untarred, you can enter the directory `iproute2` and just type **make**. You must have the kernel source code that was used to compile your current running kernel located in `/usr/src/linux`.

After you have typed `make`, the utility suite will compile. There is no `install` target for `make` so you will have to manually install the `ip` utility. The `ip` utility, as with all of the utilities in this package, should be installed into the `/sbin` directory. This is so that they are available even before your `/usr` directory is mounted. There is also a `/etc/iproute2` directory in the package that contains sample definition files. If you do not have a `/etc/iproute2/` directory on your system, create one and copy the contents of the package directory to the new directory. If an `/etc/iproute2/` directory exists and you do not know what it is being used for, you will want to find out if the files in that directory have some meaning to the system you are running. If not, replacing them with the files in the package directory will not hurt. Of course if you are ever unsure, back up the old files.

In a nutshell, you want to perform the following steps:

1. Compile the utilities by typing **make**.
2. Check `/etc/iproute2/` with `ls -l /etc/iproute2`.
3. If needed, create `/etc/iproute2/` with `mkdir/etc/iproute2/`.
4. Populate it with `cp ./etc/iproute2/* /etc/iproute2/`.
5. Change into the `ip` directory with `cd ip`.

6. `cp ifcfg ip routef routel rtacct rtmon rtpr` /sbin.
7. Change into `tc` directory with `cd ../tc`.
8. Copy it with `cp tc` /sbin.

This will compile the utility and copy the configuration files and the executables into the appropriate directories. You should now be able to execute the `ip` utility from anywhere on the system by typing **ip**. To test and see if this worked, type **ip addr** and you should get a list of the interfaces and addresses on your system.

General Command Structure

The `ip` utility has a global syntax structure that will be quite familiar to anyone that has ever configured a Cisco router using IOS. All of the commands start with `ip` followed by the appropriate object, such as `addr` or `route`, then followed by the arguments and information needed to perform the function. All IPv4 addresses and networks are specified using CIDR syntax, for example 127.0.0.1/8 for the loopback interface and network. All IPv6 addresses and network may be specified using collapsed notation (see Chapter 9, "IPv6").

This chapter presents a comprehensive description of the `ip` utility objects that you will be using. You will start by going through most of the `ip` commands in extreme detail, covering the `link`, `addr`, `route`, `rule`, `neigh`, `tunnel`, `multicast`, and `monitor` objects (detailed in Table 4.1). The most important of these are the `addr`, `route`, and `rule` objects because they form the heart of the Policy Routing implementation structure under Linux, the Triad. The other objects are included here for reference—you will be making use of them in the examples and exercises.

Table 4.1   `ip` *Utility Objects*

Object	Description
link	Network Device
addr	IP Address (Triad #1)
route	Routes (Triad #2)
rule	Rules (Triad #3)
neigh	ARP Neighbors Table
tunnel	IP Tunnels
multicast	IP Multicast
monitor	Debug and Tracking

These sections will be different from the style you have seen up to this point because of the nature of the command syntax of the `ip` command. As of August 2000 there are no man pages for `ip`, and the documentation is only available in LaTeX format. If you have read the `ip-cref.tex` document that Kuznetsov has written as included in 1999-03-08 distribution or newer of IPROUTE2, feel free to just skim through most of this section. I have extended the discussion and examples somewhat, but the core is taken from `ip-cref.tex`. If you have any questions or comments about the examples or statements in this section, please direct them to me.

IP Global Command Syntax

The generic form of the `ip` command is

`ip [ options ] object [ command [ arguments ]]`

Options

Options is a multivalued set of modifiers that affect the general behavior and output of the `ip` utility. All options begin with the - character and may be used both in long and abbreviated forms. Currently the following options are available:

- `-V, -Version`—Print the version of the `ip` utility and exit.
- `-s, -stats, -statistics`—Output more information.
  This option may be repeated to increase the verbosity level of the output. As a rule, the additional information is device or function statistics or values. In many cases the values output should be considered in the same sense as output from the `/proc/` directory, where the name of the value is not directly related to the value itself.
- `-f, -family {inet, inet6, link}`—Enforce which protocol family to use. If this option is not present, the protocol family output to use is guessed from the other command-line arguments. If the rest of the command line does not provide sufficient information to guess a protocol family, the `ip` command falls back to a default family of `inet` in the case of network protocols. `link` is a special family identifier meaning that no networking protocol is involved. There are several shortcuts for this option, as listed here:
    `-4`—Shortcut for `-family inet`.
    `-6`—Shortcut for `-family inet6`.
    `-0`—Shortcut for `-family link`.

- `-o, -oneline`—Format the output records as single lines by replacing any line feeds with the \ character.
  This option is to provide a convenient method for sending the command output through a pipe—for example, when you want to count the number of output records with `wc` or you want to `grep` through the output.
- `-r, -resolve`—Use system name resolution to output DNS names.
  Note that `ip` itself never uses DNS to resolve names to addresses. This option exists for convenience only.

Object

This is the most important part of the `ip` command line. Object is the object type on which you want to operate or obtain information. The object types understood by the current `ip` utility are `link`, `addr`, `neigh`, `route`, `rule`, `maddr`, `mroute`, and `tunnel`.

- `link`—Physical or logical network device.
- `addr`—Protocol (IPv4 or IPv6) address on a device.
- `neigh`—ARP or NDISC cache entry.
- `route`—Routing table entry.

- `rule`—Rule in routing policy database.
- `maddr`—Multicast address.
- `mroute`—Multicast routing cache entry.
- `tunnel`—Tunnel over IP.

The names of all of the objects may be written in full or abbreviated form. For example, `addr` may be abbreviated as `ad` or just `a`. Within each section as the commands are illustrated the usable abbreviations are shown. However, I strongly recommend that when you use the `ip` command within scripts, you make it a habit to always use the full command-line specification. Using the abbreviations is easy on the command line but harder to easily read and understand within scripts. Since you may not be the only person who ever has to deal with your scripts, you should strive to make them as complete as possible.

Command

Command specifies the action to perform on the object. The set of possible actions depends on the object type. Typically it is possible to `add`, `delete`, and `show` (`list`) the object(s), but some objects will not allow all of these operations and many have additional actions and commands. Note that the command syntax `help`, which is available for all objects, prints out the full list of available commands and argument syntax conventions. If no command is given, a default command is assumed. The default command is usually `show` (`list`) but if the objects of the class cannot be listed, the default is to print out the command syntax help.

Arguments

Arguments is the list of command options specific to the command. The arguments depend on the command and the object. There are two types of arguments that can be issued:

- **Flags**—These are abbreviated with a single keyword.
- **Parameters**—These consist of a keyword followed by a value.

Each command has a default parameter that is used if the arguments are omitted. For example, the `dev` parameter is the default for the `ip link` command; thus `ip link list eth0` is equivalent to `ip link list dev eth0`. Within all the following command descriptions, I distinguish default parameters with the marker (default) next to the default command.

As previously mentioned for the names of objects, all keywords may be abbreviated with the first or first few unique letters. These shortcuts are convenient when `ip` is used interactively, but they are not recommended for use in scripts, and please do not use them when reporting bugs or asking for help. Officially allowed abbreviations are listed along with the first mention of the command.

Error Conditions

The `ip` command most commonly fails for the following reasons:

The command-line syntax is wrong. This is often due to using an unknown keyword, an incorrectly formatted TCP/IP address, a wrong keyword argument for the command, and so on. In that case, the `ip` command exits without performing any actions and prints out an error message containing information about the reason for failure. In some cases it prints out the command syntax help.

The arguments did not pass self-consistency verification.

`ip` failed to compile a kernel request from the arguments due to insufficient user-provided information.

The kernel returned an error to a syscall. In that case, `ip` prints the error message as it was output from `perror(3)`, prefixed with a comment and the syscall identifier.

The kernel returned an error to a `RTNETLINK` request. In that case, `ip` prints the error message as it was output from `perror(3)`, prefixed with `RTNETLINK` answers.

NOTE

Note that all `ip` command operations are atomic. This means that if the `ip` command fails, it does not change anything in the system. One harmful exception is the `ip link` command, which may change only part of the device parameters given on the command line. I will mention this again in the section on `ip link` usage and recommend that all `ip link` actions be performed individually. This is actually a preferred use for the `ip` command in general. If you need to perform many repetitions of the command, use a script loop or a script. Then, any generated error messages can be associated with the appropriate `ip` command action.

It is difficult to list all possible error messages, especially the syntax errors. As a rule, their meaning should be clear from the context of the command that was issued. For example, if you issue the command `ip link sub eth0` with the obvious misspelling of `set`, you get the error message `Command "sub" is unknown, try "ip link help"`, which should prompt you to check your command syntax.

In using the `ip` command there are several facilities that need to be present for the command to perform its functions. The `ip` command talks to the kernel through the `NETLINK` interface. This is turned on by the `NETLINK` and `RNETLINK` options discussed in the beginning of this chapter. If the `ip` command does not work or you get an error message, you do not have the needed functions defined or your kernel is not the one you compiled. The most common mistakes are

- `NETLINK` is not configured in the kernel. The error message is `Cannot open netlink socket Invalid value`.
- `RTNETLINK` is not configured in the kernel. In that case, one of the following messages may be printed, depending on the actual command issued:

  `Cannot talk to rtnetlink Connection refused`

  `Cannot send dump request Connection refused`

Now that you have seen the overview of the command syntax it is time to delve into the details. The following sections detail the usage of the command syntax elements and give some examples.

ip link—Network Device Configuration

A link refers to a network device. The ip link object and the corresponding command set allow you to view and manipulate the state of network devices. There are just two commands for the link object: set and show.

The full help syntax which you may want to refer back to for ip link is as follows:

```
Usage: ip link set DEVICE { up | down | arp { on | off } |
                          dynamic { on | off } |
                          multicast { on | off } | txqueuelen PACKETS |
                          name NEWNAME |
                          address LLADDR | broadcast LLADDR |
                          mtu MTU }
      ip link show [ DEVICE ]
```

ip link set—Change Device Attributes

This command allows you to change device attributes.

Abbreviations: set, s

WARNING

You can request multiple parameter changes with ip link. If you request multiple parameter changes and any ONE change fails, ip aborts immediately after the failure. Thus, the parameter changes prior to the failure have completed and are not backed out on abort. This is the only case where using the ip command can leave your system in an unpredictable state. The solution is to avoid changing multiple parameters with one ip link set call. Use as many individual ip link set commands as necessary to perform the actions you want.

Arguments

- dev *NAME* (default)—*NAME* specifies the network device to operate on, for example: eth0.
- up/down—Change the state of the device to up or down.
- arp on/arp off—Change NOARP flag status on the device.
  Note that this operation is not allowed if the device is already in the up state. Since neither the ip utility nor the kernel checks for this condition, you can get very unpredictable results changing the flag while the device is running. It is better to set the device down, then issue this command.
- multicast on/multicast off—Change the MULTICAST flag on the device.
- dynamic on/dynamic off—Change the DYNAMIC flag on the device.
- name *NAME*—Change the name of the device.
  Note that this operation is not recommended if the device is running or has some addresses already configured. You can break your system's security and inadvertently modify other networking daemons and programs by changing the device name while the device is running or has addressing assigned.

- txqueuelen *NUMBER*/txqlen *NUMBER*—Change the transmit queue length of the device.
- mtu *NUMBER*—Change the MTU (maximum transfer unit) of the device.
- address *LLADDRESS*—Change the station address of the interface.
- broadcast *LLADDRESS*, brd *LLADDRESS*, or peer *LLADDRESS*—Change the link layer broadcast address (or peer address in the case of a POINTOPOINT interface).

  Note that, for most physical network devices (ethernet, token ring, and so on), changing the link layer broadcast address will break networking. Do not use this argument if you do not understand what this operation really does.

The ip command does not allow changing the PROMISC and ALLMULTI flags, which are considered obsolete and should not be changed administratively.

Examples

To change the station address of the interface dummy:

```
ip link set dummy address 000000000001
```

To start the interface dummy:

```
ip link set dummy up
```

ip link show—Look at Device Attributes

This command allows you to look at the device attributes.

Abbreviations: show, list, lst, sh, ls, l

Arguments

This command only has two arguments:

- dev *NAME* (default)—*NAME* specifies the network device to show. If this argument is omitted, the command lists all the devices.
- up—Display only running interfaces.

Example

```
kuznet@alisa~:$ ip link ls dummy
2: dummy: <BROADCAST,NOARP> mtu 1500 qdisc noop
    link/ether 00:00:00:00:00:00 brd ff:ff:ff:ff:ff:ff
```

The number followed by a colon is the interface index or *ifindex*. This number uniquely identifies the interface. If you look at the output from cat /proc/net/dev, you will see that the network devices are listed in the same order as the numbering you see here. After the ifindex is the interface name (eth0, sit0, and so on). The interface name is also unique at any given moment; however, interfaces may disappear from the list, such as when the corresponding driver module is unloaded, and another interface with the same name will be created later. Additionally, with the ip link set *DEVICE* name *NEWNAME* command, the system administrator may change the device's name.

The interface name may also have another name or the keyword NONE appended after an @ symbol. This signifies that this device is bound to another device in a master/slave device relationship. Thus, packets sent through this device are encapsulated and forwarded via the master device. If the name is NONE, the master device is unknown.

After the interface name you see the flags associated with the device. Then comes the interface mtu, which determines the maximum size of a data packet that can be sent as a single packet over this interface.

qdisc (queuing discipline) shows which queuing algorithm is used on the interface. In particular, the keyword noqueue means that this interface does not queue anything. The keyword noop indicates that the interface is in blackhole mode, in which all of the packets sent to it are immediately discarded. The queueing disciplines refer to the QoS setup for the device.

The qlen indicates the default transmit queue length of the device, measured in packets.

The flags that are shown within the angle brackets show the actual kernel associated status of the device. The most applicable flags are as follows:

- UP—This device is turned on, ready to accept packets for transmission onto the network. It also may receive packets from other nodes on the network.
- LOOPBACK—The interface does not communicate to other hosts. All the packets that are sent through it will be returned to the sender, and only bounced-back packets can be received.
- BROADCAST—This device is able to send packets to all other hosts sharing the same physical link, for example, Ethernet.
- POINTOPOINT—The network has only two ends with two nodes attached. All the packets sent to the link will reach the peer link, and all packets received are originated by the peer.
  If neither LOOPBACK nor BROADCAST nor POINTOPOINT is set, the interface is assumed to be a NBMA (Non-Broadcast Multi-Access) link. NBMA is the most generic (and also the most complicated) type of device type, because a host attached to a NBMA link cannot send information to any other host without additional manually provided configuration information.
- MULTICAST—An advisory flag noting that the interface is aware of multicasting. Broadcasting is a particular case of multicasting in which the multicast group contains all of the nodes on the link as members. Note that software must *NOT* interpret the absence of this flag as the incapability of the interface to multicast. Any POINTOPOINT or BROADCAST link is multicasting by definition, because you have direct access to all the link neighbors and thus to any particular group of them. The use of high-bandwidth multicast transfers is not recommended on broadcast-only networks because of the high expense associated with the transmission, but such use is not strictly prohibited.
- PROMISC—The device listens and feeds to the kernel all of the traffic on the link. This includes every packet on the network that passes the transceiver. Usually this mode exists only on broadcast links and is used by bridges and network monitoring devices.

- ALLMULTI—The device receives all multicast packets wandering on the link. This mode is used by multicast routers.
- NOARP—This flag is different from the other flags. It has no invariant value, and its interpretation depends on network protocols involved. As a rule, it indicates that the device does not need any address resolution and that the software or hardware knows how to deliver packets without any help from the protocol stacks.
- DYNAMIC—This is an advisory flag marking this interface as dynamically created and destroyed.
- SLAVE—This interface is bound to other interfaces in order to share link capacities.

Other flags do exist and can be seen within the angle brackets, but they are either obsolete (NOTRAILERS), not implemented (DEBUG), or specific to certain devices (MASTER, AUTOMEDIA, and PORTSEL). They do not need to be discussed here. Additionally, the values of the PROMISC and ALLMULTI flags as shown by the ifconfig utility and by the ip utility are different. The ip link list command provides the current true device state, whereas ifconfig shows the flag state that was set through ifconfig itself.

The second line of the output from the example contains information about the link layer addresses associated with the device. The first word (ether, sit) defines the interface hardware type, which then determines the format and semantics of the addresses and thus logically is part of the address itself. The default format of station and broadcast addresses (or peer addresses for POINTOPOINT links) is a sequence of hexadecimal bytes separated by colons. However, some link types may instead have their own natural address formats that are used in the presentation. For example, the addresses of IP tunnels are printed as dotted-quad IP addresses. While NBMA links have no well-defined broadcast or peer address, this field may contain useful information such as the address of a broadcast relay or the address of an ARP server. Multicast addresses are not shown by this command.

When given the option -statistics, ip will print the interface statistics as additional information in the listing. Note that you can give this option multiple times, with each repetition increasing the verbosity of output.

```
kuznet@alisa~ $ ip -s link ls eth0
3: eth0: <BROADCAST,MULTICAST,UP> mtu 1500 qdisc cbq qlen 100
    link/ether 00:a0:cc:66:18:78 brd ff:ff:ff:ff:ff:ff
    RX bytes  packets  errors  dropped overrun mcast
    2449949362 2786187  0        0       0       0
    TX bytes  packets  errors  dropped carrier collsns
    178558497  1783945  332      0       332     35172
```

The RX and TX lines summarize receiver and transmitter statistics. The information output breaks down into the following:

- bytes—The total number of bytes received or transmitted on the interface. This number wraps when the maximum length of the natural data type on the architecture is exceeded. In order to provide correct long term data from this output, these statistics should be continuously monitored. Continuous monitoring of this data requires a user-level daemon to sample the output periodically.

- packets—The total number of packets received or transmitted on the interface.
- errors—The total number of receiver or transmitter errors.
- dropped—The total number of packets dropped because of lack of resources.
- overrun—The total number of receiver overruns resulting in packet drops. As a rule, if the interface is overrun, either you have a serious problem within the kernel or your machine is too slow to handle the speed of this interface.
- mcast—The total number of received multicast packets. This option is supported only on certain devices.
- carrier—The total number of link media failures, such as those due to lost carrier.
- collsns—The total number of collision events on ethernet-like media. This number has different interpretations on other link types.
- compressed—The total number of compressed packets. It is available only for links using VJ header compression.

When you issue the -statistics option more than once, you get additional output, depending on the statistics supported by the device itself, as in the following example with ethernet:

```
kuznet@alisa~ $ ip -s -s link ls eth0
3: eth0: <BROADCAST,MULTICAST,UP> mtu 1500 qdisc cbq qlen 100
    link/ether 00:a0:cc:66:18:78 brd ff:ff:ff:ff:ff:ff
    RX bytes   packets  errors  dropped overrun mcast
    2449949362 2786187  0       0       0       0
    RX errors  length   crc     frame   fifo    missed
               0        0       0       0       0
    TX bytes   packets  errors  dropped carrier collsns
    178558497  1783945  332     0       332     35172
    TX errors  aborted  fifo    window  heartbeat
               0        0       0       332
```

In this case the error names are pure ethernetisms. Other devices may have non-zero fields in these positions, but the headers are generated independently of the device responses. It is up to the device driver to send more appropriate error messages to the system logging facility, such as is done by the token ring driver.

ip address—Protocol Address Management

address refers to a protocol (IPv4 or IPv6) address attached to a network device. Each device must have at least one address in order to use the corresponding protocol. It is possible to have several different addresses attached to one device. These addresses are not discriminated within the protocol structure, so the term *alias* is not quite appropriate for such multiple addresses. I will not refer to this situation in those terms.

Abbreviations: address, addr, a

Arguments

add, delete, flush, show (list)

The ip addr command allows you to look at the addresses and their properties on an interface. You can add new addresses and delete old ones without regard to any ordering. Later in this section you will see the concept of primary and secondary addresses as applied to Linux.

For reference as you go through the command syntax listing, here is the full ip addr help output:

```
Usage: ip addr {add|del} IFADDR dev STRING
       ip addr {show|flush} [ dev STRING ] [ scope SCOPE-ID ]
                            [ to PREFIX ] [ FLAG-LIST ] [ label PATTERN ]
IFADDR := PREFIX | ADDR peer PREFIX
          [ broadcast ADDR ] [ anycast ADDR ]
          [ label STRING ] [ scope SCOPE-ID ]
SCOPE-ID := [ host | link | global | NUMBER ]
FLAG-LIST := [ FLAG-LIST ] FLAG
FLAG  := [ permanent | dynamic | secondary | primary |
           tentative | deprecated ]
```

ip address add—Add New Protocol Address

This command is used to add a new protocol address.

Abbreviations: add, a

Arguments

- dev *NAME*—The name of the device to which you add the address.
- local *ADDRESS* (default)—The address of the interface.
  The format of the address depends on the protocol. IPv4 uses dotted quad, and IPv6 uses a sequence of hexadecimal halfwords separated by colons. *ADDRESS* may be followed by a slash and a decimal number, which encodes network prefix (netmask) length in CIDR notation. If no CIDR netmask notation is specified, the command assumes a host (/32 mask) address is specified.
- peer *ADDRESS*—The address of remote endpoint for POINTOPOINT interfaces. Again, *ADDRESS* may be followed by a slash and a decimal number, encoding the network prefix length. If a peer address is specified, then the local address cannot have a network prefix length because the network prefix is associated with the peer rather than with the local address. In other words, netmasks can only be assigned to peer addresses when specifying both peer and local addresses.
- broadcast *ADDRESS*—The broadcast address on the interface.
  The special symbols + and - can be used instead of specifying the broadcast address. In this case the broadcast address is derived either by setting all of the interface host bits to one (+) or by setting all of the interface host bits to zero (-). In most modern implementations of IPv4 networking you will want to use

the (+) setting. Unlike ifconfig, the ip command does not set a broadcast address unless explicitly requested.

- label *NAME*—Each address may be tagged with a label string.
  In order to preserve compatibility with Linux 2.0 net aliases, this string must coincide with the name of the device or must be prefixed with the device name followed by a colon (eth0:duh).
- scope *SCOPE_VALUE*—The scope of the area within which this address is valid.

The available scopes are listed in the file /etc/iproute2/rt_scopes. The predefined scope values are

- global—The address is globally valid.
- site (IPv6 only)—The address is site local, valid only inside this site.
- link—The address is link local, valid only on this link.
- host—The address is valid only inside this host.

Examples

ip addr add 127.0.0.1/8 dev lo brd + scope host adds the usual loopback address to a loopback device. The device must be enabled before this address will show up.

ip addr add 10.0.0.1/24 brd + dev eth0 adds address 10.0.0.1 with prefix length 24 (netmask 255.255.255.0) and standard broadcast to interface eth0.

ip address delete—Delete Protocol Address

This commands allows you to delete the protocol address.

Abbreviations: delete, del, d

Arguments

The arguments coincide with arguments of ip addr add. The device name is a required argument, and the rest are optional. If no arguments are given, the first address listed is deleted.

Examples

ip addr del 127.0.0.1/8 dev lo deletes the loopback address from the loopback device.

To delete all IPv4 addresses on interface eth0:

```
while ip -f inet addr del dev eth0; do
  nothing
done
```

Another method to disable all IP addresses on an interface using ip addr flush is discussed in the ip addr flush section.

ip address show—Look at Protocol Addresses

This command allows you to look at the protocol addresses.

Abbreviations: show, list, lst, sh, ls, l

Arguments

- dev *NAME* (default)—The name of the device.
- scope *SCOPE_VAL*—List only addresses with this scope.
- to *PREFIX*—List only addresses matching this prefix.
- label *PATTERN*—List only addresses with labels matching *PATTERN*. *PATTERN* is the usual shell regexp-style pattern.
- dynamic/permanent (IPv6 only)—List only addresses installed due to stateless address configuration or only permanent (not dynamic) addresses.
- tentative (IPv6 only)—List only addresses that did not pass duplicate address detection.
- deprecated (IPv6 only)—List only deprecated addresses.
- primary/secondary—List only primary (or secondary) addresses.

Example

```
kuznet@alisa~ $ ip addr ls eth0
3: eth0: <BROADCAST,MULTICAST,UP> mtu 1500 qdisc cbq qlen 100
    link/ether 00:a0:cc:66:18:78 brd ff:ff:ff:ff:ff:ff
    inet 193.233.7.90/24 brd 193.233.7.255 scope global eth0
    inet6 3ffe:2400:0:1:2a0:ccff:fe66:1878/64 scope global dynamic
       valid_lft forever preferred_lft 604746sec
    inet6 fe80::2a0:ccff:fe66:1878/10 scope link
```

The first two lines coincide with the output of ip link list, since it is only natural to interpret link layer addresses as being addresses of the protocol family AF_PACKET. The list of IPv4 and IPv6 addresses follows, accompanied by additional attributes such as scope value, flags, and address labels. Address flags are set by the kernel and cannot be changed administratively. Currently, the following flags are defined:

- secondary—This address is not used when selecting the default source address for outgoing packets. An IP address becomes secondary if another address within the same prefix (network) already exists. The first address within the prefix is primary and is the tag address for the group of all the secondary addresses. When the primary address is deleted, all of the secondarys are purged, too. See the examples in Chapter 5 "Simple Network Examples" and "Primary/Secondary Addressing Versus Multiple Addresses Explained" at the end of the ip addr section for the actual functionality of these steps.
- dynamic—The address was created due to stateless autoconfiguration. In this case, the output also contains information on the times for which the address remains valid. After the preferred lifetime (preferred_lft) expires, the address is moved to the deprecated state and, after the valid lifetime (valid_lft) expires, the address is finally invalidated.
- deprecated—The address is deprecated. It is still valid but cannot be used by newly created connections. See dynamic, above.
- tentative—The address is not used because duplicate address detection is still not complete or has failed.

`ip address flush`—Flush Protocol Addresses

This command flushes protocol addresses selected by some criteria.

Abbreviations: `flush`, `f`

Arguments

This command has the same arguments as `show`. The major difference is that this command will not run if no arguments are given. Otherwise you could delete all of your addresses by mistake. This command (and the other `flush` commands described below) are very dangerous. If you make a mistake, the command does not ask or forgive but will cruelly purge all of your addresses. Be warned!

With the option `-statistics`, the command becomes verbose and prints out the number of deleted addresses and number of processing rounds made in flushing the address list. If the `statistics` option is given twice, `ip addr flush` also dumps all of the deleted addresses in the full format, as described in the `ip addr list` section.

Examples

To delete all the addresses from private network `10.0.0.0/8`:

```
netadm@amber~ # ip -stat -stat addr flush to 10/8
2 dummy    inet 10.7.7.7/16 brd 10.7.255.255 scope global dummy
3 eth0     inet 10.10.7.7/16 brd 10.10.255.255 scope global eth0
4 eth1     inet 10.8.7.7/16 brd 10.8.255.255 scope global eth1
***Round 1, deleting 3 addresses***
***Flush is complete after 1 round***
```

Another instructive example is deleting all IPv4 addresses from all ethernet interfaces in the system:

```
netadm@amber~ # ip -4 addr flush label "eth*"
```

The last example shows how to flush all the IPv6 addresses acquired by the host from stateless address autoconfiguration after enabling forwarding or disabling autoconfiguration.

```
netadm@amber~ # ip -6 addr flush dynamic
```

Primary/Secondary Addressing Versus Multiple Addresses Explained

There are two sides to the relationship between multiple IP addresses assigned to a single device. If all of the addresses are independent of each other—in other words, they are not members explicitly of the same IP network—then they may be manipulated and used without regard to each other. If the addresses are coded to belong to the same IP network, they are considered to be in a Primary/Secondary addressing group. In such a group the first network address added will be the Primary address for that network group and all other addresses added within that group are considered Secondaries. This is best illustrated through example.

Primary/Secondary Address Groups

Consider the IPv4 network defined by 10.1.1.0/24, which contains all IPv4 addresses from 10.1.1.0 through 10.1.1.255 inclusive. On interface eth0 you define the following multiple addresses:

```
ip addr add 10.1.1.1/24 dev eth0
```

```
ip addr add 10.1.1.64/24 dev eth0
```

```
ip addr add 10.1.1.200/24 dev eth0
```

This is a Primary/Secondary addressing group. The group is the set of all addresses that belong to the IPv4 network defined by 10.1.1.0/24. The Primary address is 10.1.1.1 and all other addresses, in this case 10.1.1.64 and 10.1.1.200, are Secondary addresses. To see this you issue the **ip addr list** command for eth0.

```
ip addr list dev eth0
```

```
8: eth0: <BROADCAST,MULTICAST,UP> mtu 1500 qdisc pfifo_fast qlen 100

    link/ether 00:a0:cc:21:ee:d3 brd ff:ff:ff:ff:ff:ff

    inet 10.1.1.1/24 scope global eth0

    inet 10.1.1.64/24 scope global secondary eth0

    inet 10.1.1.200/24 scope global secondary eth0
```

Any and all other IPv4 addresses added that are defined within the IPv4 10.1.1.0/24 network through specification of an appropriate network mask are considered Secondary addresses. But the definition of the network *does not* cover all addresses within the 10.1.1.0/24 network block!

Multiple Addresses

Membership in a Primary/Secondary Address Group is defined only by administrative specification of an appropriate netmask. Thus all of the addresses assigned above are defined as belonging to the IPv4 10.1.1.0/24 network address block by virtue of the netmasks used.

So if you rerun the example above but use any other netmask then you define addresses that are not considered members of a Primary/Secondary Address Group. This is coded as follows:

```
ip addr add 10.1.1.1/24 dev eth0
```

```
ip addr add 10.1.1.64/32 dev eth0
```

```
ip addr add 10.1.1.200/16 dev eth0
```

Notice the use of a host mask (10.1.1.64/32) and a "Class B" mask (10.1.1.200/16), which should technically include the "Class C" mask (10.1.1.1/24). Now if you look at the ip addr list output you see the difference:

ip addr list dev eth0

```
8: eth0: <BROADCAST,MULTICAST,UP> mtu 1500 qdisc pfifo_fast qlen 100

    link/ether 00:a0:cc:21:ee:d3 brd ff:ff:ff:ff:ff:ff

    inet 10.1.1.1/24 scope global eth0

    inet 10.1.1.64/32 scope global eth0

    inet 10.1.1.200/16 scope global eth0
```

Note that all of these addresses are considered independent addresses. Another way of thinking about this is that each of these addresses is a Primary address for a defined IPv4 network that has no Secondary members. Thus the Primary/Secondary Address Group is only defined by administrative function.

Relationship Between Addressing Types

At this point you may be wondering why I even bother to make a distinction between these types of addressing. The reason lies both historically within the multiple addressing structure of the Linux network stack and in practical application of adding and removing addresses from interfaces.

Interface Aliases

Historically within Linux you added multiple IPv4 addresses to an interface through use of aliases. An *alias* was an interface name extension such as eth0:1. You would add an IPv4 address by defining it as the address for a specific alias. Thus in the first example of Primary/Secondary addresses above, the following definitions should exist under aliases:

```
eth0 = 10.1.1.1/24
eth0:1 = 10.1.1.64/24
eth0:2 = 10.1.1.200/24
```

And if you then took down any of the aliases you would take down all of the interfaces. This is a limitation of the ifconfig tool and the way in which IPv4 addresses are traditionally considered. This methodology has been replaced within Linux by the multiple addressing methods. But using the concept of Primary/Secondary Address Groups allows for the same behavior.

The core concept is that a Primary/Secondary Address Group is removed and treated as a single entity whereas all other multiple addresses are treated independently. Thus when you remove a Primary address from an interface you remove *all* associated Secondary addresses. As an example I will look at an interface with two Primary/Secondary Address Groups defined along with several independent multiple addresses.

First, add a Primary/Secondary Address Group for 10.1.1.0/24 to your eth0 interface:

```
ip addr add 10.1.1.1/24 dev eth0
```

```
ip addr add 10.1.1.65/24 dev eth0
```

And now you add a Primary/Secondary Address Group for 10.1.1.0/16 to your eth0 interface:

```
ip addr add 10.1.1.64/16 dev eth0
```

```
ip addr add 10.1.1.200/16 dev eth0
```

Finally, add in some other addresses within this set:

```
ip addr add 10.1.1.32/25 dev eth0
```

```
ip addr add 10.1.1.192/25 dev eth0
```

Note that these two addresses have the same netmask but are in different networks.

Now look at the address listing:

```
ip addr list dev eth0
```

```
8: eth0: <BROADCAST,MULTICAST,UP> mtu 1500 qdisc pfifo_fast qlen 100

    link/ether 00:a0:cc:21:ee:d3 brd ff:ff:ff:ff:ff:ff

    inet 10.1.1.1/24 scope global eth0

    inet 10.1.1.64/16 scope global eth0

    inet 10.1.1.32/25 scope global eth0

    inet 10.1.1.192/25 scope global eth0

    inet 10.1.1.65/24 scope global secondary eth0

    inet 10.1.1.200/16 scope global secondary eth0
```

Note that you have four (4) Primary addresses defined and two (2) Secondary addresses defined. Note also that they are not grouped together as you would think they should be. This is because the definition of a Primary/Secondary Address Group is an artificial structure imposed on the actual addressing functions.

Now remove the Primary address for the 10.1.1.0/24 network:

```
ip addr del 10.1.1.1/24 dev eth0
```

And look at the end result:

```
ip addr list dev eth0
```

```
8: eth0: <BROADCAST,MULTICAST,UP> mtu 1500 qdisc pfifo_fast qlen 100

    link/ether 00:a0:cc:21:ee:d3 brd ff:ff:ff:ff:ff:ff

    inet 10.1.1.64/16 scope global eth0

    inet 10.1.1.32/25 scope global eth0

    inet 10.1.1.192/25 scope global eth0

    inet 10.1.1.200/16 scope global secondary eth0
```

Note that both addresses belonging to the 10.1.1.0/24 Primary/Secondary Address Group were removed but that no other address was touched. That is the definition of a Primary/Secondary Address Group.

This point is deeply related to the concept of the scope when talking about the address member of the Triad. Chapter 5 covers this entire subject of scopes and Primary/Secondary groups in detail. For now you should just note that the older concept of interface aliases is dead and that some backward compatibility is retained through the Primary/Secondary groups.

ip neighbour—neighbour/ARP Table Management

The neighbour table objects establish bindings between protocol addresses and link layer addresses for hosts sharing the same physical link. neighbour object entries are organized into tables. The IPv4 neighbour object table is also known as the ARP table. These commands allow you to look at the neighbour table bindings and their properties, to add new neighbour table entries, and to delete old ones.

Abbreviations: neighbour, neighbor, neigh, n

To help with understanding the command flow, here is the output of ip neigh help:

```
Usage: ip neigh { add | del | change | replace } { ADDR [ lladdr LLADDR ]
          [ nud { permanent | noarp | stale | reachable } ]
          | proxy ADDR } [ dev DEV ]
       ip neigh {show|flush} [ to PREFIX ] [ dev DEV ] [ nud STATE ]
```

Arguments

add, a, change, chg, replace, repl, delete, del, d, flush, flu, and show (list)

The following commands create new neighbour records or update existing ones:

- ip neighbour add—Add a new neighbour entry.
- ip neighbour change—Change the existing entry.
- ip neighbour replace—Add a new entry or change the existing entry.

All of the following modify these commands:

- to *ADDRESS* (default)—The protocol address of the neighbour. It is either an IPv4 or an IPv6 address.
- dev *NAME*—The interface to which this neighbour is attached.
- lladdr *LLADDRESS*—The link layer address of the neighbour. *LLADDRESS* can be null.
- nud *NUD_STATE*—The state of the neighbour entry. nud is an abbreviation for *Neighbour Unreachability Detection*. This state can take one of the following values:
  - permanent—The neighbour entry is valid forever and can be removed only administratively.
  - noarp—The neighbour entry is valid. No attempts to validate this entry will be made, but it can be removed when its lifetime expires.
  - reachable—The neighbour entry is valid until reachability timeout expires.
  - stale—The neighbour entry is valid, but suspicious. This option to ip neighbour does not change the neighbour state if the entry was valid and the address has not been changed by this command.

Examples

```
ip neigh add 10.0.0.3 lladdr 000001 dev eth0 nud perm
```

Add permanent ARP entry for neighbour 10.0.0.3 on the device eth0.

```
ip neigh chg 10.0.0.3 dev eth0 nud reachable
```

Change its state to reachable.

ip neighbour delete—Delete Neighbour Entry

This command invalidates a neighbour entry.

Abbreviations: delete, del, d

The arguments are the same as with ip neigh add, only lladdr and nud are ignored.

Example

To invalidate the ARP entry for neighbour 10.0.0.3 on the device eth0.

```
ip neigh del 10.0.0.3 dev eth0
```

The deleted neighbour entry will not disappear from the tables immediately; if it is in use, it cannot be deleted until the last client releases it. Otherwise, it will be destroyed during the next garbage collection.

Attempts to delete or to change manually a NOARP entry created by the kernel may result in unpredictable behavior. More specifically, the kernel may start trying to resolve this address even on NOARP interfaces or change the address to multicast or broadcast.

ip neighbour show—List Neighbour Entries

This command displays neighbour tables.

Abbreviations: show, list, sh, ls

Arguments

These options select the entries to be displayed from the ARP table:

- to *ADDRESS* (default)—Prefix selecting neighbours to list.
- dev *NAME*—List only neighbours attached to this device.
- unused—List only neighbours that are not in use now.
- nud *NUD_STATE*—List only neighbour entries in this state. *NUD_STATE* takes values listed after the example or the special value all, which means all the states. This option may occur more than once. If this option is absent, ip lists all the entries except for none and noarp.

Example

```
kuznet@alisa~ $ ip neigh ls
 dev lo lladdr 00:00:00:00:00:00 nud noarp
fe80::200:cff:fe76:3f85 dev eth0 lladdr 00:00:0c:76:3f:85 router \
    nud stale
0.0.0.0 dev lo lladdr 00:00:00:00:00:00 nud noarp
193.233.7.254 dev eth0 lladdr 00:00:0c:76:3f:85 nud reachable
193.233.7.85 dev eth0 lladdr 00:e0:1e:63:39:00 nud stale
kuznet@alisa~ $
```

The first word of each line is the protocol address of the neighbour, followed by the device name. The rest of the line describes the contents of the neighbour entry identified by the pair (device, address).

lladdr is the link layer address of the neighbour.

nud is the state of Neighbour Unreachability Detection for this entry. The full list of the possible NUD states with minimal descriptions follows:

- none—The state of the neighbour is void.
- incomplete—The neighbour is in process of resolution.
- reachable—The neighbour is valid and apparently reachable.
- stale—The neighbour is valid, but probably it is already unreachable, so the kernel will try to check it at the first transmission.
- delay—A packet has been sent to the stale neighbour, and the kernel waits for confirmation.
- probe—The delay timer has expired, but no confirmation was received. The kernel has started to probe neighbour with ARP/NDISC messages.
- failed—Resolution has failed.
- noarp—The neighbour is valid, and no attempt to check the entry will be made.

- permanent—This is a noarp entry, but only the administrator can remove the entry from the neighbour table.
- A link layer address is valid in all the states except for none, failed, and incomplete.

IPv6 neighbours can be marked with the router flag, which means that that neighbour introduced itself as an IPv6 router.

Option -statistics provides some usage statistics:

```
kuznet@alisa~ $ ip -s n ls 193.233.7.254
193.233.7.254 dev eth0 lladdr 00:00:0c:76:3f:85 ref 5 used 12/13/20 \
    nud reachable
kuznet@alisa~ $
```

Here, ref is the number of users of this entry and used is a triplet of time intervals in seconds, separated by slashes. The triplet of numbers is coded as used/confirmed/updated. In this example they show that

The entry was used 12 seconds ago.

The entry was confirmed 13 seconds ago.

The entry was updated 20 seconds ago.

ip neighbour flush—Flush Neighbour Entries

This command flushes the neighbour tables. Entries may be selected to flush by various criteria.

Abbreviations: flush, f

This command has the same arguments as show. Note that it will not run when no arguments are given, and that the default neighbour states to be flushed do not include permanent or noarp.

With the option -statistics the command becomes verbose and prints out the number of deleted neighbours and number of rounds made in flushing the neighbour table. If the option is given twice, ip neigh flush also dumps all the deleted neighbours in the format described in the previous subsection as in the following example:

```
netadm@alisa~ # ip -s -s n f 193.233.7.254
193.233.7.254 dev eth0 lladdr 00:00:0c:76:3f:85 ref 5 used 12/13/20 \
    nud reachable
***Round 1, deleting 1 entries***
***Flush is complete after 1 round***
```

ip route—Routing Table Management

Abbreviations: route, ro, r

This command manages the route entries within the kernel routing tables. The kernel routing tables keep information about protocol paths to other networked nodes.

As you saw in Chapter 2, "Policy Routing Theory," there are two parts to the imple-mentation of the RPDB (Routing Policy Data Base). The `ip route` object allows spec-ification and definition of the routing information base part of the RPDB.

To understand the massive amount of information in the following section you will want to study the syntax and command flow in the `ip route help` listing. When you understand the command syntax flow, you will realize that the rest of these sections essentially walk through the command parts piece by piece. Here is the output for `ip route help`:

```
Usage: ip route { list | flush } SELECTOR
       ip route get ADDRESS [ from ADDRESS iif STRING ]
                           [ oif STRING ] [ tos TOS ]
       ip route { add | del | change | append | replace | monitor } ROUTE
SELECTOR := [ root PREFIX ] [ match PREFIX ] [ exact PREFIX ]
            [ table TABLE_ID ] [ proto RTPROTO ]
            [ type TYPE ] [ scope SCOPE ]
ROUTE := NODE_SPEC [ INFO_SPEC ]
NODE_SPEC := [ TYPE ] PREFIX [ tos TOS ]
             [ table TABLE_ID ] [ proto RTPROTO ]
             [ scope SCOPE ] [ metric METRIC ]
INFO_SPEC := NH OPTIONS FLAGS [ nexthop NH ]...
NH := [ via ADDRESS ] [ dev STRING ] [ weight NUMBER ] NHFLAGS
OPTIONS := FLAGS [ mtu NUMBER ] [ advmss NUMBER ]
           [ rtt NUMBER ] [ rttvar NUMBER ]
           [ window NUMBER] [ cwnd NUMBER ] [ ssthresh REALM ]
           [ realms REALM ]
TYPE := [ unicast | local | broadcast | multicast | throw |
          unreachable | prohibit | blackhole | nat ]
TABLE_ID := [ local | main | default | all | NUMBER ]
SCOPE := [ host | link | global | NUMBER ]
FLAGS := [ equalize ]
NHFLAGS := [ onlink | pervasive ]
RTPROTO := [ kernel | boot | static | NUMBER ]
```

ip route {add/change/replace}

This command adds, changes, or replaces routes in the routing tables.

- `ip route add`—Add new route
- `ip route change`—Change route
- `ip route replace`—Change route or add new one

Abbreviations: add, a; change, chg; replace, repl

Arguments

to *PREFIX* or to *TYPE PREFIX* (default)—The destination prefix of the route. If *TYPE* is omitted, `ip` assumes type `unicast`. Other values of *TYPE* are listed in Chapter 2 and are summarized here as follows:

- unicast—The route entry describes real paths to the destinations covered by the route prefix.
- unreachable—These destinations are unreachable; packets are discarded and the ICMP message host unreachable (ICMP Type 3 Code 1) is generated. The local senders get error EHOSTUNREACH.
- blackhole—These destinations are unreachable; packets are silently discarded. The local senders get error EINVAL.
- prohibit—These destinations are unreachable; packets are discarded and the ICMP message communication administratively prohibited (ICMP Type 3 Code 13) is generated. The local senders get error EACCES.
- local—The destinations are assigned to this host, the packets are looped back and delivered locally.
- broadcast—The destinations are broadcast addresses, the packets are sent as link broadcasts.
- throw—Special control route used together with policy rules. If a throw route is selected, then lookup in this particular table is terminated, pretending that no route was found. Without any Policy Routing, it is equivalent to the absence of the route in the routing table, the packets are dropped and ICMP message net unreachable (ICMP Type 3 Code 0) is generated. The local senders get error ENETUNREACH.
- nat—Special NAT (Network Address Translation—see Chapter 8) route. Destinations covered by the prefix are considered as dummy (or external) addresses, which require translation to real (or internal) ones before forwarding. The addresses to translate to are selected with the attribute via.
- anycast (not implemented currently)—The destinations are anycast addresses assigned to this host. They are mainly equivalent to local addresses, with the difference that such addresses are invalid to be used as the source address of any packet.
- multicast—Special type, used for multicast routing. It is not present in normal routing tables.

PREFIX is an IPv4 or IPv6 address optionally followed by a slash and prefix length. If the length of the prefix is missing, ip assumes full-length host route. Also, there is one special PREFIX—default—that is equivalent to IP 0/0 or to IPv6 /0.

- tos TOS or dsfield TOS—Type of Service (TOS) key. This key has no mask associated and the longest match is understood as to first compare the TOS of the route and the packet; if they are not equal, then the packet still may match a route with zero TOS. TOS is either an 8-bit hexadecimal number or an identifier from /etc/iproute2/rt_dsfield.
- metric NUMBER or preference NUMBER—Preference value of the route. NUMBER is an arbitrary 32-bit number.
- table TABLEID—The table to add this route. TABLEID may be a number or a string from the file /etc/iproute2/rt_tables. If this parameter is omitted, ip assumes table main, with the exception of local, broadcast, and nat routes, which are put to table local by default.

- dev *NAME*—The output device name.
- via *ADDRESS*—The address of the nexthop router. Actually, the sense of this field depends on route type. For normal unicast routes it is either a true nexthop router or, if it is a direct route installed in BSD compatibility mode, it can be a local address of the interface. For nat routes it is the first address block of translated IP destinations.
- src *ADDRESS*—The source address to preferentially use when sending to the destinations covered by route prefix. This address must be defined on a local machine interface. This preference comes into play when routes and rules are combined with Masquerade and NAT functions as provided by other utilities.
- realm *REALMID*—The realm this route is assigned to. *REALMID* may be a number or a string from the file /etc/iproute2/rt_realms.
- mtu MTU or mtu lock MTU—The MTU along the path to destination. If the lock modifier is not used, MTU may be updated by the kernel due to path MTU discovery. If the lock modifier is used, then no path MTU discovery will be performed, and all the packets will be sent without the DF bit set for the IPv4 case or fragmented to the MTU for the IPv6 case.
- window *NUMBER*—The maximum advertised window for TCP to these destinations, measured in bytes. This parameter limits the maximum data bursts your TCP peers are allowed to send to you.
- rtt *NUMBER*—The initial RTT (Round Trip Time) estimate.
  Actually, in Linux 2.2 and 2.0 it is not RTT but the initial TCP retransmission timeout. The kernel forgets it as soon as it receives the first valid ACK from a peer. Alas, this means that this attribute affects only the connection retry rate and is hence useless.
- nexthop *NEXTHOP*—The nexthop of a multipath route. *NEXTHOP* is a complex value with its own syntax, as follows:
  via *ADDRESS* is the nexthop router.
  dev *NAME* is the output device.
  weight *NUMBER* is the weight of this element of multipath route reflecting its relative bandwidth or quality.

- scope *SCOPE_VAL*—The scope of the destinations covered by the route prefix. *SCOPE_VAL* may be a number or a string from the file /etc/iproute2/rt_scopes. If this parameter is omitted, ip assumes scope global for all gatewayed unicast routes, scope link for direct unicast routes and broadcasts, and scope host for local routes.
- protocol *RTPROTO*—The routing protocol identifier of this route. *RTPROTO* may be a number or a string from the file /etc/iproute2/rt_protos. If the routing protocol ID is not given, ip assumes the protocol is boot—in other words, "this route has been added by someone who does not understand what he is doing." Several of these protocol values have a fixed interpretation as in the following list:
  - redirect—Route was installed due to ICMP redirect.
  - kernel—Route was installed by the kernel during autoconfiguration.

- boot—Route was installed during bootup sequence. If a routing daemon will start, it will purge all of them. This is the value assigned to manually inserted routes that do not have a protocol specified.
- static—Route was installed by administrator to override dynamic routing. Routing daemon(s) will respect them and advertise them if it is so configured.
- ra—Route was installed by Router Discovery protocol.
  Note that the rest of the values of RTPROTO are not reserved, and the administrator is free to assign or not assign protocol tags. Routing daemons at least should take care of setting some unique protocol values for themselves such as they are assigned in rtnetlink.h or in the rt_protos database.
- onlink—Pretend that the nexthop is directly attached to this link, even if it does not match any interface prefix. One application of this option may be found in IP tunnels between dissimilar addresses.
- equalize—Allow packet-by-packet randomization on multipath routes. Without this modifier, route will be frozen to one selected nexthop, so that load splitting will occur only on per-flow base. equalize works only if the appropriate kernel configuration option is chosen or if the kernel is patched. Note that the presence or absence of this modifier determines how load balancing is performed and also how traffic flows are policy routed in some situations.

Two more commands, prepend and append, exist. prepend does the same thing as the classic route add command by adding the route even if another route to the same destination already exists. The opposite is append, which adds the route to the end of the list. I strongly recommend that you avoid using these commands.

Unfortunately, IPv6 currently understands only the append command correctly, with all the rest of the command set translating to append. Certainly, this will change in the future.

ip route add Examples

To add a plain route to network 10.0.0/24 via gateway 193.233.7.65:

```
ip route add 10.0.0/24 via 193.233.7.65
```

To change it to a direct route via device dummy:

```
ip ro chg 10.0.0/24 via 193.233.7.65 dev dummy
```

To add default multipath route, splitting load between ppp0 and ppp1:

```
ip route add default scope global nexthop dev ppp0 nexthop dev ppp1
```

Note the scope value, which is not necessary but prompts the kernel that this route is gatewayed rather than direct. Actually, if you know the addresses of the remote endpoints, it would be better to specify them using the parameter via.

To nat the address 192.203.80.144 to 193.233.7.83 before forwarding:

`ip route add nat 192.203.80.142 via 193.233.7.83`

Note that the reverse nat translation is set up with policy rules, as described in the `ip rule` Policy Routing section.

ip route delete

Abbreviations: `delete, del, d`

`ip route del` has the same arguments as `ip route add`, but their semantics are a bit different.

Key values (`dest, tos, preference`, and `table`) select the route to delete. If any optional attributes are present, `ip` verifies that they coincide with attributes of the route to delete. If no route was given, the key and attributes are not found, and `ip route del` fails.

Linux kernel 2.0 had the capability to delete a route selected only by the prefix address while ignoring its netmask. This option does not exist anymore, due to the ambiguous nature of the selection. If you wish to have such functionality, look at the `ip route flush` command, which provides a richer set of capabilities.

ip route delete Examples

To delete the multipath route created by the `add` example previously:

`ip route del default scope global nexthop dev ppp0 nexthop dev ppp1`

ip route show

This format of the command allows viewing the routing table contents and looking at route(s) as selected by some criteria.

Abbreviations: `show, list, sh, ls, l`

Arguments

These are the selection arguments that allow you to select routes to show:

- `to` *SELECTOR* (default)—Select routes only from the given range of destinations. *SELECTOR* has optional modifiers (`root, match`, and `exact`) and a prefix.
- `root` *PREFIX*—Selects routes with prefixes not shorter than *PREFIX*. For example, `root 0/0` selects all the routing table.
- `match` *PREFIX*—Selects routes with prefixes not longer than *PREFIX*. `match 10.0/16` selects `10.0/16, 10/8`, and `0/0`, but it does not select `10.1/16` and `10.0.0/24`.
- `exact` *PREFIX* (or just *PREFIX*)—Selects routes with exactly this prefix.

Note that if none of these options are present, then the `ip` command assumes `root 0/0`, which lists the entire table. The rest of the selection arguments are:

- `tos` *TOS* or `dsfield` *TOS*—Select only routes with given TOS.

- table *TABLEID*—Show routes from this table(s). Default setting is to show table main (ID 254). *TABLEID* may be either the ID of a real table or one of the special values:
    all—List all the tables.
    cache—Dump the routing cache.

Note that IPv6 has only a single route table. However, splitting into main, local, and cache is emulated by the ip utility.

- cloned or cached—List cloned routes that are dynamically forked off of other routes because some route attribute (like MTU) was updated. It is equivalent to table cache.
- from *SELECTOR*—The same syntax as to *SELECTOR* but bounds the source address range rather than the destination. Note that the from option works only with cloned routes.
- protocol *RTPROTO*—List only routes of this protocol.
- scope *SCOPE_VAL*—List only routes with this scope.
- type *TYPE*—List only routes of this type.
- dev *NAME*—List only routes going via this device.
- via *PREFIX*—List only routes going via selected *PREFIX* nexthop routers.
- src *PREFIX*—List only routes with preferred source addresses selected by *PREFIX*.
- realm *REALMID* or realms *FROMREALM/TOREALM*—List only routes with these realms.

Using this command is best explained by running through an example.

Example

First you need to count the routes of protocol gated/bgp on a router.

```
kuznet@amber~ $ ip route list proto gated/bgp | wc
    1413    9891    79010
kuznet@amber~ $
```

To count the size of the routing cache, you have to use option -o, because cached attributes can take more than one line of output.

```
kuznet@amber~ $ ip -o route list cloned | wc
    159    2543    18707
kuznet@amber~ $
```

The output of this command consists of per route records separated by line feeds. However, some records may consist of more than one line, particularly when the route is cloned or you have requested additional statistics. If the option -o is given, line feeds separating lines inside records are replaced with backslash signs.

The output has the same syntax as arguments given to ip route add, so it can be understood easily.

```
kuznet@amber~ $ ip route list 193.233.7/24
193.233.7.0/24 dev eth0  proto gated/conn  scope link \
    src 193.233.7.65 realms inr.ac
kuznet@amber~ $
```

If you list cloned entries, the output contains other attributes, which are evaluated during route calculation and updated during route lifetime. An example of the output is

```
kuznet@amber~ $ ip route list 193.233.7.82 table cache
193.233.7.82 from 193.233.7.82 dev eth0  src 193.233.7.65 \
  realms inr.ac/inr.ac
    cache <src-direct,redirect>  mtu 1500 rtt 300 iif eth0
193.233.7.82 dev eth0  src 193.233.7.65 realms inr.ac
    cache  mtu 1500 rtt 300
kuznet@amber~ $
```

This route looks a bit strange, doesn't it? Did you notice that this is the path from 193.233.7.82 back to 193.233.82? In the section on ip route get, you will see how this route is created.

The second line, which starts with the word cache, shows the additional attributes that normal routes do not possess. The cache flags contained within the angle brackets are

- local—Packets are delivered locally. It stands for loopback unicast routes, for broadcast routes, and for multicast routes if this host is a member of the corresponding group.
- reject—The path is bad. Any attempt to use it results in an error. See the error attribute below.
- mc—The destination is multicast.
- brd—The destination is broadcast.
- src-direct—The source is on a directly connected interface.
- redirected—The route was created by an ICMP Redirect.
- redirect—Packets going via this route will trigger ICMP redirect.
- fastroute—The route is eligible to be used for fastroute.
- equalize—Make packet-by-packet randomization along this path.
- dst-nat—Destination address requires translation.
- src-nat—Source address requires translation.
- masq—Source address requires masquerading.
- notify (not implemented)—A change or deletion of this route will trigger RTNETLINK notification.

The following are optional attributes that may be present:

- error—On reject routes this is the error code returned to local senders when they try to use this route. These error codes are translated to ICMP error codes sent to remote senders according to the rules described in the section on route types.
- expires—This entry will expire after this timeout.

- iif—The packets for this path are expected to arrive on this interface.

The option -statistics will show further information about this route:

- users—Number of users of this entry.
- age—Shows when this route was last used.
- used—Number of lookups of this route since its creation.

ip route flush—Allows Group Deletion of Routes

This command allows flushing routes as selected by some criteria. The arguments have the same syntax and semantics as the arguments of ip route show, but the routing tables are purged rather than listed. The only difference is the default action performed. Where the ip route show command dumps the main IP routing table, ip route flush prints the help page.

With the option -statistics, the command becomes verbose and prints out the number of deleted routes and the number of rounds needed to flush the routing table. If the option is given twice, ip route flush also dumps all deleted routes in the format described in the previous subsection.

Abbreviations: flush, f

ip route flush Examples

The first example flushes all the gatewayed routes from table main, such as after a routing daemon crash.

```
netadm@amber~ # ip -4 ro flush scope global type unicast
```

This option deserved to be put into the scriptlet routef, available within the IPROUTE2 utility distribution. This option was described in the route(8) man page as borrowed from BSD but was never implemented in Linux.

The second example is flushing all IPv6 cloned routes:

```
netadm@amber~ # ip -6 -s -s ro flush cache
3ffe:2400::220:afff:fef4:c5d1 via 3ffe:2400::220:afff:fef4:c5d1 \
  dev eth0  metric 0
    cache  used 2 age 12sec mtu 1500 rtt 300
3ffe:2400::280:adff:feb7:8034 via 3ffe:2400::280:adff:feb7:8034 \
  dev eth0  metric 0
    cache  used 2 age 15sec mtu 1500 rtt 300
3ffe:2400::280:c8ff:fe59:5bcc via 3ff:2400::280:c8ff:fe59:5bcc \
  dev eth0  metric 0
    cache  users 1 used 1 age 23sec mtu 1500 rtt 300
3ffe:2400:0:1:2a0:ccff:fe66:1878 via 3ffe:2400:0:1:2a0:ccff:fe66:1878 \
  dev eth1  metric 0
    cache  used 2 age 20sec mtu 1500 rtt 300
3ffe:2400:0:1:a00:20ff:fe71:fb30 via 3ffe:2400:0:1:a00:20ff:fe71:fb30 \
  dev eth1  metric 0
    cache  used 2 age 33sec mtu 1500 rtt 300
```

```
ff02::1 via ff02::1 dev eth1  metric 0
    cache  users 1 used 1 age 45sec mtu 1500 rtt 300
***Round 1, deleting 6 entries***
***Flush is complete after 1 round***
netadm@amber~ # ip -6 -s -s ro flush cache
Nothing to flush.
```

The third example is flushing BGP routing tables after gated death.

```
netadm@amber~ # ip ro ls proto gated/bgp | wc
   1408    9856    78730
netadm@amber~ # ip -s ro f proto gated/bgp
***Round 1, deleting 1408 entries***
***Flush is complete after 1 round***
netadm@amber~ # ip ro f proto gated/bgp
Nothing to flush.
netadm@amber~ #
```

Note that there is one usage of ip route flush you will become very familiar with and it is worth mentioning now:

ip route flush cache

This command flushes out the routing cache and should be run whenever you manually manipulate the routing table on a running machine. If you do not flush the cache after adding, deleting, or changing a route, there may be a delay of up to several minutes before the routing manipulation takes effect. This is due to the current routing process being optimized for usage. A datastream that has created a routing decision through the route process will cause the routing decision to be cached for the life of the stream plus a timeout period. Thus in order for a route manipulation to be immediately effective you will want to flush out the cache. At this time there is no mechanism for flushing a specific part of the routing cache but there is little penalty in most situations when a complete cache flush is performed.

ip route get—Obtain Route Pathing

This command gets a single route to a destination and prints its contents exactly as the kernel sees it. This is not the same as a physical traceroute style lookup nor is it equivalent to ip route show. ip route show shows the existing routes; ip route get resolves them and creates new clones if necessary.

Essentially, ip route get is equivalent to actually sending a packet along this path. If the argument iif is not given, the kernel creates a route to output packets toward the requested destination. This is equivalent to pinging the destination then running ip route list cache. However, in the case of ip route get, no packets are actually sent. With the argument iif present, the kernel pretends that a packet has arrived from this interface and searches for a path to forward the packet. This command outputs routes in the same format as ip route ls.

Abbreviations: get, g

Arguments

These are the options to define what route to get:

- to *ADDRESS* (default)—The destination address.
- from *ADDRESS*—The source address.
- tos *TOS* or dsfield *TOS*—Type Of Service.
- iif *NAME*—The device this packet is expected to arrive from.
- oif *NAME*—Enforce output device on which this packet will be routed out.
- connected—If no source address (option from) was given, look up the route again, with the source address set to the preferred address as received from the first lookup. If Policy Routing is used, this may be a different route.

`ip route get` Examples

To find a route to output packets to 193.233.7.82:

```
kuznet@amber~ $ ip route get 193.233.7.82
193.233.7.82 dev eth0  src 193.233.7.65 realms inr.ac
   cache  mtu 1500 rtt 300
kuznet@amber~ $
```

To find a route to forward packets arriving on eth0 from 193.233.7.82 and destined to 193.233.7.82:

```
kuznet@amber~ $ ip route get 193.233.7.82 from 193.233.7.82 iif eth0
193.233.7.82 from 193.233.7.82 dev eth0  src 193.233.7.65 \
  realms inr.ac/inr.ac
   cache <src-direct,redirect>  mtu 1500 rtt 300 iif eth0
kuznet@amber~ $
```

This is the operation that created the funny route in the examples to ip route list with 193.233.7.82 looped back to 193.233.7.82. Note the redirect flag present on the output.

To find multicast route for packets arriving on eth0 from host 193.233.7.82 and destined to multicast group 224.2.127.254 assuming that a multicast routing daemon is running (in this case running pimd).

```
kuznet@amber~ $ ip route get 224.2.127.254 from 193.233.7.82 iif eth0
multicast 224.2.127.254 from 193.233.7.82 dev lo  \
  src 193.233.7.65 realms inr.ac/cosmos
   cache <mc> iif eth0 Oifs eth1 pimreg
kuznet@amber~ $
```

This route differs from the ones seen before. It contains a normal part and a multicast part. The normal part is used to deliver or not deliver the packet to local IP listeners. In this case the router is not acting as a member of the multicast group, so the route has no local flag and only forwards packets. The output device for such entries is always loopback. The multicast part consists of an additional Oifs list showing the output interfaces.

Now it is time for a more complicated example, adding an invalid gatewayed route for a destination that is really directly connected

```
netadm@alisa~ # ip route add 193.233.7.98 via 193.233.7.254
netadm@alisa~ # ip route get 193.233.7.98
193.233.7.98 via 193.233.7.254 dev eth0  src 193.233.7.90
    cache  mtu 1500 rtt 3072
```

and probing it with ping:

```
netadm@alisa~ # ping -n 193.233.7.98
PING 193.233.7.98 (193.233.7.98) from 193.233.7.90  56 data bytes
From 193.233.7.254 Redirect Host(New nexthop 193.233.7.98)
64 bytes from 193.233.7.98 icmp_seq=0 ttl=255 time=3.5 ms
From 193.233.7.254 Redirect Host(New nexthop 193.233.7.98)
64 bytes from 193.233.7.98 icmp_seq=1 ttl=255 time=2.2 ms
64 bytes from 193.233.7.98 icmp_seq=2 ttl=255 time=0.4 ms
64 bytes from 193.233.7.98 icmp_seq=3 ttl=255 time=0.4 ms
64 bytes from 193.233.7.98 icmp_seq=4 ttl=255 time=0.4 ms
^C
--- 193.233.7.98 ping statistics ---
5 packets transmitted, 5 packets received, 0% packet loss
round-trip min/avg/max = 0.4/1.3/3.5 ms
```

What occurred? The router at 193.233.7.254 understood that you have a much better path to the destination and sent an ICMP redirect message. Now retry ip route get to see what you have in your routing tables.

```
netadm@alisa~ # ip route get 193.233.7.98
193.233.7.98 dev eth0  src 193.233.7.90
    cache <redirected>  mtu 1500 rtt 3072
```

ip rule—Routing Policy Database Management

This command manipulates the third part of the Policy Routing Triad: rules.

As discussed in Chapter 2, there are three parts to the implementation of the RPDB. The ip rule object allows specification and definition of the policy rules part of the RPDB.

Abbreviations: rule, ru

To understand the logic of the commands section you will want to understand the logic of the commandline. The output for ip rule help is as follows:

```
Usage: ip rule [ list | add | del ] SELECTOR ACTION
SELECTOR := [ from PREFIX ] [ to PREFIX ] [ tos TOS ] [ fwmark FWMARK ]
            [ dev STRING ] [ pref NUMBER ]
ACTION := [ table TABLE_ID ] [ nat ADDRESS ]
          [ prohibit | reject | unreachable ]
```

```
             [ realms [SRCREALM/]DSTREALM ]
TABLE_ID := [ local | main | default | NUMBER ]
```

ip rule add—Insert New Rule

Use this command to insert a new rule.

Abbreviations: add, a; delete, del, d

Arguments

The following list of arguments to the rule command will add or delete the appropriate rule:

- type *TYPE* (default)—The type of rule. The list of valid types was specified in Chapter 2 and is summarized here for reference:
  - unicast—The rule prescribes returning the route found in the routing table referenced by the rule.
  - blackhole—The rule prescribes to drop a packet silently.
  - unreachable—The rule prescribes generating the error Network is unreachable (ICMP Type 3 Code 0).
  - prohibit—The rule prescribes generating the error Communication is administratively prohibited (ICMP Type 3 Code 13).
  - nat—The rule prescribes translating the source address of the IP packet to some other value.
- from *PREFIX*—Select the source prefix to match.
- to *PREFIX*—Select the destination prefix to match.
- iif *NAME*—Select the incoming device to match. If the interface is loopback, the rule matches only packets originated by this host. It means that you may create separate routing tables for forwarded and local packets and, hence, completely segregate them.
- tos *TOS* or dsfield *TOS*—Select the TOS value to match.
- fwmark *MARK*—Select the value of fwmark to match.
- priority *PREFERENCE*—The priority of this rule. Each rule should have an explicitly set unique priority value. Priority is an unsigned 32-bit number, thus you have 4,294,967,296 possible rules.
- table *TABLEID*—The routing table identifier to look up if the rule selector matches.
- realms *FROM/TO*—Realms to select if the rule matches and routing table lookup succeeds. Realm *TO* is used only if the route returned did not select any realm.
- nat *ADDRESS*—The base IP address block to translate to a source address. The *ADDRESS* may be either the start of a block of nat addresses as selected by nat routes, a local host address, or even zero. In the last two cases the Linux router does not nat translate the packets but masquerades them to this address.

Changes to the RPDB made with these commands do not become active immediately. You should run ip route flush cache to flush out the routing cache after inserting rules.

<table>
<tr><td>

NOTE

For historical reasons, `ip rule add` does not require any priority value and allows the priority value to be non-unique. If the user has not supplied a priority value, one is assigned by the kernel. If the user asked to create a rule with a priority value that already exists, the kernel did not reject the request and added the new rule before all old rules of the same priority. This is a mistake in the current design, nothing more. It should be fixed by the time you read this, so please do not rely on this feature. You should always use explicit priorities when creating rules.

</td></tr>
</table>

ip rule add Examples

To route packets with source addresses from 192.203.80/24 according to routing table inr.ruhep:

```
ip rule add from 192.203.80.0/24 table inr.ruhep prio 220
```

To translate packet source 193.233.7.83 to 192.203.80.144 and route it according to table 1 (Table 1 is defined in /etc/iproute/rt_tables as inr.ruhep):

```
ip rule add from 193.233.7.83 nat 192.203.80.144 table 1 prio 320
```

To delete an unused default rule:

```
ip rule del prio 32767
```

ip rule show—List Policy Rules

Use this command to list policy rules.

Abbreviations: show, list, sh, ls, l

Good news—This is the only command that has no arguments. Here is the example:

```
kuznet@amber~ $ ip rule list
0:      from all lookup local
200:    from 192.203.80.0/24 to 193.233.7.0/24 lookup main
210:    from 192.203.80.0/24 to 192.203.80.0/24 lookup main
220:    from 192.203.80.0/24 lookup inr.ruhep realms inr.ruhep/radio-msu
300:    from 193.233.7.83 to 193.233.7.0/24 lookup main
310:    from 193.233.7.83 to 192.203.80.0/24 lookup main
320:    from 193.233.7.83 lookup inr.ruhep map-to 192.203.80.144
32766:    from all lookup main
```

In the first position is the rule priority value, followed by a colon. Then the selectors follow, with each key prefixed by the keyword used to create the rule.

The keyword lookup is followed by the routing table identifier as recorded in the file /etc/iproute2/rt_tables.

If the rule does nat, as in rule #320, it is shown by the keyword map-to, followed by the start of the block of addresses to map.

The sense of this example is pretty simple. The prefixes `192.203.80.0/24` and `193.233.7.0/24` form an internal network, but each prefix is routed differently. Additionally, the host `193.233.7.83` is translated to another prefix as `192.203.80.144` when talking to the outer world.

`ip tunnel`—IP Tunnelling Configuration

Abbreviations: `tunnel`, `tunl`

The `tunnel` objects encapsulate packets within IPv4 packets and sends them over the IP infrastructure.

As with the other sections this will make more sense if you understand the logic of the command line. The output of `ip tunnel help` is as follows:

```
Usage: ip tunnel { add | change | del | show } [ NAME ]
          [ mode { ipip | gre | sit } ] [ remote ADDR ] [ local ADDR ]
          [ [i|o]seq ] [ [i|o]key KEY ] [ [i|o]csum ]
          [ ttl TTL ] [ tos TOS ] [ [no]pmtudisc ] [ dev PHYS_DEV ]

Where: NAME := STRING
       ADDR := { IP_ADDRESS | any }
       TOS  := { NUMBER | inherit }
       TTL  := { 1..255 | inherit }
       KEY  := { DOTTED_QUAD | NUMBER }
```

`ip tunnel add`—Creating Tunnels

Use this command to create IPIP, GRE, or SIT tunnels.

Abbreviations: `add`, `a`

Arguments

These options define how to setup a tunnel.

- `name` *NAME* (default)—Select the tunnel device name.
- `mode` *MODE*—Set the `tunnel` mode. Three modes are available: `ipip`, `sit`, and `gre`.
- `remote` *ADDRESS*—Set the remote endpoint of the tunnel.
- `local` *ADDRESS*—Set the fixed local address for tunneled packets. It must be an address on another interface of this host.
- `ttl` *N*—Set fixed TTL N on tunneled packets. *N* is a number in the range 1–255. `0` is a special value, meaning that packets inherit TTL value. Default value is `inherit`.
- `tos` *TOS* or `dsfield` *TOS*—Set fixed TOS on tunneled packets. Default value is `inherit`.
- `dev` *NAME*—Bind the tunnel to device *NAME*, so that tunneled packets will be routed only via this device and will not able to escape to another device when the route to an endpoint changes.

- `nopmtudisc`—Disable Path MTU Discovery on this tunnel. It is enabled by default. Note that a fixed TTL is incompatible with this option. A tunnel with fixed TTL always performs `pmtu` discovery.
- `key` *K*, `ikey` *K*, `okey` *K* (GRE only)—Use keyed GRE with key *K*. *K* is either a number or an IP address-like dotted quad. The parameter `key` sets `key` to use in both directions; `ikey` and `okey` allow setting different keys for input and output.
- `csum`, `icsum`, `ocsum` (GRE only)—Checksum tunneled packets. The flag `ocsum` orders the checksumming of outgoing packets, and `icsum` requires that all the input packets have a correct checksum. `csum` is equivalent to the combination `icsum ocsum`.
- `seq`, `iseq`, `oseq` (GRE only)—Serialize packets. The flag `oseq` enables sequencing outgoing packets, and `iseq` requires that all input packets be serialized. `seq` is equivalent to the combination `iseq oseq`.

ip tunnel add Examples

To create `POINTOPOINT` IPv6 tunnel with maximum TTL of 32:

```
ip tunl add Cisco mode sit remote 192.31.7.104 local 192.203.80.142 ttl 32
```

ip tunnel show—List Tunnel Attributes

Use this command to list tunnel attributes.

Abbreviations: `show`, `list`, `sh`, `ls`, `l`

Example

```
kuznet@amber~ $ ip tunl ls Cisco
Cisco: ipv6/ip  remote 192.31.7.104  local 192.203.80.142  ttl 32
```

The line starts with the tunnel device name terminated by a colon, then the tunnel mode follows. The parameters of the tunnel are listed with the same keywords used at tunnel creation.

```
kuznet@amber~ $ ip -s tunl ls Cisco
Cisco: ipv6/ip  remote 192.31.7.104  local 192.203.80.142  ttl 32
RX Packets    Bytes       Errors CsumErrs OutOfSeq Mcasts
    12566     1707516     0      0        0        0
TX Packets    Bytes       Errors DeadLoop NoRoute  NoBufs
    13445     1879677     0      0        0        0
```

Essentially these numbers are the same as those printed using `ip -s link show`, but the tags are different to reflect tunnel-specific features. These features are

- `CsumErrs`—The total number of packets dropped because of checksum failures for a GRE tunnel with enabled checksumming.
- `OutOfSeq`—The total number of packets dropped because they arrived out of sequence for a GRE tunnel with enabled serialization.
- `Mcasts`—The total number of `multicast` packets received on a `broadcast` GRE tunnel.

- DeadLoop—The total number of packets that were not transmitted because the tunnel is looped back to itself.
- NoRoute—The total number of packets that were not transmitted because there is no IP route to a remote endpoint.
- NoBufs—The total number of packets that were not transmitted because the kernel failed to allocate the buffer.

ip monitor and rtmon—Route State Monitoring

The ip utility allows the continuous monitoring of the state of devices, addresses, and routes. This option has a different format in that the command monitor is first on the command line, followed by the object list.

```
ip monitor [ file FILE ] [ all  OBJECT-LIST ]
```

OBJECT-LIST is the list of object types that you want to monitor. It may contain link, address, and route. If no file argument is given, ip opens RTNETLINK, listens to it, and dumps the state changes in the format, as described in the previous sections.

If a filename is given, ip does not listen to RTNETLINK but opens the file that is assumed to contain RTNETLINK messages saved in binary format and dumps them. Such a history file can be generated with the utility rtmon. This utility has a command-line syntax similar to ip monitor. Ideally, rtmon should be started before the first network configuration command is issued. It is possible to start rtmon at any time, as it prepends the history with the system state snapshot dumped at the moment of startup.

Summary

The ip utility is part of the IPROUTE2 utility suite. This utility replaces the old ifconfig and route utilities you saw in Chapter 1. It not only allows complete duplication of the functionality of those utilities but adds depth and atomicity to the operation set.

This utility contains the mechanisms for manipulating the RPDB under Linux. The RPDB is the core of the Linux Policy Routing mechanism as you saw in Chapter 3 "Linux Policy Routing Structures." Now that you have seen the theory of Policy Routing (Chapter 2), the Linux implementation (Chapter 3), and the Linux utility (the current chapter), it's time to jump into two chapters on examples and exercises using these concepts and utilities to implement Policy Routing under Linux.

PART II

Policy Routing Implementations

CHAPTER 5

Simple Network Examples

This chapter will take you through a series of implementation examples for Policy Routing. These examples primarily draw upon the use and configuration of Policy Routing under Linux. You will see the various uses of the ip utility, which was illustrated in Chapter 4. In some instances I will use and refer to other utilities and methods for configuring the structure, but will not be explaining those utilities in this book.

This chapter starts off with the Policy Routing core subjects of addresses, routes, and rules. As you saw in Chapter 3, "Linux Policy Routing Structures" these subjects comprise the core of the RPDB. In most cases I start with the overall theory and delve deeper into the ramifications of implementing that theory. Interspersed throughout are practical examples intended to reinforce the theory and usage. The examples create an ever-increasing complexity and illustrate many of the concepts of Policy Routing. You will see how the limitations of the protocols come into play especially when considering implementations within a finite network structure.

After covering the fundamentals of addressing, routes, and rules, you will jump into the interactions and manipulation of multiple routing tables. This covers the more esoteric structures using tables with some simple rule structures. Then all of the basics are applied to illustrate the complex interactions that can be created with simple steps. In this scenario you will explore the full gamut of addressing, routes, and rules all multiply interacting. At the end of this chapter you will have full control of the basics, a black belt of Policy Routing in Linux.

IP Addressing

The first and most basic of the Policy Routing structure elements is the addressing structure. This fundamental part of an IP network is often completely taken for granted. In the many sessions I have given on using Policy Routing in Linux, I am always asked why I even bother discussing addresses. In reply, I usually ask if anybody there can explain what an IP address is. With your own answer to this question in mind, let me begin.

When looking at a Policy Routing setup you should start by considering the IP addressing structure. The use and interactions of addressing in an IPv4 network often indicate the fundamental data flow of the network structure. To fully understand how these addresses interact with the routing structure of the network, I will first discuss some of the theory of addressing under IPv4 with some forward references to IPv6 as well. From this basis you can see why some of the problems within routed networks currently exist.

Fundamental IP Address Concept

The fundamental design notion behind IPv4 addresses is that an address uniquely identifies the source of a set of services. Most people consider an IP address as identifying a single network interface on a particular machine. But that is a misperception of the address. Think deeper of the actual sequence of events defining how you would locate a given address on a particular network segment.

When considering the communication on a given physical network, say an Ethernet or Token Ring hub, under IPv4 the IP address is not used in direct communication. Any two network devices under IPv4 communicate over a physical network using their respective Media Access Control (MAC) addresses. This is the reason behind Address Resolution Protocol (ARP). On any physical network you can have as many different IPv4 networks as you want coexistent and unaware of each other. Under such a network scheme you may talk of routing structures required between two machines on the same physical network.

A physical network structure that has coexistent, independent IPv4 networks defined and operational provides a good perspective for understanding the divorce of addressing from physical structure. In those conditions you may have multiple complete IPv4 networks defined as matching identical MAC addresses. When you communicate under such a network setup you use the IP address that is appropriate for the network you want to communicate with. Consider the following information and setup:

```
Machine A - eth0:
MAC Address - 00:11:22:33:44:AA
IP Address - 192.168.1.1/24

Machine B - eth0:
MAC Address - 00:11:22:33:44:BB
IP Address - 10.1.1.1/8

Machine C - eth0:
MAC Address - 00:11:22:33:44:CC
IP address - 192.168.1.254/24, 10.254.254.254/8
```

Since Machine C has two IP addresses assigned it is probably the router. Now look at the arp tables on Machine A and Machine B and you will see two different IP addresses associated with the same MAC address. Machine A's arp table lists IP address 192.168.1.254 as having MAC address 00:11:22:33:44:CC and Machine B's arp table lists IP address 10.254.254.254 as having MAC address 00:11:22:33:44:CC.

By seeing the IP address as simply a pointer to the location of a set of services you can see why many of the tricks of IP become a normal conclusion. Spoofing, loopback, and hijacking, along with load balancing, proxy ARP, and NAT, are all functions of the "free" nature of IPv4 addresses.

Consider how you match up a human-readable network name such as www.policyrouting.org with the associated IPv4 address. The DNS service provides a correlation between these two items. Then when you want to see what information is available under the http protocol on that network node, your browser queries the IP address returned from the DNS lookup with a specific request for the "well-known" service port. In this case the IP address is providing a reference platform for obtaining the service. But what is that reference platform?

Now the notion that an IP address is associated with a particular interface becomes hazardous. When you consider what reference platform is associated with the IP address you must take into account the fact that there is no reliable association of the IP address to any particular physical system. Indeed, if the http service considered here were behind a hardware load balancer, the notion of that IP address as "belonging" to any particular hardware system is ludicrous. The only definition of the service relies on the provision of many systems feeding a common output.

Implausible and confusing as this may seem at first glance, the type of setup required to implement this scenario is all too familiar. Consider a standard NAT firewall or any IPv4 load balancing system and you will see that the IP addressing mechanisms are used to define a service without reference to any physical interface. When I speak of an IP address, then, I refer to the services and usage of that address and not to any particular physical manifestation of that address.

Now that an IP address no longer belongs to a physical interface you can start to look at the various methods of using it. This is where you start to play with the IP address structure of the network. By defining the IP address structure you can implement additional methods of Policy Routing.

Example 5.1: Multiple IP Addressing

The following exercise in implementing multiple IP addresses will help you further understand the parts of the IP address functions. This hands-on exercise will then be used as the basis for the rest of the addressing structure explanations.

You will create multiple IP addresses and explore several of the additional device structures provided under Linux. All of the features are available under Kernel 2.1.32 or higher. The utility is ip from the IPROUTE2 package.

Your machine has two network interface cards (NICs) installed. One is Ethernet (eth0) and the other is Token Ring (tr0). Additionally you have the Dummy, Tap, and several flavors of Tunnel interface. You start with no addresses configured with the lone exception of loopback. So your system output from ip addr list looks like Listing 5.1.

Listing 5.1   Output of ip addr list

```
1: lo: <LOOPBACK,UP> mtu 3924 qdisc noqueue
    link/loopback 00:00:00:00:00:00 brd 00:00:00:00:00:00
    inet 127.0.0.1/8 brd 127.255.255.255 scope host lo
    inet6 ::1/128 scope host
2: dummy: <BROADCAST,NOARP> mtu 1500 qdisc noop
    link/ether 00:00:00:00:00:00 brd ff:ff:ff:ff:ff:ff
3: eth0: <BROADCAST,MULTICAST,UP> mtu 1500 qdisc pfifo_fast qlen 100
    link/ether 00:11:22:33:44:aa brd ff:ff:ff:ff:ff:ff
    inet6 fe80::211:22ff:fe33:44aa/10 scope link
4: tr0: <BROADCAST,MULTICAST,UP> mtu 2000 qdisc pfifo_fast qlen 100
    link/ether 00:11:22:33:44:bb brd ff:ff:ff:ff:ff:ff
    inet6 fe80::211:22ff:fe33:44bb/10 scope link
5: tap0: <BROADCAST,MULTICAST,NOARP> mtu 1500 qdisc noop
    link/ether fe:fd:00:00:00:00 brd ff:ff:ff:ff:ff:ff
6: tunl0@NONE: <NOARP> mtu 1480 qdisc noop
    link/ipip 0.0.0.0 brd 0.0.0.0
7: gre0@NONE: <NOARP> mtu 1476 qdisc noop
    link/gre 0.0.0.0 brd 0.0.0.0
8: sit0@NONE: <NOARP> mtu 1480 qdisc noop
    link/sit 0.0.0.0 brd 0.0.0.0
9: teql0: <NOARP> mtu 1500 qdisc noop qlen 100
    link/generic
```

Now you will configure your eth0 interface to have three IPv4 addresses: 10.1.1.1/8, 172.16.1.1/16, and 192.168.1.1/24. Your tr0 interface will have the following three addresses: 10.1.1.2/8, 172.16.1.2/16, and 192.168.1.2/24. This is accomplished through the following command sequence:

```
ip addr add 10.1.1.1/8 dev eth0 brd +
ip addr add 172.16.1.1/16 dev eth0 brd +
ip addr add 192.168.1.1/24 dev eth0 brd +
ip addr add 10.1.1.2/8 dev tr0 brd +
ip addr add 172.16.1.2/16 dev tr0 brd +
ip addr add 192.168.1.2/24 dev tr0 brd +
```

Listing 5.2 is the output from ip addr list.

Listing 5.2   Revised ip_addr list Output

```
1: lo: <LOOPBACK,UP> mtu 3924 qdisc noqueue
    link/loopback 00:00:00:00:00:00 brd 00:00:00:00:00:00
    inet 127.0.0.1/8 brd 127.255.255.255 scope host lo
    inet6 ::1/128 scope host
```

Listing 5.2   continued

```
2: dummy: <BROADCAST,NOARP> mtu 1500 qdisc noop
   link/ether 00:00:00:00:00:00 brd ff:ff:ff:ff:ff:ff
3: eth0: <BROADCAST,MULTICAST,UP> mtu 1500 qdisc pfifo_fast qlen 100
   link/ether 00:11:22:33:44:aa brd ff:ff:ff:ff:ff:ff
   inet 10.1.1.1/8 brd 10.255.255.255 scope global eth0
   inet 172.16.1.1/16 brd 172.16.255.255 scope global eth0
   inet 192.168.1.1/24 brd 192.168.1.255 scope global eth0
   inet6 fe80::211:22ff:fe33:44aa/10 scope link
4: tr0: <BROADCAST,MULTICAST,UP> mtu 2000 qdisc pfifo_fast qlen 100
   link/ether 00:11:22:33:44:bb brd ff:ff:ff:ff:ff:ff
   inet 10.1.1.2/8 brd 10.255.255.255 scope global tr0
   inet 172.16.1.2/16 brd 172.16.255.255 scope global tr0
   inet 192.168.1.2/24 brd 192.168.1.255 scope global tr0
   inet6 fe80::211:22ff:fe33:44bb/10 scope link
5: tap0: <BROADCAST,MULTICAST,NOARP> mtu 1500 qdisc noop
   link/ether fe:fd:00:00:00:00 brd ff:ff:ff:ff:ff:ff
6: tunl0@NONE: <NOARP> mtu 1480 qdisc noop
   link/ipip 0.0.0.0 brd 0.0.0.0
7: gre0@NONE: <NOARP> mtu 1476 qdisc noop
   link/gre 0.0.0.0 brd 0.0.0.0
8: sit0@NONE: <NOARP> mtu 1480 qdisc noop
   link/sit 0.0.0.0 brd 0.0.0.0
9: teql0: <NOARP> mtu 1500 qdisc noop qlen 100
   link/generic
```

You may recall the various items of information in this printout from the discussion of the ip utility in Chapter 4. An important one is the definition of the addresses on the inet lines. For example, the eth0 address 10.1.1.1/8 has a scope global toward the end of the line. This scope parameter is the second important topic of IP addressing.

IP Address Scoping

Many operating systems have methods of assigning multiple IP addresses to an interface. These multiple assignments often code the assignment in terms of fragmented interfaces. A fragmented interface, often referred to as a *coloned* interface or IP alias, is a subinterface defined as a virtual part of the primary interface. You usually see these addresses and assignments in terms of being allocated one to one with a specific interface fragment. Recalling the multiple IP addresses from Example 5.1 you would have seen that eth0 = 10.1.1.1/8, eth0:1 = 172.16.1.1/16, and eth0:2 = 192.168.1.1/24. This tying of the IP address to a virtual interface fragment violates the fundamental consideration of IP addresses being independent of assignment.

What sets the Policy Routing usage apart, especially under Linux, is the concept of addressing scopes. When you assign multiple IP addresses to a single interface under the fragmented interface setup, you treat the first entered address as the primary and the rest of the addresses as secondaries. If you delete the primary address the interface goes away and you lose all other addresses. The interface is paramount in this scenario.

In Policy Routing the treatment of IP addresses obeys the fundamental disassociation of address from physical assignment. Thus when you assign multiple IP addresses to an interface in Policy Routing, you have complete independence of the addresses. There is no fragmented interface to which the address is associated. Instead, all addresses are treated equal and capable of being used independently. However, this brings up the question of how an IP address is defined with respect to the IP network structure.

The definition of an IP address scope ties together the concept of the address and the network. An address exists independently of the network and other addresses. Defining which addresses fit into which network spaces is purely a matter of definition with respect to the IP address itself. This definition is coded through the Classless Inter Domain Routing (CIDR) mask value.

A CIDR mask specifies the masking bits used on an IP network. This is the subnet mask when referencing the network itself. In Policy Routing addressing, this mask specifies the scope of the address space by defining the network coverage. Thus when you have a CIDR mask of /24, you define a network originally referred to as a Class C network. The address scope is then defined as having that address being a member of that network.

This sounds convoluted but is very simple. An example should clarify this somewhat. Consider the addressing structure you implemented in Example 5.1. Each of the addresses in that example had an independent scope. Thus if you look at the addressing for eth0 from that example you have three scopes—call them A, B, and C.

```
10.1.1.1/8      =    Scope A
172.16.1.1/16      =    Scope B
192.168.1.1/24      =    Scope C
```

To show the extent of the scope, consider a simple quiz. Which of the following addresses belong to which scope listed above?

```
10.1.1.2/16
172.16.1.2/24
192.168.1.2/24
```

The answers, in order, are: D (new), E (new), C. Both of the first two addresses and CIDR masks define new scopes, D and E. Only the last one is a member of a preexisting scope. Yes, 10.1.1.2 as an independent address can be considered as belonging to the range of addresses defined by 10.1.1.1/8, but the addition of the /16 CIDR mask defines it as belonging to a new scope. Ditto on the 172.16.1.2 address. In the 192.168.1.2 address the mask also agrees and thus defines that address as belonging to the previously defined scope.

The reason I belabor this point is that the scope has a direct bearing on how the address is treated. In the preceding quiz, the address 192.168.1.2/24 would become a secondary address on the interface. As I discussed in the beginning of this section, a secondary address is removed when the corresponding primary address is removed. Thus if you deleted the original 192.168.1.1/24 address from eth0, then both of the 192.168.1. addresses would disappear. Conversely, since the 10.1.1.2/16 address defines a different scope, deleting the 10.1.1.1/8 address would not affect it. To see this in action work the following example.

Example 5.2: Primary/Secondary IP Addressing

Assume this example starts where Example 5.1 left off. You have two interfaces, each having three addresses defined. See Listing 5.2 for details. Now you define the three new addresses onto eth0 as in the scope discussion. This could be done using the following command sequence:

```
ip addr add 10.1.1.3/16 dev eth0 brd +
ip addr add 172.16.1.3/24 dev eth0 brd +
ip addr add 192.168.1.3/24 dev eth0 brd +
```

Now you have defined several new addresses onto eth0 and one of these addresses is a secondary address. Your `ip addr list dev eth0` would look like the Listing 5.3.

Listing 5.3   Output of ip addr list dev eth0

```
3: eth0: <BROADCAST,MULTICAST,UP> mtu 1500 qdisc pfifo_fast qlen 100
    link/ether 00:11:22:33:44:aa brd ff:ff:ff:ff:ff:ff
    inet 10.1.1.1/8 brd 10.255.255.255 scope global eth0
    inet 172.16.1.1/16 brd 172.16.255.255 scope global eth0
    inet 192.168.1.1/24 brd 192.168.1.255 scope global eth0
    inet 10.1.1.3/16 brd 10.1.255.255 scope global eth0
    inet 172.16.1.3/24 brd 172.16.1.255 scope global eth0
    inet 192.168.1.3/24 brd 192.168.1.255 scope global secondary eth0
    inet6 fe80::211:22ff:fe33:44aa/10 scope link
```

Now delete the address 192.168.1.1/24 with the following command:

```
ip addr del 192.168.1.1/24 dev eth0
```

You will see the following listing of addresses on eth0:

```
3: eth0: <BROADCAST,MULTICAST,UP> mtu 1500 qdisc pfifo_fast qlen 100
    link/ether 00:11:22:33:44:aa brd ff:ff:ff:ff:ff:ff
    inet 10.1.1.1/8 brd 10.255.255.255 scope global eth0
    inet 172.16.1.1/16 brd 172.16.255.255 scope global eth0
    inet 10.1.1.3/16 brd 10.1.255.255 scope global eth0
    inet 172.16.1.3/24 brd 172.16.1.255 scope global eth0
    inet6 fe80::211:22ff:fe33:44aa/10 scope link
```

As expected, both of the 192.168.1.x addresses are gone. If you want to prove to yourself that this is due to scoping, just try deleting any of the other addresses and see which ones go away.

What you have seen through these examples is the two primary concepts of IP addresses within Policy Routing. The first concept is the divorce of usage where an IP address refers to the provision of a set of services and is independent of any particular physical manifestation. The second concept is the grouping of addresses as defined by the scope of the address, which ties together the address with the provision of the network as an entity.

IP Routes

The second major building block of Policy Routing is the usage and concept of IP routes. Under traditional routing this is the only element that is considered, and it is relegated to a single use. Traditionally, all routes were destination based. As discussed in Chapter 2 and fit into the Policy Routing hierarchy in Chapter 3, routes may be based on any and all parts of an IP network packet. Additionally, routes no longer just specify where a packet may be forwarded, but specify additional actions as well.

The full coverage of Policy Routing allows actions on the route both at the host and at the router level. The router level is obvious but why would a host have any participation? The host level is often where the initial participation in the network can be very fruitful. If you recall the analogy to the driveway as used in the beginning of Chapter 2, then you see the place for the host system to participate in the routing structure.

When you consider the host system participation you may assume one of several network configurations. The simplest is the multiple router scenario, where you are interested in placing the policy logic on the host because you may have several traditional routers in place. Additionally, you may have to consider the multiple network scenario where your host system has one interface but there are several logical IP networks coexistent on the physical network. You saw a limited example of this in the IP addressing earlier.

Example 5.3: Host Routing

To illustrate both of these scenarios, consider that you have a host system with a single Ethernet interface. This interface is configured as in Example 5.1, so you have a single interface with the following three IP addresses defined:

```
etho:
10.1.1.1/8
172.16.1.1/16
192.168.1.1/24
```

You happen to know that most of the other machines are addressed within the 10/8 network scope because that is the defined corporate standard network. The 172.16/16 scope is used by the system administration group and the 192.168.1/24 scope is used by the engineering testing lab group.

The core router for the corporation connecting to the outside world has an address of 10.254.254.254. It should be the default router for all traffic to the Internet. Additionally, you know that this core router also has an address of 172.16.254.254, which is used as the management address for the router by the administrative group. A second router exists with address 192.168.1.254 and it connects to the engineering test lab systems, which exist within scope 192.168.2/24.

At this point with only the addresses defined on your eth0 interface you can ping and receive responses from all of the routers you know about on the network. But why can you ping, for example, the 172.16.254.254 router interface and receive a response? Or indeed why do any of the addresses respond to you?

This is a function of the automatic route creation that occurs whenever you add an IP address to the system that defines a scope with more than one member. Earlier when you defined your IP addressing scopes you used a CIDR mask that as a network mask defined more than just your sole IP address. In other words, 192.168.1.1/24 defines a scope that includes any address from 192.168.1.0/24 through 192.168.1.255/24 inclusive. Under Linux Policy Routing, this automatically defines the corresponding network route to the route table. This is why the scope is what ties together the notion of address and network.

Look at the current routing table on this system as shown by `ip route list`:

```
10.0.0.0/8 dev eth0  proto kernel  scope link  src 10.1.1.1
172.16.0.0/16 dev eth0  proto kernel  scope link  src 172.16.1.1
192.168.1.0/24 dev eth0  proto kernel  scope link  src 192.168.1.1
127.0.0.0/8 dev lo  scope link
```

Note especially how the routes for the additional addresses are coded. In all of these cases there is a field that tells the system which source address to use on the packet. So when you ping 10.254.254.254, you use a source address of 10.1.1.1. What if you wanted complete control over the route creation? Think then of the definition of scope. The address scope is what ties together the address with the network. The smallest definable network then consists of a single address, and the route to a single address is the address itself. So to turn off automatic route creation you can simply specify all of your addresses as host addresses.

To try this, run through the following command sequence. First you will clear all your addresses, then you will add in your addresses with full /32 scopes, and then you will view the output of your route table.

```
ip addr flu dev eth0
ip addr add 10.1.1.1/32 dev eth0 brd 10.255.255.255
ip addr add 172.16.1.1/32 dev eth0 brd 172.16.255.255
ip addr add 192.168.1.1/32 dev eth0 brd 192.168.1.255
ip ro list
127.0.0.0/8 dev lo  scope link
```

Note that the output of your route table contains only the loopback device route. None of the addresses you entered are in the route table. Now you want to add the routes that had been autocreated before. This will show you what the full standard route commands do.

```
ip ro add 10/8 proto kernel scope link dev eth0 src 10.1.1.1
ip ro add 172.16/16 proto kernel scope link dev eth0 src 172.16.1.1
ip ro add 192.168.1/24 proto kernel scope link dev eth0 src 192.168.1.1
```

Now if you do a `ip ro list` you will see that your routing table is exactly the same as when you ran `ip route list`. Just for kicks, what do you suppose will happen if you change the `src` parameter? Try the following commands:

```
ip ro del 172.16/16 proto kernel scope link dev eth0 src 172.16.1.1
ip ro add 172.16/16 proto kernel scope link dev eth0 src 192.168.1.1
```

When you look at your route table with `ip ro list` you see that the route to 172.16.0.0/16 is coded using a `src` of 192.168.1.1. Now could you ping the 172.16.254.254 router? Probably not. As you recall from the intro to this exercise it only had a 10/8 and a 172.16/16 address defined. So when your packet with a source address of 192.168.1.1 hits it, it does not know how to respond—that is, if your packet even gets to the router interface in the first place. And yes this is a complicated way to spoof an address.

The most important part of this illustration is that you can now play what I refer to as loopy routing. For example, suppose the core router, 10.254.254.254, had a connection to the engineering 192.168.2.0/24 network and that it had a route to 192.168.1.0/24 via the engineering router. So when you now send out your ping to 172.16.254.254 it responds by sending back a packet to you through the engineering network. Your packet travels through the network to the router one way and returns by a completely different path. That is Policy Routing using addresses and routes.

Example 5.4: Basic Router Filters

You have seen some of the ways you can use the route commands to change the outgoing source address on your host system. Turning to the other half, the router or multiconnected host, you see how the route command can do more than just indicate destination. You can use simple route commands to implement security and other advanced policies using Policy Routing as you will see in the following examples.

Recall from Chapter 4 that the `route` subcommand had several types that could be defined for routes. The `unicast`, `local`, `broadcast`, and `multicast` types are for specific use as you will see when using multiple routing tables and rules. The `nat` type will be covered in Chapter 8. What you will use here are the `throw`, `unreachable`, `prohibit`, and `blackhole` types.

These four types of routes have the following attributes:

```
throw         -    returns ICMP Type 3 Code 0 (net unreachable)
unreachable   -     returns ICMP Type 3 Code 1 (host unreachable)
prohibit      -    returns ICMP Type 3 Code 13 \
                        (communication administratively prohibited)
blackhole     -    drops the packet with no message
```

Since each ICMP error code returned has a different message, what you use depends on whether you have a specific purpose for denying the route. Considering the router setup from Example 5.3, what if you are in charge of the core, accounting, and engineering routers as shown in Figure 5.1. The engineering router connects to the engineering test network, 192.168.2.0/24. The accounting router connects to the accounting network, 172.17.0.0/16. All the client devices have a default route pointing to the core router, 10.254.254.254. The core router then has routes that point to the engineering, 10.254.254.253, and the accounting, 10.254.254.252, routers.

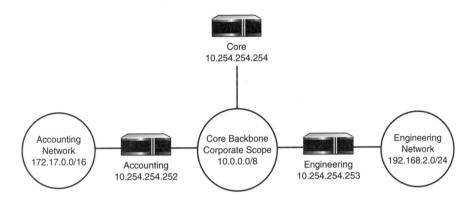

Figure 5.1

Basic router filter's network diagram.

Most traffic from the main 10/8 network is not allowed onto either of these networks. The accounting network is to be administratively denied to anyone with the exceptions that the range of addresses 10.2.3.32/27 and 10.3.2.0/27 are allowed to access the accounting network. The engineering test network may be accessed by anyone on 10.10.0.0/14. All others do not even know the network exists.

This set of network security policies sounds like a firewall type of decision, but this is a common routing security structure. This is very easily done through routes on a policy router. First, you have to decide what messages you want to send back to the originating machine. In the case described above I would use the following setups (see Listing 5.4).

Listing 5.4   Basic Router Filter's Simple Planner

```
From accounting network - 172.17.0.0/16
10.2.3.32/27        -    full route
10.3.2.0/27         -    full route
10/8             -    prohibit
172.16/16        -    prohibit

From Engineering test network    - 192.168.2.0/24
10.10/14         -    full route
10/8             -    blackhole
172.17/16        -    blackhole
172.16/16        -    blackhole
```

Note that these are coded in terms of "From" the respective network. This is due to the routes you are using still operating in terms of destination-based routing. Even though the types are Policy Routing, the routes themselves only code for destinations. This usage serves two purposes: First, these routes can operate on a non-Policy Routing system; second, the routing structure within the OS itself can remain streamlined in operation. As you saw in Chapter 3, the less structure placed into any one segment of the packet path, the faster the routing decision.

To apply these routes to the routers you need to consider the current connectivity of the routers. Each of the engineering and accounting routers has two interfaces: eth0 on the corporate backbone and tr0 on the respective private network. You will start from the bare system without any addressing and set up the routers.

Starting with the engineering system first you have two addresses assigned and the security policy as stated in the beginning of this example. You can set up this router in several different ways. Consider first the following command sequence:

```
ip addr add 192.168.2.254/24 dev tr0 brd +
ip addr add 10.254.254.253/32 dev eth0 brd 10.255.255.255
ip ro add 10.10/14 scope link proto kernel dev eth0 src 10.254.254.253
```

Now you have added in the IP addresses and turned off the autoroute configuration for only the 10/8 network by using the /32 scope mask. Then you define a route for all traffic returning to 10.10/14 networks. The autoroute is installed for the 192.168.2.0/24 network as you wanted. Since no other routes are defined, then any other packet, such as for 172.17/16 or other 10/8 addresses, would not be routed by the system. But what happens when a router does not have a route for a packet? It will return an ICMP Type 3 Code 0, which is a "Net unreachable" message. But you do not want any errors returned to any of your other networks or to the engineering network itself. So you then add the following routes:

```
ip ro add blackhole 10/8
ip ro add blackhole 172.17/16
ip ro add blackhole 172.16/16
```

Now any packets that specifically try to return to any of those networks are silently dropped.

Now you consider the accounting router setup. Again you have two interfaces with addresses and the security policy statement. But in the security policy statement for this network you want to send back an ICMP Type 3 Code 13 "communication administratively prohibited" message. So you set up the accounting router as follows:

```
ip addr add 10.254.254.252/32 dev eth0 brd 10.255.255.255
ip addr add 172.17.254.254/16 dev tr0 brd +
ip ro add 10.2.3.32/27 scope link proto kernel dev eth0 src 10.254.254.252
ip ro add 10.3.2.0/27 scope link proto kernel dev eth0 src 10.254.254.252
ip ro add prohibit 10/8
ip ro add prohibit 172.16/16
ip ro add prohibit 192.168.2/24
```

As noted previously, all of these routes take effect on communications that are exiting from the subnetwork. So the ICMP errors are actually returned to the systems that exist in the subnetwork itself. This is due to the routes being valid for forwarding operations only. They are destination based. When you start working with the final member of the Policy Routing triad, rules, you will see where the other packet selection mechanisms come into play.

Example 5.5: Multiple Routes to Same Destination

Now that you have set up the security policies using the Policy Routing route structure, you turn to the setup on the core router. Recently your company has obtained two Internet connections from two different service providers. Each connection is a T1 with an independent router and an independent assigned address scope. You want to set up load balancing for the Internet traffic.

The global information you will need is about the two different ISPs, and you will set up the multiple addresses you need on your router's external interface, eth1, as shown in Listing 5.5.

Listing 5.5 Multiple Address Assignments

```
ISP #1:
Router Interface = 1.1.1.30/27
ISP #2:
Router Interface = 2.2.2.30/27

Your router eth1
ip addr add 1.1.1.1/27 dev eth1 brd +
ip addr add 2.2.2.1/27 dev eth1 brd +
```

Even though you have two different routes to the Internet, you would think that you can only have one default route. But you can have as many default or other routes as you would like. There are several different ways to code multiple routes to the same destination. Each method depends on the behavior you would like to have.

The first method is to use a per-packet method of multiple default routes. Under this scenario each packet entering the router will go out a different route. The main drawback to this format is that the paths to the final destination may vary in transit time enough to cause problems with packet reassembly queuing, especially with certain server types. But this is a very simple method to implement.

The route subcommand of the ip utility contains the methods allowing for multiple routers. This is coded using the equalize and nexthop commands. The nexthop command itself defines multiple gateways to send packets to and can take an optional weight command, which allows packets to be differentially balanced. The equalize command tells the route structure to send on a per-packet basis.

For example, if you decide to send each packet independently through each router, you would use the following command:

```
ip route add equalize default \
      nexthop via 1.1.1.30 dev eth1 \
      nexthop via 2.2.2.30 dev eth1
```

This will send each packet out through a different router. The first packet will go to 1.1.1.30, the second to 2.2.2.30, the third to 1.1.1.30, and so on ad nauseaum.

What if the router 1.1.1.30 was two T1s and the router 2.2.2.30 was a 512K fractional T1? Then you would want to weight the routes so as to send 4 packets to 1.1.1.30 for every 1 packet sent to 2.2.2.30. The easy way is to use the packet counts as weights. You would then use the following version of the command:

```
ip route add equalize default \
      nexthop via 1.1.1.30 dev eth1 weight 4 \
      nexthop via 2.2.2.30 dev eth1 weight 1
```

Now another way you might want to load balance is to allow each traffic flow sequence to go by one of the routes. But you do not want to inspect packets or code half the addresses one way and half the other. Instead you simply remove the equalize modifier from your multiple hop default route. Now traffic will be routed to one or the other route on a per-flow basis rather than a per-packet basis. Again you can use weights in this sense to load balance the flows themselves. Note that the per-flow is for tcp sessions while udp is treated per packet.

Example 5.6: Troubleshooting Unbalanced Multiple Loop Routes

You can also use the loopy routing feature to force one of the router connections to be treated as a pure input router and the other router as a pure output router. This method is often used with unbalanced connections to provide for the core site usage.

For example, suppose that you want to start providing a Web site for your corporation. You will contract with two different ISPs to provide connections. One of them will provide a T1 with a subnet of addresses for use. The other will provide 5 T1 lines with 2 IP addresses and they also agree to allow your subnet IPs from the other ISP to be sent through their connection. So you have a configuration as follows (illustrated in Figure 5.2):

```
ISP #1:
Router 1.1.1.30/27
Subnet 1.1.1.0/27
ISP #2:
Router 2.2.2.2/30
Your usable IP - 2.2.2.1/30
```

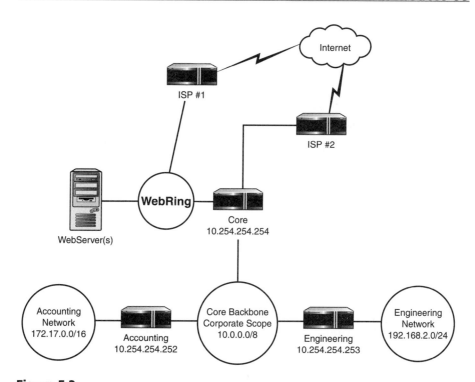

Figure 5.2

Web server load balancing.

You set up a network, WebRing, to contain several Web and other Internet servers. They are assigned real IP addresses from the 1.1.1.0/27 network address space. The router from ISP #1 also connects into this network. All of your servers have a single default route pointing at your router's tr0 interface 1.1.1.1. Your other interface is connected by a crossover cable to ISP #2's router. Now the route structure is that all outgoing traffic will be routed to the Internet through ISP #2's router. Since this traffic contains the addresses given by ISP #1, the return requests will come down to your network through ISP #1's router.

Your router is not doing any real work here. The route you use simply allows all traffic from tr0 to flow out through eth0. Now your Web site gets very popular. Your notice that the uplink through ISP #2 is often running at capacity while the downlink through ISP #1 is barely cracking 256K bursts. So you decide to funnel some of the traffic through to use up some of the ISP #1 bandwidth. No problem, you simply use the weights in your router to send some traffic upward through the ISP #1 router.

And whammo, your Web site slows to a crawl. As soon as you remove the weighted routes everything is great. Upon investigation with your Ethereal brand packet sniffer you see that the Web machines are confused by the route redirects and that all the Web traffic now tries to go up through ISP #1's router.

Now you see why the placement of Policy Routing structures becomes important. In this scenario you would want to recode the default routes on the Web systems themselves to have weights. When you recode the route on your router it then informs the Web sites through a redirect to use the router from ISP #1. But since the redirect has no provision for weight, all packets then go through the ISP #1 router. When you code policy routes on the Web servers themselves, the packets are appropriately balanced and the maximum bandwidth is appropriately used.

If you had been assigned the block of IP addresses from ISP #1 and they were independent of the router, you could place the Web servers on a third network behind your router and you could then use the Policy Routing to balance the traffic flows. This type of setup also provides security to the systems as well and will be revisited later.

IP Rules

One of the topics that you have not seen is the supposed original basis for using Policy Routing in the first place—the ability to route based on source, TOS, packet data, and other packet features. This is where the final member of the Policy Routing triad, rules, enters the scene.

As you saw in Chapter 3, rules are what provide the decision structure in the RPDB. Rules function not just as logical packet selectors, but also possess the capability to act upon a selected packet. In this sense the true power becomes apparent. Rules have much the same set of actions as routes when acting directly on a packet. Unlike routes, they cannot specify any forwarding actions but only the blocking actions. To illustrate, consider Example 5.7.

Example 5.7: Basic Router Filters v2.0

Consider the setup you have running from Example 5.4 as illustrated by Figure 5.1. The security structure provided by the routes acts upon the traffic, leaving the subnets only. Since you have control of the core router and the subnet routers, you would like to reimplement the security structure so that the requesting client is returned the appropriate error message.

The logic revisited is that the accounting network is to be administratively denied to all except the range of addresses 10.2.3.32/27 and 10.3.2.0/27. The engineering test network may only be accessed by anyone in 10.10.0.0/14, with all others not even knowing the network exists. To summarize the logic tree:

```
To accounting network - 172.17.0.0/16
10.2.3.32/27      -     allowed
10.3.2.0/27       -     allowed
0/0          -     prohibit

To Engineering test network   - 192.168.2.0/24
10.10/14      -     allowed
0/0          -     blackhole
```

Note that this logic is supposed to be from the point of view of the core router. Looking back at Listing 5.4 from Example 5.4 you can see that the implemented logic is on the subnet routers. To ensure that your new structure is not prone to the hackery that could be done under the implementation of Example 5.4, you also need to look at the logic from the point of view of the subnet routers. In that manner anyone trying to subvert the global security by directly pointing at the subnet routers would be forced to obey the same rules. So the subnet router's logic would then look like

```
# Accounting Network Router
10.2.3.32/27        -    allow
10.3.2.0/27         -    allow
0/0            -    blackhole

# Engineering test network Router
10.10/14       -    allow
0/0            -    blackhole
```

Note that this is essentially the same as the core router logic with the exception that on the accounting router and the engineering router all traffic not allowed is silently discarded. In this manner you can essentially make the accounting and engineering routers invisible. Whether the end user workstation is coded for a default route to the core router or has entered a route directly to the accounting or engineering routers, the logical behavior of the network is consistent.

You then set about implementing this policy using the rules on the core, accounting, and engineering routers. Starting with the core router first, you allow for the default rules (see Chapter 4) and code in the following rule set:

```
# For the Accounting Network
ip rule add from 10.2.3.32/27 to 172.17/16 prio 16000
ip rule add from 10.3.2.0/27 to 172.17/16 prio 16010
ip rule add from 0/0 to 172.17/16 prio 16020 prohibit

# For the Engineering Test Network
ip rule add from 10.10/14 to 192.168.2/24 prio 17000
ip rule add from 0/0 to 192.168.2/24 prio 17010 blackhole
```

This allows all traffic from the allocated subnets to be passed into the routes while returning or dropping those packets not allowed. Of course you still have the routes themselves pointing to the accounting and engineering subnets. The ordering of the rules is important and you have allowed space to add rules later by spacing out the priority number. It would have sufficed to not put the to section in the first two rules or in the fourth. But you usually will want to err on the side of exact specification, especially when you end up placing rules into play that you come back to look at several months later. Also note that you are not specifying the interface on which the packets arrive or leave. This allows these rules to act globally. If you were certain that the traffic would be confined in transit to specific interfaces, then you would also specify the interface here. Conversely, by using an interface specification on a multi-interfaced router you can allow some traffic without having to specify any rules.

In this setup there is no restriction on any of the 10.10/14 addresses accessing the accounting network or on any of the 10.2.3.32/27, 10.3.2.0/27 addresses accessing the engineering test network. That is why you want to be able to specify Policy Routing structures on the accounting and engineering routers. By so spreading the logic, you allow for better traffic flow and also ensure that there is no one point of catastrophic failure.

You then continue on to configure the accounting router. As specified in the logic tree for Example 5.7, the accounting router will have the following rule set.

```
ip rule add from 10.2.3.32/27 dev eth0 prio 16000
ip rule add from 10.3.2.0/27 dev eth0 prio 16010
ip rule add from 0/0 dev eth0 prio 16020 blackhole
```

Note that in this case you do specify the interface on which the packets arrive. You make the assumption that if any packets originate from within the accounting network with an incorrect source address, there are other methods to deal with them.

Having coded the accounting router you turn to the engineering test network router. Again following the logic tree, you install the following rule set:

```
ip rule add from 10.10/14 dev eth0 prio 17000
ip rule add from 192.168.2/24 dev tr0 prio 17010
ip rule add from 0/0 prio 17020 blackhole
```

Now here you decide that because the engineers are wont to play with various attack programs, especially ones that use spoofing, you will limit the traffic both into and out of the network. So you allow the traffic on interface eth0 from the allowed addresses into the network. Then you allow out only the traffic with the appropriate IP address from the internal interface. Finally, you silently discard all other traffic. You essentially use the source address rules to only allow allocated addresses into and out of the network.

Multiple Route Tables

Up to this point you have been using the single master route table available within Policy Routing. All of the examples and uses have assumed that you only have a single global route structure. This is true for all known Policy Routing capable devices with the exception of Linux. At this point I will diverge into the enhanced world of Policy Routing structures under Linux.

As you saw in Chapter 3, within the Linux Policy Routing structure there is provision for 255 independent routing tables. The standard structure allocation provides a default structure. Recalling this information from Chapters 3 and 4, you have the following default table structure:

```
Table #253   =   DEFAULT (created by the default rule #32767)
Table #254   =    MAIN (default master route table)
Table #255   =   LOCAL (broadcast & local addresses)
```

As you recall from Chapter 3, of these tables the LOCAL table should not be modified or used normally. It has a special functionality with respect to the broadcast and local route structures.

The naming of these tables is handled by a lookup reference file. This file is /etc/iproute2/rt_tables. While you can always reference the tables by number from 1 to 255, it is easier to read your scripts if you name the tables. I usually will place a comment at the beginning of my scripts that states the names and numbers association so that the file still makes sense if someone changes the rt_tables mapping.

Example 5.8: Basic Router Filters v3.0

In order to use the flexibility immediately accorded to you by the specification of multiple routing tables, you decide to recode your security structure from Example 5.7 in terms of simpler rules. You start with the core router. You decide to create two new route tables that contain the routes for the accounting and engineering networks. First you edit the rt_tables file and name the tables appropriately (see Listing 5.6).

Listing 5.6   The Edited rt_tables File

```
#
# reserved values
#
255     local
254     main
253     default
0       unspec
#
# Policy Routing Example 5.8
#
1       accounting
2       engineering
#
# end rt_tables
```

Now you start to populate the route tables and rules.

Note that the specification of the complete routing and security structure can now be fulfilled on the core router. In Example 5.7 you were limited because of the rules. In that setup any traffic selected for either the engineering or accounting network could be routed to the other network. That is, any traffic from 10.10/14 could be routed to the accounting network due to being selected for fall through to the main table by the Engineering rule. And vice versa, the Accounting-allowed rule traffic would fall through to the main table and could be routed to the engineering network.

Now you see that you can specify exactly that all traffic to either of these networks be segregated into a table by the appropriate rule. Thus you only need three rules to specify all the traffic flow. You need to create the rules first by starting fresh on the core router without any routes or rules referring to the accounting or engineering networks.

```
#For the Accounting Network
ip rule add from 10.2.3.32/27 to 172.17/16 prio 16000 table accounting
ip rule add from 10.3.2.0/27 to 172.17/16 prio 16010 table accounting

#For the Engineering Test Network
ip rule add from 10.10/14 to 192.168.2/24 prio 17000 table engineering
```

This sends the traffic destined for the respective network to a route table for that network, and only such traffic will get to the table. Now you need to code the accounting and engineering route tables.

```
# The accounting table #1
ip route add 172.17/16 table accounting via 10.254.254.252 proto static
ip route add prohibit default

# The engineering table #2
ip route add 192.168.2/24 table engineering via 10.254.254.253 proto static
ip route add blackhole default
```

Now all traffic flowing to these networks is segregated and you have implemented the security policy. Or have you?

Recall that the original security policy stated that all traffic to the accounting network that was not permitted was to be returned an ICMP Administratively Denied message, and that no one was to be able to determine that the engineering test network existed if they were not permitted to access it. Does this setup still follow those maxims? Upon further inspection you determine that it does not. Why?

You added to the accounting and engineering routing tables default routes that specified the appropriate actions to take. For accounting you prohibit and for engineering you blackhole. But what if someone from the 10/8 network who is not allowed onto engineering—in other words, someone sourced outside 10.10/14—decides to try to get to 192.168.2/24? From the rules above they would end up in the main table. Now the main table does not have a route to the engineering network so by default the router will return a ICMP Network Unreachable. This is not the same as a blackhole where the packets are dropped. So the default route in the engineering table is never reached or used. Ditto for the accounting network.

The trick then is to still use the rules to control the flow of alternate traffic. You do note that you had purposely allocated space in the rule priority selection so that you could also insert rules later on. To complete the Policy Routing structure, you add the rules to control the unwanted traffic streams:

```
#For Accounting network
ip rule add from 0/0 to 172.17/16 prio 16050 prohibit

# For Engineering test network
```

```
ip rule add from 0/0 to 192.168.2/24 prio 17050 blackhole
```

Now you have the security policy completely specified on the core router. Turning to the accounting and engineering routers you see that the setups as specified in Example 5.7 are sufficient for the current security structure.

At this point you review the total Policy Routing structure. The core router has the main role in the routing structure. It provides the appropriate error messages and allowed traffic control to the accounting and engineering networks. This policy structure is supported by the implementation on the accounting and engineering routers. These sub-network routers reinforce the security policy by allowing only the traffic that is allowed. While in this type of setup you could have dispensed with implementing any policy on the core router, you want to stress that the core router should always be the default. The subnetwork routers merely prevent internal hackery.

You can see how without the multiple routing tables on the core router you would not have been able to lock down the traffic to the subnetworks as accurately. This is true of many situations in Policy Routing. Since each routing table is completely independent of the others, there can be no crossover bleed of misdirected routes.

All Together Now

Having tackled the setup required for implementing this Policy Routing structure you want to move on to bigger projects. Luckily you have been selected to assist in incorporating a recently acquired company into the corporate network fabric.

This company has three different connections into the core network:

- The first connection is the Internet and is mediated from an existing firewall you have no control over.
- The second connection is the primary vendor who has provided a connection to their ordering system.
- The third connection is the primary transport supplier who has provided a connection into their scheduling system.

The network connections all terminate into a single Token Ring network. Currently there are four small Token Ring-Ethernet routers installed between the internal Ethernets and the Token Ring. Additionally, there is a translating bridge between the two Ethernets and the Token Ring for the Internet connection. Your job is to fix and secure this mess.

The networks and connections from the three outside networks are shown in Listing 5.7.

Listing 5.7   All Together Now Initial Notes

```
# Internet
Allocated DMZ Address Space from Firewall: 172.16.1.0/24
Firewall TokenRing Interface: 172.16.1.254, 192.168.1.254, 192.168.2.254
Provides NAT for all addresses in the 192.168.0/22 range
```

Listing 5.7   continued

```
# Vendor
Allocated DMZ Addresses: 192.168.100.0/24
Router TokenRing Interface: 192.168.100.254
Provides Connection to 172.18/16
Allows routes to 192.168.1/24 and 192.168.2/24

# Supplier
Allocated DMZ Addresses: 192.168.200.0/24
Router TokenRing Interface: 192.168.200.254
Provides Connection to 10.10/16
Allows routes to 192.168.1/24 and 192.168.2/24
```

You find out the two internal Ethernets use 192.168.1.0/24 and 192.168.2.0/24. Now some of the allowances from the routers make sense. Digging further you find out that only some people are supposed to be allowed into either or both of the Vendor and Supplier networks. And there are several groups of computers that management would like to not have Internet access.

You write down all of the information and distill it into Listing 5.8.

Listing 5.8   All Together Now Routing/Security Policy

```
# Allowed to Vendor network
192.168.1.0/24
192.168.2.32/27

# Allowed to Supplier network
192.168.2.0/24
192.168.128/29

# Denied Internet
192.168.1.128/25
192.168.2.32/27
```

Fairly simple so far. You take out all four small routers and both of the translating bridges so that nothing now connects the Token Ring with the internal Ethernets. You decide to use a single Policy Routing core router between the internal Ethernets and the Token Ring DMZ. While determining where to install the Ethernet cables you discover that the two Ethernets are actually only two different hubs with a backplane connection, thus making them one physical network. Therefore, you only need one physical Ethernet interface. Well, this will be even easier, you think, hoping that nothing else pops up to surprise you.

You start configuring your core router by notating the addresses and primary routes (see Listing 5.9).

Listing 5.9   All Together Now Address and Routes Notes

```
# tr0
172.16.1.1/24
192.168.100.1/24
192.168.200.1/24

# eth0
192.168.1.254/24
192.168.2.254/24

# Primary Routes
172.18.0.0/16 through gateway 192.168.100.254 (Vendor)
10.10.0.0/16 through gateway 192.168.200.254 (Supplier)
Default through gateway 172.16.1.254 (Internet)
```

You now have both your configuration and your security policy. You decide to create one script to implement the corresponding Policy Routing structure. This script with comments is shown in Listing 5.10.

Listing 5.10   All Together Now—The Script

```
# Begin script for CORPALL V1.0
#
# Vendor Net:
#     172.18/16 / router 192.168.100.254/24
# Supplier Net:
#     10.10/16 / router 192.168.200.254/24
# Internet Firewall:
#     default / router 172.16.1.254/24
#
# Implement Multiple IP Addresses
#
# TokenRing 0 - DMZ
ip addr add 172.16.1.1/24 dev tr0 brd +
ip addr add 192.168.100.1/24 dev tr0 brd +
ip addr add 192.168.200.1/24 dev tr0 brd +
#
# Ethernet 0 - Internal Ethernets
ip addr add 192.168.1.254/24 dev eth0 brd +
ip addr add 192.168.2.254/24 dev eth0 brd +
#
# Implement Routing Tables
#     Table 1 = vendor
#     Table 2 = supplier
#     Table 3 = inet
#
# To Internet - use inet table
ip route add default via 172.16.1.254 proto static table inet
#
```

Listing 5.10   continued

```
# To Vendor Net - use vendor table
ip route add 172.18/16 via 192.168.100.254 proto static table vendor
#
# To Supplier Net - use supplier table
ip route add 10.10/16 via 192.168.200.254 proto static table supplier
#
# Implement Rules
#    15000 - 15999 use for Vendor
#    16000 - 16999 use for Supplier
#    17000 - 17999 use for Internet
#
# To Vendor Net
ip rule add from 192.168.1.0/24 to 172.18/16 prio 15000 table vendor
ip rule add from 192.168.2.32/27 to 172.18/16 prio 15100 table vendor
#
# To Supplier Net
ip rule add from 192.168.2.0/24 to 10.10/16 prio 16000 table supplier
ip rule add from 192.168.1.128/29 to 10.10/16 prio 16100 table supplier
#
# To Internet
ip rule add from 192.168.1.0/25 to 0/0 prio 17000 table inet
ip rule add from 192.168.2.0/27 to 0/0 prio 17100 table inet
ip rule add from 192.168.2.64/26 to 0/0 prio 17200 table inet
ip rule add from 192.168.2.128/25 to 0/0 prio 17300 table inet
#
# Force Policy Routing Structure Update
ip route flush cache
#
# end CORPALL version 1.0
```

You can then run this configuration script on your Policy Routing core router and you will have a complete implementation. This one script ties together all of the parts of basic Policy Routing implementation. You have multiple IP addresses, multiple routing tables, rules, and a defined structure for implementation.

Just to prove to yourself that this is not the only way to implement this structure, you create an alternate script (see Listing 5.11).

Listing 5.11   All Together Now—The Other Script

```
# Begin script for CORPALL V1.0 Alternate
#
# Vendor Net:
#    172.18/16 / router 192.168.100.254/24
# Supplier Net:
#    10.10/16 / router 192.168.200.254/24
# Internet Firewall:
#    default / router 172.16.1.254/24
```

Listing 5.11   continued

```
#
# Implement Multiple IP Addresses
#
# TokenRing 0 - DMZ
ip addr add 172.16.1.1/24 dev tr0 brd +
ip addr add 192.168.100.1/24 dev tr0 brd +
ip addr add 192.168.200.1/24 dev tr0 brd +
#
# Ethernet 0 - Internal Ethernets
ip addr add 192.168.1.254/24 dev eth0 brd +
ip addr add 192.168.2.254/24 dev eth0 brd +
#
# Implement Routing Tables
#     Table 1 = external
#
# To Internet - use main table default route
ip route add default via 172.16.1.254 proto static
#
# To Vendor Net - use external table
ip route add 172.18/16 via 192.168.100.254 proto static table external
#
# To Supplier Net - use external table
ip route add 10.10/16 via 192.168.200.254 proto static table external
#
# Implement Rules
#     15000 - 15999 use for Vendor
#     16000 - 16999 use for Supplier
#     17000 - 17999 use for Internet
#
# To Vendor Net
ip rule add from 192.168.1.0/24 to 172.18/16 prio 15000 table external
ip rule add from 192.168.2.32/27 to 172.18/16 prio 15100 table external
ip rule add from 0/0 to 172.18/16 prio 15999 table external blackhole
#
# To Supplier Net
ip rule add from 192.168.2.0/24 to 10.10/16 prio 16000 table external
ip rule add from 192.168.1.128/29 to 10.10/16 prio 16100 table external
ip rule add from 0/0 to 10.10/16 prio 16999 table external blackhole
#
# To Internet
ip rule add from 192.168.1.128/25 to 0/0 prio 17000 table main blackhole
ip rule add from 192.168.2.32/27 to 0/0 prio 17100 table main blackhole
# Default AntiSpoof
ip rule add from 192.168.1.0/24 to 0/0 dev eth0 prio 17200
ip rule add from 192.168.2.0/24 to 0/0 dev eth0 prio 17300
ip rule add from 0/0 dev eth0 prio 17999 blackhole
#
```

Listing 5.11   continued

```
# Force Policy Routing Structure Update
ip route flush cache
#
# end CORPALL version 1.0 Alternate
```

Upon careful study, you determine that this script would also correctly implement the Policy Routing structure you want. The first script uses three additional routing tables and simple rules. The second script uses only one additional table and more complex rules. But both will work identically from the point of view of the traffic through the router.

Summary

You now have your black belt in basic Policy Routing implementation. You see from the final example that there is usually more than one correct implementation method. You see how the three elements of Policy Routing—address, route, and rule—support, intermingle, and interact with each other.

You are now ready to start considering the advanced implications of Policy Routing structures. You wonder how the core triad interacts with other network structures, especially when you start considering dynamic routing, NAT, firewalling, QoS, and packet filters. These subjects are the next you start to study as you begin to see the larger network picture emerge.

CHAPTER 6

Complex Network Examples

With your newly acquired Policy Routing Black Belt you feel you can take on the world. So you decide you want to try some of the outer limits of Policy Routing structures. You start from the consideration of the Triad: Address, Route, and Rule. The definitions of the basic elements of Policy Routing are broad statements of use. You wonder what hidden assumptions and applications are covered within those definitions.

You start by considering how services define addressing and how to manipulate those services from the origin. You look at the service structure of an individual host as it relates to the overall provision of services within the network, then to how those network services are interoperative under the same set of rules.

This leads you into the complex interactions between routes and rules. How you ensure that the multiple priorities and structures are implemented within the host defines the implementation of the security and network policies. Making sure that services within a host are integrated into the network structure leads you to consider the network scopes.

Considering where your host's services fit into the larger network structures brings up the question of packet-level functions. You want to ensure that the core packet considerations are driven by the security and network policies and are not limited by the hosts providing the services. This drives the mechanism of network-level Policy Routing structures.

Finally, looking at the full scope of the network-level Policy Routing structures you ponder the function of the interface between your network and the greater conglomeration of networks of which your network is a member. As with star clusters and galaxies, the interactions function on a basic level and how you define those interactions at the border interfaces drives the usage of the internetwork. This brings you full circle to considering that the implementation of Policy Routing, as with any fractal feature set, is scaleless in the viewing. At any level, the same principles and operations function. Whether you consider the internal services within a host system or the Internet itself, the same ruleset and application structure define your Policy Routing.

Local Service Segregation

An address defines a set of services. This simple statement provides a powerful tool that can define how any system on a network is viewed. In the one extreme a system may be invisible because it provides no services. In the other it may be seen to contain the network.

Consider a system with perhaps just one or two services. If you assign multiple addresses to this system, in what way are the services defined to the system? This raises the question of how the actual implementations of both services and addresses are performed by a Policy Routing structure.

Within Policy Routing, an address does not define any particular physical device. While traditional practice is to always assign an address to a device, there is no requirement. What happens if an address is defined not to a particular hardware interface but to a virtual interface defined only in software? More precisely, what should happen?

With these questions scrolling through your mind you decide to set up a little testing environment and see what happens when these and other questions are implemented. Your setup consists of a machine you call net1, which connects to Network A. A full Policy Routing–compliant system you call router1 is connected between this network and another network, Network B. host1 and host2 reside on Network B. You have an independent machine running Ethereal or any other packet capture utility you are familiar with that is connected to both networks so that you can see the details of the packets themselves. This setup is illustrated in Figure 6.1.

This is the testing environment you will use throughout this chapter as you explore advanced Policy Routing topics. The setup is quite flexible and can be added to easily.

Example 6.1—The Art of Ping

To start your testing you set up the testing environment with the following addressing:

```
net1        192.168.1.1/24
router1     192.168.1.254/24
            10.1.1.1/24
host1       10.1.1.2/24
host2       10.1.1.3/24
```

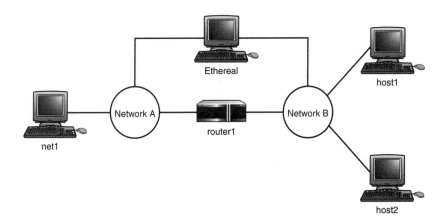

Figure 6.1

Policy Routing testing network.

This setup defines Network A as 192.168.1.0/24 and Network B as 10.1.1.0/24. The two host machines have their default routes pointing at router1. The net1 machine only has a network route for 10.1.1.0/24 pointing at router1. And router1 has no default route set.

Under this setup, you can ping from net1 to all three devices, router1, host1, and host2. On the packet capture you can see that the arps are correctly answered on both sides of router1. This is traditional standard networking.

Now you want to see what happens if you start adding addresses to router1. First you try adding addresses to the physical interfaces on router1. You add 172.16.1.254/16 to the Network B interface of router1. Then you try pinging this interface from host1 and verify that is does respond. So router1 is routing between the two addresses on the single interface.

Now you decide to use a virtual interface on router1 to perform the same test. Looking through the list of available interfaces you decide to try the dummy interface set. On the system is a dummy0 interface, which looks like the following:

```
[root@router1 /root]# ip link ls dev dummy0
5: dummy0: <BROADCAST,NOARP> mtu 1500 qdisc noop
    link/ether 00:00:00:00:00:00 brd ff:ff:ff:ff:ff:ff
```

Now you delete the 172.16.1.254/24 address from the Network B interface and add it to the dummy interface. Then you set the dummy interface active. Now your dummy0 interface looks as follows:

```
[root@router1 /root]# ip addr ls dev dummy0
5: dummy0: <BROADCAST,NOARP,UP> mtu 1500 qdisc noqueue
    link/ether 00:00:00:00:00:00 brd ff:ff:ff:ff:ff:ff
    inet 172.16.1.254/24 scope global dummy0
    inet6 fe80::200:ff:fe00:0/10 scope link
```

Finally you try pinging this address from host1. The ping output looks exactly like the output from when you had assigned the address to the physical device interface. Now you see that the address is truly independent of the physical devices.

Curious, you look at the routing table on router1 to see if there is anything different about this setup:

```
[root@router1 /root]# ip route
192.168.1.0/24 dev eth0  proto kernel  scope link  src 192.168.1.254
172.16.1.0/24 dev dummy0  proto kernel  scope link  src 172.16.1.254
10.1.1.0/24 dev eth1  proto kernel  scope link  src 10.1.1.254
```

Everything looks perfectly normal. Just for grins you try pinging 172.16.1.254 from the net1 machine. And you get the `connect: Network is unreachable` message response from net1. Of course, net1 only has a route to the 10.1.1.0/24 network via router1 and has no route to the 172.16.1.0/24 network, thus the ping packets never go anywhere.

Example 6.2—Loopback Dummy

You think some more about how router1 can respond to the ping for 172.16.1.254 when the interface that contains the address is internal to the system itself. Indeed, you wonder how router1 responds to any type of ping. This leads to considering again how the Routing Policy Database (RPDB) works in this situation.

Considering how the system is responding you determine that since the address belongs to the system, then the system responds due to ownership. This is true for any address owned by the system. The response follows the output procedures as specified through the RPDB. To consider the simple one-packet ping from host1 to router1 for the 172.16.1.254 address, you have the following simplified steps:

1. host1 checks its routing table and determines that it has no specific route to 172.16.1.254. Thus, it should send the packet to the default gateway, router1.
2. router1 receives the packet and determines that it owns the 172.16.1.254 address and so it should respond.
3. router1 consults its RPDB to determine the method of response. Since in this case there is a route with a provided source address it uses the `src` address to respond. Additionally, there is no defined route response so router1 responds using the local table route to host1.
4. host1 receives the response coded with the 172.16.1.254 source address.

Now statement 3 is deliberate in scope. The tangled logic is best illustrated by going through the following example. You really need to pay careful attention to the details to understand how the responses are generated.

First, you delete all addresses from dummy0 on router1 using the `flush` command, **ip addr flush dev dummy0**. Then you add back in the address to dev dummy0 using the host mask to prevent auto-route creation, **ip addr add 172.16.1.254/32 dev dummy0**. You then test this setup by pinging the address from host1 and note that you get a response.

Now you look at the routing table on router1. The route to 172.16.1.254 is coded only in the `local` table. This is as it should be because the local table contains all broadcast and interface routes. You note that this is the only location for this route.

You create a table called table2, which refers to routing table 2, by adding a line to `/etc/iproute2/rt_tables`. Then you add a default route through net1 to table2, which specifies using the src of 172.16.1.254, `ip route add default via 192.168.1.1 src 172.16.1.254 table table2`.

So far you are not using this table, so a ping from host1 will still get a response. To use the table you create a rule. This rule is different and explained in just a bit:

```
ip rule add from 172.16.1.254 dev lo table 2 prio 2000
```

To ensure that this rule is used by the system immediately, you issue the route cache flush, `ip route flush cache`.

Fire up the Ethereal capture on Network A and ping from host1 to 172.16.1.254. The capture looks like the following:

```
172.16.1.254 -> host2        ICMP Echo (ping) reply
172.16.1.254 -> host2        ICMP Echo (ping) reply
172.16.1.254 -> host2        ICMP Echo (ping) reply
172.16.1.254 -> host2        ICMP Echo (ping) reply
```

Note that you are listening on Network A, not on Network B where the ping originated from. The response packet was exactly as you suspected but sent to a different network. This is why the format of the rule statement is very important.

You dissect the rule statement by considering the actions in order. First, the rule is added with a `from` clause that specifies the address you added to `dev dummy0`, 172.16.1.254. This rule will look at all packets with source address 172.16.1.254. There is an additional qualifier, `dev lo`, that states that the interface through which the packet is originated must be `lo`, the loopback interface. But the interface to which the packet was supposedly destined and replied from is `dummy0`. This is the strange part.

You wonder if maybe this is due to `dev dummy0` being somehow different from the physical interfaces. So you try the same sequence only this time you add the address to `dev eth1`, which is the Network B interface. All the rest of the commands are the same. And now when you ping, you get the same result.

What you see is that an address exists only to define a service—just as required by the tenets of Policy Routing. Yes, it seems weird to consider that an address assigned to a physical interface can be routed back through a different interface, but the really weird part is even thinking that the address is "assigned" to the interface.

At first glance this may seem to be a convoluted and theoretical example, but think back to "loopy" routing and consider the following setup.

Example 6.3—Reality Is Loopy

You have a Policy Routing firewall system, router1, similar to Example 5.6, "Troubleshooting Unbalanced Multiple Loop Routes," from Chapter 5, "Simple Network Examples." This system has three different interfaces defined on the system, as illustrated in Figure 6.2. The first interface, eth0, is connected to Network A, a legal IP network (real Internet routable addressing), provided through a 256K Frame connection. The second interface, eth1, is connected to Network B, which has a connection to the Internet through a full T1 frame. The third interface, sat0, is connected to a high downlink speed satellite connection, which has a 64Kbps uplink and a 3Mbps downlink. The addressing is similar to the following (substituting private addresses):

```
eth0    192.168.1.254/24
        gateway from Inet = 192.168.1.253/24
eth1    172.16.1.1/30
        gateway to Inet = 172.16.1.2/30
sat0    10.1.1.1/30
        gateway from/to Inet = 10.1.1.2/30
```

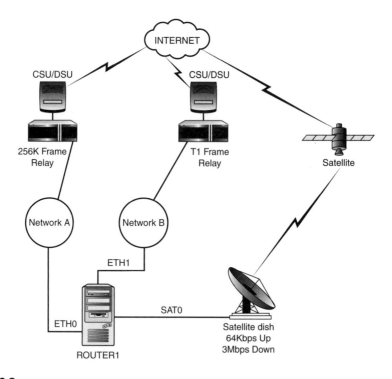

Figure 6.2

Reality is loopy.

What you have is all of your Internet accessible devices on network 192.168.1.0/24. The default route for those devices is the router1 eth0 interface, 192.168.1.254. The uplink to the Internet for these devices is 172.16.1.2. This is so far just a simple example of asymmetrical routing.

The router1 is also running named for DNS. This is a service being provided by router1 on all of its interfaces. Recalling how the outputs are seen from Example 6.2, you would think that there is only one way that the DNS server could be located. But you want DNS queries coming in the link from ISP #1, who provides the 256K link to go back out the 256K link with the address of eth0. Also, you want the DNS queries coming in from the link to ISP #2, the T1 provider, to return out that link with the address from eth1. Finally, you want DNS queries from the satellite link to go out the link to ISP #2 but using the sat0 address as source. Using the constructs from Example 6.2, this is easy.

You create a setup to handle these requirements. First you define three routing tables in /etc/iproute2/rt_tables. These are DMZ, Inet, and Sat. In each of these tables you place the following routes:

```
ip route add default via 192.168.1.253 table DMZ src 192.168.1.254
ip route add default via 172.16.1.2 table Inet src 172.16.1.1
ip route add default via 172.16.1.2 table Sat src 10.1.1.1
```

Now you define the rules to interact with these route tables. Note that in this case you only need deal with the source address because the incoming packet would already have been routed to the system.

```
ip rule add from 192.168.1.254 dev lo table DMZ prio 15000
ip rule add from 172.16.1.1 dev lo table Inet prio 15100
ip rule add from 10.1.1.1 dev lo table Sat prio 15200
```

Now you have your loopy routing and you get to DNS too.

All of these setups rely on the provision of addresses as independent from any physical definition. The address merely defines the location of a service.

Bounce Table Walking

There are times when being able to define the table to which you will send a packet is simply not enough. To this point you have specified uses of the RPDB that end in the final routing table destination. You wonder about additional interactions between the rules and route tables.

Example 6.4—Throw Routes

Returning to your test network setup you decide to make the two hosts, host1 and host2, appear as two different networks. To make the packet traces obvious, you use 172.16.1.1/24 for host2 and leave host1 on 10.1.1.3/24. On router1 you assign 10.1.1.254/24 and 172.16.1.254/24 to dev eth1 on Network B. After setting up these addresses you verify that host2 can ping all other systems.

So your test setup now has the following machines, addresses, and routes:

```
net1      192.168.1.1/24
          No Default Route
          Static route to 10.1.1.0/24 and 172.16.1.0/24 via router1
router1   eth0: 192.168.1.254/24
          eth1: 10.1.1.254/24, 172.16.1.254/24
          No additional routes
host1     10.1.1.1/24
          Default route to 10.1.1.254
host2     172.16.1.1/24
          Default route to 172.16.1.254
```

In order to see how the rules interact with the routing tables you first try a little experiment.

On host2 you add a few additional /32 addresses from the network, say 172.16.1.2-5. These will be the test addresses sending out data to see how the throw route works. You will use the traceroute utility to test using these extra addresses.

What you want to see is how the throw route can be used to bounce out of a routing table back to the rules. To this end on router1 you set up two tables. Each table has a default route pointing to a different router. Then you set up rules that take two of the extra addresses from host2 and send them to different tables. The command setup for this is as follows:

```
ip route add default via 10.1.1.2 src 10.1.1.254 table 2
ip route add default via 192.168.1.1 src 192.168.1.254 table 3
ip rule add from 172.16.1.2/32 table 2 prio 15000
ip rule add from 172.16.1.3/32 table 3 prio 15100
ip route flush cache
```

Now on host2 you issue two different traceroute commands to the same location using the two different addresses. The commands and output you get are as follows:

```
[root@host2 /etc]# traceroute -s 172.16.1.2 192.168.1.1
traceroute to 192.168.1.1 (192.168.1.1) from 172.16.1.2, \
        30 hops max, 40 byte packets
 1  router1 (10.1.1.254)  20.091 ms  0.566 ms  0.461 ms
 2  * * *
(and so on)
[root@host2 /etc]# traceroute -s 172.16.1.3 192.168.1.1
traceroute to 192.168.1.1 (192.168.1.1) from 172.16.1.3, \
        30 hops max, 40 byte packets
 1  router1 (10.1.1.254)  0.976 ms  0.510 ms  0.458 ms
 2  net1 (192.168.1.1)  0.700 ms  0.599 ms  0.576 ms
```

Just as you suspected, the traceroute that uses the 172.16.1.2 source address is sent into routing table 2 on router1. And that routing table contains a default route to host1, which has no knowledge of the destination so the probes just die off. If you look at the packet trace on Network B you will eventually see that an ICMP Destination Unreachable is sent back to 172.16.1.2. Unfortunately, in this case the traceroute program does not ever receive this message but you know that is a problem with the traceroute program itself.

Now you add a throw route to table 2 for the specific traceroute address destination. From Chapter 4 you know that the action of a throw route is to return from the routing table as though the routing lookup has failed. This throw route is added as follows:

```
ip route add throw 192.168.1.1/32 table 2
```

When you now retry that traceroute, it succeeds just like the other address did.

```
[root@host2 /etc]# traceroute -s 172.16.1.2 192.168.1.1
traceroute to 192.168.1.1 (192.168.1.1) from 172.16.1.2, \=
        30 hops max, 40 byte packets
 1  router1 (10.1.1.254)  0.982 ms  0.610 ms  0.478 ms
 2  net1 (192.168.1.1)  0.679 ms  0.623 ms  0.583 ms
```

What you logically deduce is that the throw route, being the best match in the routing table, is used for these packets. If you only had a single routing table, this action would have effectively terminated the routing and the packet would have been immediately returned unreachable. But due to the RPDB, the action instead is to evaluate the next rule in the list. In this case the next matching rule is the default rule 32766, which sends the lookup into table main. This table has a route to the destination and the lookup succeeds, with the result that the traceroute then succeeds.

At this point you may be asking yourself why you would ever want to use a throw route. After all, if the routing is set up correctly and Policy Routing is implemented, you should never need to use such a route.

Consider, then, the meshing of Example 6.3 with Example 6.4. What if you had a Web server that was running on a system with multiple addresses and multiple interfaces and routes? Most of the time you want this particular server to route each Web request via a different route depending on the address and interface.

For example, you know that the number one Web server in the Internet, Apache, can assign virtual hosts both to a single address and to multiple addresses. So say you had an Apache server that had two interfaces and each interface had three addresses. The Apache treats each of the six addresses as belonging to a different domain. Furthermore, you have several virtual servers on top of two of the addresses.

Here you are running ten virtual Web servers. Each of these servers has a different set of output files. All of the servers are required to be visible to the corporate network through a single router connection on one of the two networks. This router is specifically set up to only see one of the addresses assigned to the Web server. What you have on the server is a routing table for each address using the loopback rules as in Example 6.3 because each address gets routed through a different router.

You could add a specific route to the corporate network to each router table, but you know that corporate is considering different network schemes for that router and might also add other routers to other parts of the corporate network. In order to simplify your life when corporate changes their mind yet again, you decide to add throw routes to all of these tables for the corporate network. Then you create a new table containing the current routes to corporate and assign a rule after all the other rules that sends the traffic into that table. Now when corporate decides to add routers or change the existing router, you simply change the one table and everything continues to work.

By the way, that is a somewhat real example that I ended up implementing a few years back for a Web server that was both the corporate intranet server and the corporate Internet server. This setup is quite simple and easy to do and highly secure.

Tag Routing with TOS and fwmark

Of course using internal services and routing them differentially is great when you have access to a Policy Routing–capable system. But most of the server systems running over IPv4 today do not implement much of the basic IPv4 suite, let alone the advanced networking portions. There are several facilities available to deal with these types of systems.

The first facility that comes to mind is the QoS (Quality of Service) umbrella of protocols. Many of the items within this scope were originally intended to provide very specific types of routing and queuing services. But what is more interesting, and relevant to this discussion, is the design as a whole.

When you consider most of the various items commonly lumped under the QoS umbrella, such as DiffServ, IntServ, or RSVP, you see that they were designed to prioritize packet traffic flows. A packet is classified and then queued and routed based on that classification. The important part to note is that the packet itself, in part or in whole, is used to make a classification decision about the packet—not unlike the decision made to route a packet based on source address.

This general view is true of all facets of Policy Routing. After all, Policy Routing is routing based on the entire packet itself. And, when you start to consider the actual realities of implementing a routing interface, you quickly realize that queuing is an integral part of the actual act of interfacing to the network—thus the statement that QoS is an integral part of the scope of Policy Routing.

As with any large and complicated system, the various parts of Policy Routing as a whole have unique and specific roles that do not seem to be a part of the intent of the general system. Those roles of the QoS spectrum include traffic flow service levels and the various mechanisms for implementing the queuing structures, among others. That entire scope of usage would require another book and will not be discussed here.

The interesting part of the QoS family, in reference strictly to routing the packet, lies in the mechanisms for classification. As you learned in Chapter 3, "Linux Policy Routing Structures," one of the mechanisms for specifying a route within the RPDB is to use the TOS (Type of Service) tag within the packet header to select a route or drive a rule. Since almost all QoS classification mechanisms are designed to use this field, either in the original format or in various other methods (for example, DiffServ architecture), these classification mechanisms can be used to select packets using very specific parameters.

The specification of the TOS field for use in Policy Routing is best made with a broadly scoped and yet very precise mechanism. Within the Linux implementation this description fits the classifier known as u32. The u32 classifier is a binary-based selection mechanism. It essentially uses two parameters to operate upon a packet. The first parameter is the binary offset into the packet, and the second parameter is the binary match. Because the offset is specified as a binary location, you can look at any given part of the packet. The binary match is specified as a pattern and a mask so that you can look for specific signature patterns or even very specific bits. Thus you have a comprehensive packet selection mechanism over the entire packet.

Packet selection mechanisms bring up the other facility of mention: packet filtering. Packet filtering mechanisms are usually considered a function of network security and control mechanisms. As with the QoS family, the essential nature of packet filtering is the important concept.

Packet filtering relies on the ability to select packets for perusal. Most of the packet filtering schemes use an internal representation of the selection mechanism to differentiate the packets. This selection mechanism representation usually takes the form of a tag field added to the packet during the period that the packet traverses the filtering device. Using the native tag field as a selector for routing provides the link to Policy Routing.

Within the Linux kernel, the packet filtering mechanisms ensconced during the 2.1 kernel development provide a mechanism for exposing this tag to the general networking structure. This is the fwmark, called nfmark in the NetFilter architecture. This mark is a specifically provided mapping from the internal tagging mechanism to the general network structures. The mark is administratively assigned as needed by a specific packet filter selection rule. This mark was in all of the 2.2 series kernels and was recently added into the new 2.3/2.4 series kernels.

Either of these two mechanisms, QoS classification or packet filter mark, allow you to specify a tag that decides the routing. These mechanisms can coexist within a single system and can even coexist with their original functionality. You get the best of both worlds.

Example 6.5—Mark My Route

The first of these two facilities you decide to examine is the firewall mark, fwmark. This facility exists in different but related implementations depending on which kernel you use. For the 2.1/2.2 series of kernels you would use the ipchains utility to fwmark the packet. For the 2.3/2.4 series you would use the iptables utility of NetFilter to provide the fwmark. You decide to check out both facilities because some of your older machines are running 2.2 kernels, while many of your newer test machines run the 2.4 series kernels.

Returning to your testing network setup you decide to install a 2.2.12 series kernel on router1 along with the ipchains utility. Then you set up a Web server on host2 along with three different addresses. You will use the fwmark facility of ipchains to tag packets entering router1 from net1. You will then use these tags to selectively allow access to specific addresses of host2.

The addresses assigned on host2 along with the Web aliases are as follows:

```
host2    10.1.1.3/24
         web1    10.1.1.5/32
         web2    10.1.1.6/32
         web3    10.1.1.7/32
```

Now on the eth0 interface of router1 you will place your fwmark rules. Recall from Chapter 3 that the INPUT chain is where you would put your tagging rules. The FORWARD chain is after the RPDB along with the OUTPUT chain.

You decide for clarity that you will tag the inbound packets using a fwmark that is the same as the final octet of the destination address. So you implement the following set of chain rules on router1:

```
ipchains -A input -p tcp -s 0/0 -d 10.1.1.5 80 -m 5
ipchains -A input -p tcp -s 0/0 -d 10.1.1.6 80 -m 6
ipchains -A input -p tcp -s 0/0 -d 10.1.1.7 80 -m 7
```

This will tag any packets entering router1 from any interface that is destined for the host2 addresses. There are some additional specifications you can add to the ipchains command to further specify the interface and even the source. If you are interested in those features you know you can look them up in the man pages, but for now you only want to see how the fwmark tag works.

Now you set about using some rules to select routing tables for these fwmarked packets. You note that in the extended listing of the fwmark from ipchains using **ipchains -L -n -v** that the fwmark is coded as a hex value. Thus, you see that if you had used a fwmark of 10, the corresponding actual tag would be 0xa. With this in mind you set up the rules noting that the ip utility uses hex only in referring to the fwmark. You end up with the following set of rules:

```
ip rule add fwmark 5 table 5 prio 15000
ip rule add fwmark 6 table 6 prio 16000
ip rule add fwmark 7 table 7 prio 17000
```

Of course, you need to populate the tables with the appropriate routes. One of the features of this style of selection is that you can tag different types of packets with the same fwmark. So, for example, when implementing the chain rules on router1 you could have marked both 10.1.1.5 and 10.1.1.6 with the same fwmark. Then the rules would select tables based on this mark. Thus you can tie together disparate packet types into the same routing structure.

Now that you have tried out the fwmark facility in kernel 2.2.12, you decide to try kernel 2.4.0 on router1 and implement the same fwmark setup. Since you already know how the rules will look, you only need to figure out how to use the iptables utility under NetFilter. You come up with the following set of iptables commands that operate as the ipchains rules you set up on router1 operated. Note that you have to specify these rules as operating on the mangle table because you are actually modifying the packet.

```
iptables -t mangle -A PREROUTING -p tcp -s 0/0 -d 10.1.1.5/32 --dport 80 \
       -j MARK --set-mark 5
iptables -t mangle -A PREROUTING -p tcp -s 0/0 -d 10.1.1.6/32 --dport 80 \
       -j MARK --set-mark 6
iptables -t mangle -A PREROUTING -p tcp -s 0/0 -d 10.1.1.7/32 --dport 80 \
       -j MARK --set-mark 7
```

In Chapter 3 you learned that the NetFilter architecture allows you to specify two different locations for packet mangling operations. Since you want to see packets entering router1 from the network you choose the PREROUTING hook. The rules that act on this setup are the same as before.

Now both the ipchains and the iptables commands can be used to set marks within the OUTPUT hook location. This location sets the mark for packets that are exiting from the localhost or loopback interface. Thus you can use all of the dev lo rules you saw in Example 6.2 to route the marked packets.

Linux DiffServ Architecture

Now that you have tried out the packet filtering techniques for marking the packets, you decide to turn your attention to the QoS classification routines. These routines are designed to tag packets for use with queuing structures. These tags are often in the form of actual changes to the TOS field within the packet header.

To date, most implementations of QoS tend to implement classification and flow control on the output, called the egress, interface. This is purely due to the general viewpoint from the development time in the early 1990s that you were only performing traditional routing. Since in traditional routing a decision about the packet destination is not performed until just before the packet leaves the system, the general consensus was that any queuing must take place after the routing decision was made. The arrival of Policy Routing has revealed that this idea, as with the traditional routing structure, is limited.

Fortunately, the Linux DiffServ architecture provides an ingress (input) queuing discipline that can meet your needs. This ingress queuing discipline (qdisc) is currently only capable of tagging and policing packets on the ingress. But the plans and future hopes are that it will grow to become a regular full-function qdisc. Additionally, there is an idea floating around to associate the entire DiffServ architecture on Linux with the services rather than the physical interface, similar in thought to the way an address within Policy Routing belongs to a service and not a physical device. Since the entire structure of QoS, including DiffServ, is considered a part of the full Policy Routing structure, this move would align all network mechanisms in the same generalized structure. And that would be best all the way around.

To use the ingress qdisc you need to understand a little of the DiffServ architecture with respect to the various terms and mechanics. In a nutshell, the qdisc is the core function that provides a method for queuing the packets. The class is the group into which the packet is placed and by which the qdisc is selective of packets. The filter is attached to the qdisc and is the selector of the packet. Basically you enable a qdisc, attach filters to the qdisc, and provide classes within the qdisc. For your purposes the actual classification will be done by the filter because the filter is the tagging mechanism.

Qdisc

There is a difference between a queue and a queuing discipline. Each particular network device has a queue that feeds packets to it. Within that device queue you may have several queuing disciplines at work. Think of a store where there is only one register at which you actually purchase your item and leave the store. That register is the device queue. From that register there are several lines that start within the store at a single point, and branch out into several lines that then converge again on the single register. Think of the entire system, beginning with the single entry point into the lines and ending at the single register, as the device queue itself. Then the various lines represent various possible queuing disciplines.

For the ingress qdisc you need only consider that there is only one possible line. Hopefully when the newer generalized structures are implemented, perhaps in 2.5 series Linux development kernels, there will be more possible lines to choose from.

Class

Queuing disciplines and classes are fundamentally intertwined. A queuing discipline may contain several classes of service. These classes and their semantics are fundamental properties of that queuing discipline. Thinking again of the store register lines, each originating line within the whole queue can be a class of the queuing discipline. Each class can contain other queuing disciplines within it, which then can contain classes, and so on and so on. In the end all of the machinations serve merely to differentiate the service received by the various packets.

A queuing discipline does not necessarily have classes. For example, the TBF queuing discipline does not allow classes. If you use TBF you essentially have a single overall class for the entire queuing discipline. In the ingress qdisc there is no real need for classes because the current function is only to provide a mechanism for tagging a packet on reception.

Filter

Filters provide the method for checking and tagging packets. These tags can then be used by the classes to determine the membership in the class. Filters may be combined arbitrarily with queuing disciplines. Thinking again about the store analogy, the point where a single line splits into several parallel lines indicates the location of a filter application. The actual split mechanism could be a class decision based on an earlier filter tag. Consider the case where everybody who has less than five items and wants to pay cash will be put into the "less than five items & pays cash" line. There is a filter entity that checks each person and if they are a "less than 5 & cash," they are given a tag. Either then or later on another entity, think of class or RPDB, moves the person to another line based on the tag.

Now that you have an idea of how the basic set up works within the Linux DiffServ mechanism, you decide to play with using the ingress qdisc for routing tags.

Example 6.6—Class Wars

In order to test this model you decide to use the 2.4 kernel with the classid-to-mark DiffServ extension. This extension will be part of the regular DiffServ code within the 2.4 series kernels. It provides an internal conversion map between a classid tag from a filter to an fwmark. In this way you can use the ultimate packet tagging power tool, the u32 classifier.

You go to router1 and make sure it is running a 2.4 kernel without any of the NetFilter architecture turned on. Then you set up the ingress qdisc on the Network B interface, eth1:

```
tc qdisc add dev eth1 handle ffff: ingress
```

Now you need to consider how the u32 filter works.

u32 Filter

The most powerful filter available in Linux is the u32 filter. This filter allows you to actually make a choice based on any data within the packet itself. As with all of the DiffServ implementations for Linux, you will use the tc utility from IPROUTE2. (The complete syntax and use of the tc utility will not be covered in this book. Please refer to the IPROUTE2 documentation for details.) Looking at the tc utility help for this filter gives a faint glimpse of this power:

```
root@router1# tc filter add u32 help
Usage: ... u32 [ match SELECTOR ... ] [ link HTID ] [ classid CLASSID ]
              [ police POLICE_SPEC ] [ offset OFFSET_SPEC ]
              [ ht HTID ] [ hashkey HASHKEY_SPEC ]
              [ sample SAMPLE ]
or        u32 divisor DIVISOR

Where: SELECTOR := SAMPLE SAMPLE ...
       SAMPLE := { ip | ip6 | udp | tcp | icmp | u{32|16|8} } SAMPLE_ARGS
       FILTERID := X:Y:Z
```

The actual heavy-duty selection mechanisms are in the SELECTOR. But all you are told is that the SELECTOR is a series of SAMPLE sections. And nowhere are you told what the SAMPLE_ARGS would have to be. But by reading through the source and looking around the Internet you amass some of the needed information for using u32 in the context of this book.

The u32 selectors are simply binary patterns with binary masks that are used to match any set of data within the packet. The most common usage is to perform matches within the packet header. There are two main types of selectors that are deeply interrelated. The human interface selectors are those that are specified using linguistic aliases for the actions specifying specific protocol and field matches, such as the IP destination address or protocol 4. Then there are the bitwizard selectors that are specified in terms of the bit pattern length. These selectors are the u32, u16, and u8 selectors themselves. Within the `tc` utility all of the human selectors are translated into bitwizard selectors.

For example, if you specify matching the human selector `match ip tos 0x10 0xff`, the `tc` utility actually matches against the packet as `match u8 0x10 0xff at 1`. Note from the human specification that you are trying to match TOS 10h. Now the TOS field within an IP header is one byte long, which is 8 bits and thus a u8 general length selector, and located at a one byte offset into the IP packet. Thus you can specify matching a one byte set of bits with a full mask located at one byte into the packet header, which is `match u8 0x10 0xff at 1`. Or you can say `match ip tos 0x10 0xff`.

Now you can see why this is bitwizard work: There is no man page or other help, you have to know your packet binary structure and hexadecimal conversions, and even the human interface is somewhat cryptic. But the power available using this filter is incredible. The ability to specify any binary data pattern means that you can pick out individual data streams for routing. Suppose that you are browsing several different Web sites from your machine. To the router, all the data streams look as though they originate from the same address to the same protocol. By using u32, you could look for data patterns that indicate SSL encryption on either the sent or returned packets and route them through a secure link. And that is without looking at the header at all.

Additionally, you can look for certain types of patterns by using the mask portion of the specification. In the TOS example from the previous paragraph you were looking for exactly TOS 16 decimal, which is 0x10 hex. But what if you wanted to consider all TOS decimal levels from 16 through 19 inclusive? You would just change the mask portion of the specification and would then have a command like `match u8 0x10 0xf3 at 1`. Thus between the specification of the length of pattern, the pattern itself, and the offset into the packet you can isolate any unique portion of the packet. You can also stack several selectors together to obtain any combination of selections you require.

As you work with the u32 filter you note some tricky behaviors on the part of the selectors. You consider the filter snippet—`match tcp src 0x1234`. This human filter is coded by `tc` as `match u16 0x1234 0xffff nexthdr+0`, which means to match a 16-bit 0x1234 pattern within the internal protocol header at offset 0. But what is contained within the offset 0 of the internal protocol header is simply the IPv4 source port for the packet.

Thus, if you were expecting the `match tcp` part to only match TCP packets, you would be surprised. The filter snippet will actually match UDP packets as well because they also have the source port contained at offset 0 within the internal protocol header. If you want to specify only matching TCP packets with source port 0x1234, then you have to stack up selectors. You would then use `match tcp src 0x1234 match ip protocol 0x6`. The additional selector `match ip protocol 0x6` states to also only look at packets of protocol 6 hex, which is TCP. Table 6.1 is the full table of selectors as known at this time.

Table 6.1 u32 Selectors

Command	Option	Data
match <ip,tcp,udp>	src	<ip source address/mask CIDR>
match <ip.tcp,udp>	dst	<ip dest address/mask CIDR>
match ip	tos	<original IPv4 TOS field in hex> <hex mask>
match ip	dsfield	<8bit entire TOS field> <hex mask>
match ip	precedence	<precedence part of TOS field> <hex mask>
match ip	ihl	<8 bit ip header length in hex>
match ip	protocol	<hex protocol number> <hex mask>
match ip	nofrag	only match non fragmented ip packets
match ip	firstfrag	only match first ip fragment
match ip	df	possibly Data Fragments (no documentation exists)
match ip	mf	possibly Matching Fragments (no documentation exists)
match <ip,tcp,udp>	sport	<source port in hex> <hex mask>
match <ip,tcp,udp>	dport	<dest port in hex> <hex mask>
match ip	icmp_type	<icmp type in hex> <hex mask>
match ip	icmp_code	<icmp code in hex> <hex mask>
match icmp	type	<icmp type in hex> <hex mask>
match icmp	code	<icmp code in hex> <hex mask>

As you can see, there are many ways in which you can look into the packet headers and determine your selection. When you combine these facilities with the ability to also specify any exact bit pattern at any offset into the packet that you want, you can see the power of the Linux DiffServ architecture.

Within the u32 filter there is another kind of selector available—the `sample` command. The `sample` command takes the same kinds of arguments as `match`. However, the `sample` command normally takes only a single argument for type. So where you would use `match ip protocol 0x6 0xff`, you can use `sample tcp` instead.

With your newly acquired knowledge of the u32 filter usage you first decide to try a simple test of the ingress filter. You know you have the ingress qdisc set up on router1 on the Network B interface. You decide to try tagging all incoming packets from 10.1.1.0/24 with classid 1. Then you will use a rule that sends those packets into table 1 and assign them additionally to realms 3/4 for tracking. You end up with the following sequence of commands:

```
tc filter add dev eth1 parent ffff: protocol ip prio 1 u32 \
     match ip src 10.1.1.0/24 classid :1
ip rule add fwmark 1 table 1 prio 15000 realms 3/4
```

```
ip route add default via 192.168.1.1 table 1 src 192.168.1.254
ip route flush cache
```

Then you run a ping from net1 to host1 and look at the output of the qdisc statistics and the realms:

```
[root@router1 root]# tc -s qdisc ls dev eth1
qdisc ingress ffff: ----------------
 Sent 0 bytes 0 pkts (dropped 0, overlimits 0)
 [root@router1 root]# rtacct 3
Realm      BytesTo     PktsTo     BytesFrom  PktsFrom
3          0           0          504        6
[root@router1 root]# rtacct 4
Realm      BytesTo     PktsTo     BytesFrom  PktsFrom
4          504         6          0          0
```

You note that the qdisc statistics do not show any traffic. That is expected because you are not using the classid anywhere on egress for DiffServ. You are only using the ingress qdisc to be able to tag packets with the u32 filter. You know that the filter is working because you have your ping packets showing up balanced on the realms. The only way the realms would list the packets is if they were acted upon by that rule. So your quick test was successful. You decide to create a listing for this just because it would be coded as follows:

```
You are playing with the MARK of the BEST ... ;-}
```

Interactions with Packet Filters

In your testing of the u32 qdisc you came to wonder what interactions exist between the NetFilter mangle and the u32 filter. You know from testing the fwmark that the mangle table can select and mark packets on input using the PREROUTING hook. You know from your u32 testing that the u32 filter can select and mark packets on ingress. Does one override the other or can they coexist?

Example 6.7—Double Play Packet

You decide to try a quick test now that you have seen good examples of both types of packet tagging. You have router1 set up with a 2.4 kernel and both the NetFilter and the DiffServ running. You then run the following set of commands to set up the tagging mechanisms for both iptables and u32:

```
tc qdisc add dev eth1 handle ffff: ingress
tc filter add dev eth1 parent ffff: protocol ip prio 1 u32 \
        match ip src 10.1.1.0/24 classid :2

/usr/local/bin/iptables -t mangle -i eth1 -A PREROUTING -s 10.1.1.0/24 -d 0/0 \
        -j MARK --set-mark 1

ip rule add fwmark 1 table 1 prio 15000 realms 1/2
ip rule add fwmark 2 table 2 prio 15100 realms 3/4
```

```
ip route add default via 192.168.1.1 src 192.168.1.254 table 1
ip route add default via 192.168.1.1 src 192.168.1.254 table 2
```

Now you try a ping from net1 to host2 and look at your realms. The only ones with any traffic are realms 1/2:

```
[root@router1 root]# rtacct
Realm      BytesTo     PktsTo      BytesFrom  PktsFrom
1          0           0           336        4
2          336         4           0          0
[root@router1 root]# rtacct 3
Realm      BytesTo     PktsTo      BytesFrom  PktsFrom
3          0           0           0          0
[root@router1 root]# rtacct 4
Realm      BytesTo     PktsTo      BytesFrom  PktsFrom
4          0           0           0          0
```

You know that the rtacct utility will only list out the realms that have actual counts in them. Just to make sure, you manually listed realm 3 and realm 4 and found them empty.

Now you wonder if this lack of traffic through fwmark 2 is due to the priority of the rule for fwmark 1 being a higher priority, 15000, than the rule for fwmark 2, 15100. So just to make sure you reverse the order of the commands, change the priorities on the rules, reboot router1, and try again. Your command listing looks like this:

```
/usr/local/bin/iptables -t mangle -i eth1 -A PREROUTING -s 10.1.1.0/24 -d 0/0 \
     -j MARK --set-mark 1

tc qdisc add dev eth1 handle ffff: ingress
tc filter add dev eth1 parent ffff: protocol ip prio 1 u32 \
      match ip src 10.1.1.0/24 classid :2

ip rule add fwmark 2 table 2 prio 15000 realms 3/4
ip rule add fwmark 1 table 1 prio 15100 realms 1/2

ip route add default via 192.168.1.1 src 192.168.1.254 table 1
ip route add default via 192.168.1.1 src 192.168.1.254 table 2
```

You try this setup and it gives the exact same output as the first. So you correctly conclude that the NetFilter parts are at a lower level within the packet tagging structures than the ingress qdisc, and that the one does not override the other.

Now you decide quickly to test out the coexistence. To this end you set up the following script, which uses u32 to tag host1 and iptables to mark host2:

```
/usr/local/bin/iptables -t mangle -i eth1 -A PREROUTING -s 10.1.1.3/32 -d 0/0 \
     -j MARK --set-mark 2

tc qdisc add dev eth1 handle ffff: ingress
```

```
tc filter add dev eth1 parent ffff: protocol ip prio 1 u32 \
        match ip src 10.1.1.2/32 classid :1

ip rule add fwmark 2 table 2 prio 15000 realms 3/4
ip rule add fwmark 1 table 1 prio 15100 realms 1/2

ip route add default via 192.168.1.1 src 192.168.1.254 table 1
ip route add default via 192.168.1.1 src 192.168.1.254 table 2
```

When you run this script you get output for all four realms. Recalling that earlier the two tagging mechanisms were set to tag the same packets, you realize that you can now have the best of both worlds. The NetFilter mark can be used on the packet headers and the u32 classifier can be used on arbitrary binary data from the packet. This allows for a truly powerful system.

Summary

What you have learned are some of the deeper workings of the usage of Policy Routing. The actions of any single part of the system are uniquely consistent across all scales. You have seen how the basic principles extend consistently to more complicated problems. When the problem is broken down into the components and their needs, the setup of the system is simple logic.

The inconsistencies are found not from within Policy Routing but from the preconceptions and interactions with other systems. As in the finest arts, a thorough understanding of the basic mechanisms produce the finest products when combined.

You look forward to implementing and extending your structure to the rest of your networks. First you want to conquer the dynamic routing setups already present within your network (Chapter 7, "Dynamic Routing Interactions") and deal with the need under IPv4 to change your addressing (Chapter 8, "NAT Functions"). Then you wonder how the new IPv6 structures work within these contexts (Chapter 9, "IPv6"). To those and other goals you set your sights.

CHAPTER 7

Dynamic Routing Interactions

Considering the methods for applying dynamic routing to Policy Routing brings up several points of contention. The obvious points regard how to utilize and propagate routing structures that are based on more than the traditional destination-based routing. The more subtle points deal with the actual intricate structures within the implementations of various dynamic routing protocols.

To this end you need to consider how the actual routing engines differ in the location of the structures. To illustrate this you need to first consider how the various parts of the routing engine are distributed within Linux as opposed to a hardware-based device such as a Cisco router. Then you need to consider the actual implementations of the dynamic routing protocols themselves as evidenced by the available source code.

With this understanding you can then begin to implement the uses of both the dynamic protocols and the Policy Routing structure. The interactions between these systems are mostly within the rules and tables used to structure the information. As these mechanisms progress in use there will hopefully be more interactions possible within the greater Internet itself. But that is another subject entirely.

Realms and Information Bases

To start with you need to consider how an actual routing engine works. Up to this point you only considered the Routing Policy Database (RPDB) as containing the state of the routing, more particularly the Policy Routing, structure. But this structure has several components.

Recalling the discussion of the RPDB from Chapter 3, "Linux Policy Routing Structures," the concept of the actual Routing Information Base (RIB) describes what you would call a routing structure. This RIB consists of all the elements necessary to describe how to propagate a packet based on the destination address. It contains many items of information including such details as the interface, MTU, nexthop router, TOS tag, and other information that may be needed to forward the packet. In most routers this is the complete routing table itself.

When you begin to think in terms of Policy Routing structures, especially when you consider the independent uses of the various Triad members, you can see that this single amorphous RIB itself is too large and unwieldy to use as a single entity. Considering that the core concept of routing is to send packets to the appropriate destination, most of the mass of information becomes extraneous and irrelevant. Except when you need to actually make decisions based on those additional items of information. So what if you were to consider splitting the RIB into a database of information and a simple routing mechanism?

Now you are looking at the fundamental change implemented in the RPDB: the concept of the RIB as a split entity where you have the information database and the Forwarding Information Base (FIB). The information contained in the information base can be used to influence and select from the paths coded into the FIB. Think again of the use of the u32 classifier from Chapter 6, "Complex Network Examples." You can use any binary information (information base) to determine what TOS tag to set. The TOS tag then selects the route to use (FIB).

It is this divorce of the information from the forwarding that gives Policy Routing power and flexibility. In either extreme, from using all of the information to traditional destination-only routing, the selection mechanism based on the information database is independent of the forwarding mechanism in the FIB. And by establishing that functionality throughout the spectrum between those extremes, Policy Routing can provide all of the uses both in today's Internet and in tomorrow's.

Splitting up these functions makes sense when you consider the complexity driven by routing structures in use. But when you need to think about a complex routing structure, the sheer enormity of the routes that may be present can quickly overwhelm you. Step back and consider what it is that you really want to know.

Within any given complex routing environment there are typically several groupings to consider. These are "meta-routes" that describe larger scale destination groups. The wording used in the ip utility is *realm*. A realm is best considered as defining a set of routes as selected by human logic. You are not selecting these routes for any network protocol level logic structure, but in order to classify them for your own understanding.

The best way to visualize this is to consider a simple example (see Figure 7.1). Suppose you have a router that has four interfaces. One is the primary connection from the Internet, one is the connection from the Internet2 project, one is to your corporate WAN, and the last one is to the local government. You know that your corporate WAN spans three continents when you factor in the vendors and customers who are also connected. The local government is interconnected with all the other local governments throughout your state, which includes some 750 individual government entities. Your boss just came down and asked how much actual bandwidth is being used from local governments to Internet2. What is your answer?

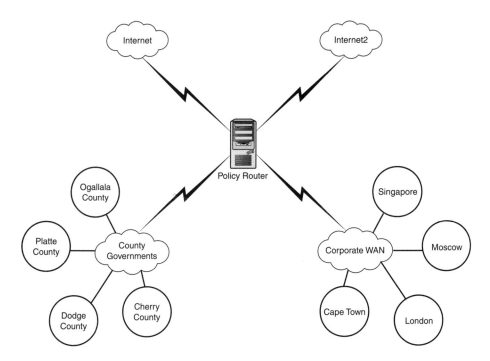

Figure 7.1

Tracking the traffic.

You know that you have OSPF running on the corporate WAN with your router providing the connection to your defined stub area within the corporate OSPF scheme. The link to the local government defines a different OSPF stub area within the state's OSPF routing scheme. You also have independent Border Gateway Protocol (BGP) peerages running on each Internet connection. All of these instances dump into different routing tables and then you have a whole set of rules for implementing your Policy Routing. But you know you can define a realm whose source scope is the local government OSPF area and whose destination scope is the Internet2 BGP peer. Then you simply can issue a command to look at the traffic amounts for that realm.

With this example in mind you should consider what Alexey Kuznetsov has to say about the implementation of realms in the IPROUTE2 utility suite. Remember that the IPROUTE2 suite includes both the `ip` utility and the `tc` utility.

`rtacct`—Route Realms and Policy Propagation

On routers using OSPF ASE (Autonomous System External) or especially the BGP protocol, the routing tables may be huge. If you want to classify or account for the packets per route, you will have to keep lots of information. Even worse, if you want to distinguish the packets not only by their destinations but also by their sources, the task presents a quadratic complexity, and its solution is physically impossible.

One approach for propagating the policy from routing protocols to the forwarding engine has been proposed. Essentially, Cisco Policy Propagation via BGP is based on the fact that dedicated routers have the entire RIB (Routing Information Base) close to the forwarding engine so that Policy Routing rules can check all the route attributes, including ASPATH (Autonomous System PATH) information and community strings.

Within the Linux architecture, where we have a split RIB as maintained by a user-level daemon and the kernel-based FIB (Forwarding Information Base), we cannot allow such a simplistic approach.

Fortunately, there exists another solution that allows an even more flexible policy with rich semantics. Routes can be clustered together in user space based on their attributes. For instance, a BGP router knows the route ASPATH or its community, whereas an OSPF router knows the route tag or its area. A network administrator adding routes manually knows the nature of those routes. Providing that the number of such aggregates, which we call realms, is low, the task of full classification both by source and destination becomes quite manageable.

So each route may be assigned to a realm. It is assumed that this identification is made by a routing daemon, but static routes may also be assigned manually through `ip route`.

Currently there exists a patch to `gated`, allowing it to classify routes to realms over all the set of policy rules. See the later section, "`gated` and Zebra," for more information. This classification is implemented within `gated` by prefix, ASPATH, origin, tag, and so on.

To facilitate this construction in the case when the routing daemon is not aware of realms, missing realms may be completed with routing policy rules.

For each packet, the kernel calculates the tuple of realms (source realm and destination realm) using the following algorithm:

1. If a route has a realm, the destination realm of the packet is set to it.
2. If a rule has a source realm, the source realm of the packet is set to it.
3. If the destination realm was not obtained from route, and the rule has a destination realm, set the destination realm from rule.
4. If at least one of the realms is still unknown, the kernel finds a reversed route to the source of the packet.
5. If the source realm is still unknown, get it from a reversed route.
6. If one of the realms is still unknown, swap realms of reversed routes and apply step 2 again.

After this procedure is completed, we know what realm the packet arrived from and the realm where it is going. If any of the realms is unknown, it is initialized to zero (or `realm unknown`).

The main application of realms is in conjunction with the tc route classifier, where they are used to help assign packets to traffic classes for accounting, policing, and scheduling them according to the classification.

A much simpler but still very useful application is packet path accounting by realms. The kernel gathers a packet statistics summary that can be viewed with the rtacct utility.

```
kuznet@amber~ $ rtacct russia
Realm      BytesTo    PktsTo    BytesFrom  PktsFrom
russia     20576778   169176    47080168   153805
```

This output shows that this router has received 153,805 packets from realm russia and forwarded 169,176 packets to russia. The realm russia consists of routes with ASPATHs not leaving russia.

Note that locally originated packets are not accounted here, since rtacct shows ingoing packets only. Using the route classifier, you can get even more detailed accounting information about outgoing packets, optionally summarizing traffic not only by source or destination but by any pair of source and destination realms.

The important point is that the classification of the routes into bundles can be done by any of the associated metadata for the route. This metadata can be the area for OSPF, the community for BGP, or simply the source address from a rule. This classification into realms follows the logic of the administrator who set up the router. As you saw in the preceding example of accounting, the realm russia is defined by the administrator as the set of all routes whose ASPATH membership does not leave russia.

gated and Zebra

This discussion of the methods of classification of routes into realms depends on the cooperation of the dynamic routing utility. In UNIX, all dynamic routing that was not simple RIP was traditionally done by the gated daemon. The gated daemon handles all types of routing. The protocol listing includes OSPF, BGP, RIP, HELLO, STATIC, ISIS, and methods of importing and exporting selected sets of information from one protocol to another.

Since the gated daemon was handed off to the MERIT consortium things have changed somewhat. The source code is no longer freely available and the license has changed to academic and non-commercial use only. Now gated has been spun off into a corporation, which will provide a commercial version for sale. The source code to the older versions is still available, however, and version 3.5.10 with patches by Alexey Kuznetsov is the one used with the Linux RPDB.

There is also a new source for routing daemons that has full GPL source code. This is the Zebra project based at http://www.zebra.org. Zebra pursues the concept of independent routing daemons for each protocol. These are all tied into a core zebra daemon, which actually manipulates the FIB inside the kernel. This setup provides a good analogy for the split between the Routing Information such as is provided by a routing protocol and the FIB, which does the actual forwarding action.

You will want to consider both of these daemons. The `gated` daemon is stable and works quite well. The Zebra suite is rapidly evolving and represents the likely face of dynamic routing in the future.

The `gated` Utility

The `gated` source that you will use is an older one, 3.5.10. Under Linux you will need to patch it to run under glibc 2.1 and to run with the `ip` utility. The patched version is on the CD and available from the Web site. For now I will assume that you have obtained the patched source and compiled it.

The most difficult part of getting `gated` to work is setting up the configuration file. The are a few quirks that you should know about. First of all, the order in which the objects are specified in the configuration file are absolute. If you do not have them in the correct order and list only the ones that are compiled into the `gated` binary, you get a lot of complaints about parse errors and statements out of order. The second most common problem is forgetting a semicolon for terminating lines. Semicolons are also required for terminating braces. See the examples.

The best way to put together a config file is to get one that works from someone else and then carefully modify it. Otherwise go slowly and set up the sections one by one and test each time. Thankfully, the `gated` daemon itself can be called with a command-line option (`-C`) to check the config file and also one to specify the file (`-f conffilename`). So, you can at least verify that your syntax is correct.

You decide that you want to run OSPF on your corporate network. In order to see how to set up `gated`, you decide to test it first by running it on a single connected machine. You know that the routers are already running OSPF under area 0.0.0.0. This area is usually referred to as the backbone area. So you set up the following `gated.conf` file:

```
routerid 192.168.1.1;
ospf yes {defaults {ospfarea backbone;}; };
```

This simply tells your system to run OSPF with all the standard defaults and join `area backbone`. Note that the `routerid` must correspond with an interface on the system and that that interface must be running when you start `gated`. Also note carefully where and how the semicolons are placed.

Now you simply run `gated` from the command line. To check on the operation you look at your main routing table with **ip route list**:

```
127.0.0.1 dev lo proto gated/conn scope host
192.168.1.0/24 dev eth0 proto gated/conn scope link src 192.168.1.1
```

Note that your default route, which you knew you had entered earlier, is gone. Also, the routes to loopback and the local ethernet are now protocol `gated/conn`. If you look in `/etc/iproute2/rt_protos` you will see that this is protocol 248. But you do not see anything from the OSPF yet. So you wait a few minutes and look again. Now you see the routes that are on some of the routers:

```
127.0.0.1 dev lo  proto gated/conn  scope host
192.168.1.0/24 dev eth0  proto gated/conn  scope link  src 192.168.1.1
128.1.1.0/24 via 192.168.1.2 dev eth0  proto gated/ospf
128.1.2.0/24 via 192.168.1.4 dev eth0  proto gated/ospfase
```

You note that one of the routers is reporting a directly learned route. It is the 192.168.1.2 router and it is telling your machine about a route it has to 128.1.1.0/24. You know it is directly connected to that network. You also see that router 192.168.1.4 is reporting a route that it has imported from some other protocol (gated/ospfase). You happen to know that is a static route on that router and that static route is all it is supposed to report via OSPF. So all is working well.

Now you know that you have several areas in your network. So you decide to quickly set up a multi-area configuration to see how it works. The machine you use has two ethernet interfaces, one of which is in the backbone and one of which is in area 172.16.1.0. The interfaces are 192.168.1.1/24 and 172.16.1.1/24. So you generate the following configuration:

```
routerid 192.168.1.1;
ospf yes {
   area 172.16.1.0 {
      authtype none;
    networks {
       172.16.1.0 mask 255.255.255.0;
      };
   interface 172.16.1.1
      cost 2 {
        priority 1;
      };
   };
   backbone {
      authtype none;
   interface 192.168.1.1
      cost 1 {
        priority 1;
      };
   };
};
```

When you fire it up and look at your routing tables you see the same routes with the addition of the local connection for 172.16.1.0/24. This is puzzling because you see no difference with the exception of the locally connected area. So you start looking for a utility that will give you the information on the OSPF areas and what is going on with the dynamic routing.

You find out that you can specify a log file for gated within the configuration file. Additionally for OSPF there is an ospf_monitor utility that enables you to talk with your OSPF routers all throughout your network. Since your gated seems to be running fine, you decide to try the ospf_monitor utility.

Upon reading the documentation you need to create a database file with the IP addresses and names of the various OSPF routers along with the authentication type if authentication is used. Since at the moment you are not using authentication, you decide to quickly create a simple file named ospf.db located in the same directory as ospf_monitor, which contains the following text:

```
192.168.1.1   mygated
192.168.1.254  core
```

This file lists both your local gated router as well as the core OSPF router. And since the names are only used to identify the device to you, you can use names that make sense.

Now that you have the file created you run the ospf_monitor utility. This utility takes the name of the database file on the command line. It has its own set of commands that can be seen by entering a ? once you are in the utility. The initial start and commands look like the following:

```
root# ospf_monitor ospf.db
listening on 0.0.0.0.1026
[ 1 ] dest command params > ?
Local commands:
   ?: help
   ?R: remote command information
   d: show configured destinations
   h: show history
   x: exit
   @ <remote command>: use last destination
   @<dest index> <remote command>: use configured destination
   F <filename>: write monitor information to filename
   S: write monitor information to stdout (default)
[ 2 ] dest command params > ?R
Remote-commands:
   a <area id> <type> <ls id> <adv rtr>: show link state advertisement
   c: show cumulative log
   e: show cumulative errors
   l: <retrans> dump lsdb (except for ASEs)
   A: <retrans> dump ASEs
   W: <retrans> dump ASEs with LSID's
   v: dump all verticies
   o: print ospf routing table
   I: show interfaces
   h: show next hops
   N <r>: show neighbors - if r is set will print retrans lst
[ 3 ] dest command params >
```

You note that the commands are sequentially numbered and that issuing commands is divided into local and remote. Since you know the order in which you input lines into your database file, you know that the dest index is for issuing remote commands. So you decide to look at your local OSPF information:

```
[ 3 ] dest command params > @1 o
   remote-command <o> sent to 192.168.1.1


        Source <<192.168.1.1     mygated>>
AS Border Routes:
Router          Cost AdvRouter      NextHop(s)
- - - - - - - - - - - - - - - - - - - - - - - - - - - - - - - - - - - - -
Area 0.0.0.0:
192.168.1.1       0 192.168.1.1
192.168.1.254     1 192.168.1.254    192.168.1.254

Area 172.16.1:
192.168.1.1       0 192.168.1.1

Total AS Border routes: 3

Area Border Routes:
Router          Cost AdvRouter      NextHop(s)
- - - - - - - - - - - - - - - - - - - - - - - - - - - - - - - - - - - - -
Area 0.0.0.0:
192.168.1.1       0 192.168.1.1

Area 172.16.1:
192.168.1.1       0 192.168.1.1

Total Area Border Routes: 2

Summary AS Border Routes:
Router          Cost AdvRouter      NextHop(s)
- - - - - - - - - - - - - - - - - - - - - - - - - - - - - - - - - - - - -

Networks:
Destination      Area           Cost Type NextHop        AdvRouter
- - - - - - - - - - - - - - - - - - - - - - - - - - - - - - - - - - - - - - - - - - - -
192.168.1        0.0.0.0           1 Net   192.168.1.1    192.168.1.1
ASEs:
Destination      Cost E     Tag NextHop        AdvRouter
- - - - - - - - - - - - - - - - - - - - - - - - - - - - - - - - - - - - - - - - - - - -
0.0.0.0            2   2       3 192.168.3.254   192.168.1.254
Total nets: 1
       Intra Area: 1   Inter Area: 0   ASE: 1
done

[ 4 ] dest command params >
```

Here you see the details of all of the areas that you have configured on your router. You can also look at any of the other OSPF routers running as long as you enter them into the ospf.db file. This is a good tool for troubleshooting an OSPF network, especially when you do not have physical access to the other routers.

Note that gated itself can participate in many types of dynamic protocols. All of these protocols may be entered into the configuration file along with the appropriate parameters. In this case you only bothered with your OSPF network. But you can have the same machine participate in BGP, RIP v1/v2, and also the newer IPv6 versions of these protocols.

NOTE

Route Weights and Selectors

If you are familiar with other routers, such as Cisco or Bay or Proteon, and have run multiple dynamic routing protocols on them, such as OSPF and RIP and BGP, then you may be wondering how Linux deals with such multiple routing structures. Remember that you can think of Linux as having two modes of routing: the traditional style and Policy Routing. While Policy Routing does provide for backward compatibility, for much of traditional routing the use of multiple dynamic routing protocols is one area where you have choices.

Consider the concept that is employed by most modern routers when dealing with multiple routes to the same destination, as learned from different routing protocols. Under traditional routing, and indeed in IPv4 routing in general, you only want one route to any given destination to be used. If you learn of a route to the same destination from two different protocols, which one do you use? To solve this problem, there is the concept of "believability" or weighting that is applied to the inputs from the protocols. In a Cisco or Proteon router, this is referred to as the Administrative Distance assigned to the routes from the given protocol. This Administrative Distance number provides a method of selecting the most "believable" route from several presented. For example, a static route has a distance of 1 whereas an OSPF route to the same destination would have a distance of 50, thus the static route would be selected as "best." In most cases this distance number can be manually changed in the configuration. The important point is that this mechanism ensures that there is one used route to the destination with all the other routes either becoming backups or standbys or simply being dropped.

In Linux, when you use the one main routing table this mechanism of distance or weighting is enforced with specified defaults in the RPDB. See the source for details on the various weights. The really key part is that with the RPDB you do not have to use only one routing table! As illustrated later in this chapter, when you allow the specific dynamic protocol to use a routing table all its own, then you control the route selection through the rules. So in Linux you can have all of the routes from all of the protocols available and then use the rules to select which route you want to use. Combine this facility of multiple routing tables for multiple routing protocols with the fact that you may have multiple routes to the same destination in the same table, as long as the TOS for the route is different, and you have a true multitude of ways to route a packet.

In summary, Linux defaults to using a configurable Administrative Distance concept when using one routing table. Multiple routing tables and the use of TOS tagged routes allow you to completely override the selection of only one "believable" route and use whatever routes you want from whatever protocols you want. This includes overriding static and local routes if you want.

The Zebra Routing Suite

For now you are interested in how the newer Zebra dynamic routing suite works. To start working with it, you obtain the newest source and compile it for your platform. The best way to get the latest code is to use the cvs repository. Check out http://www.zebra.org for details. In this case you instead go get the latest code as a tarball. The version you will use is 0.89a. This version is on the CD and in the PakSecured distribution.

Once the Zebra suite is compiled you find that there are several executables and related configuration files. Since Zebra consists of independent executables for each routing protocol, you can run any set of the protocols. Each protocol has its own configuration file that sets the parameters for the protocol.

The core daemon is zebra. It has the master configuration for all of the interfaces and system static routes. This configuration tells the other daemons which interfaces are available and performs the actual interfacing to the FIB. Each of the protocol daemons maintains a RIB unique to the protocol. This is a very nice implementation of the split between the Routing Information and the FIB as implemented in Linux itself.

One interesting part about Zebra is that the entire interface structure is modeled after the Cisco IOS command line. This makes it quite simple to manage for those who have been exposed to the Cisco-style interface. Each daemon will listen on a known port for telnet connections. There is a user-mode interface that allows viewing the routing tables and configurations, and an enable mode that allows setting parameters.

For now you want to explore how Zebra will work within your OSPF network. Returning to the setups worked through in testing gated, you start the same way with a single interface into the network. You want to set up OSPF for listening-only for now.

First, you need to configure the core zebra daemon to know about your interfaces. Remembering how your static route disappeared in the first gated test (you ran it earlier in the "gated" section of this chapter), you decide to make sure that the static route is entered into the system. Since the zebra daemon is responsible for interfaces and static routes, you create the following zebra.conf configuration file, by default located in /usr/local/etc:

```
! -*- zebra -*-
!
! zebra zebra.ospf.1.0 configuration file
!
hostname myzebra
password zebra
enable password zebra
!
interface eth0
  ip address 192.168.1.1/24
!
! Static default route
```

```
!
ip route 0.0.0.0/0 192.168.1.254
!
log file /tmp/zebra.log
```

Then you can just run the zebra daemon. Once it is running you can check your routing table with **ip route list** to see if there are any differences:

```
192.168.3.0/24 dev eth0  proto kernel  scope link  src 192.168.3.13
default via 192.168.3.254 dev eth0 proto zebra
```

Note that the default route is coded as from `proto zebra`. As you recall from the `gated` output, the kernel knows who put the route into the FIB. Note, however, that the actual interface was not recoded into a Zebra interface. This is in contrast to the `gated` setup where the interfaces ended up coded as `proto gated/conn`.

Now that you are satisfied that the `zebra` daemon is working, you leave it running and turn to configuring OSPF. For this you use the Zebra OSPF daemon, `ospfd`. The configuration file, `ospfd.conf` located in `/usr/local/etc`, is similar to the `zebra` daemon file but with OSPF-specific options. To set up for running on OSPF only you can use a simple configuration file as follows:

```
! -*- ospf -*-
!
! OSPFd zebra.ospf.1.2 configuration file
!
hostname myzebra
password zebra
enable password zebra
!
router ospf
  network 192.168.1.0/24 area 0
!
```

And then you run the `ospfd` daemon. It will receive the configuration information about the interfaces from the `zebra` daemon. So once it is running you check your routing tables again:

```
192.168.1.0/24 dev eth0  proto kernel  scope link  src 192.168.1.1
128.1.1.0/24 via 192.168.1.2 dev eth0  proto zebra
128.1.2.0/24 via 192.168.1.4 dev eth0  proto zebra
default via 192.168.1.254 dev eth0 proto zebra
```

Now you note one of the differences between Zebra and `gated`. In the same listing from `gated` you saw that there was a difference both in the name of the protocol and in whether it was a remote route or a remote static route. Here you only see that the protocol is zebra. You do not know if this route was added from a static, as the default route should be coded, or from OSPF, as 128.x.x.x/24 should be.

This is partially due to Alexey's gated patches allowing for different inputs from the gated daemon. Additionally, the gated daemon itself tracks internally which route is from which protocol. Remember that gated is monolithic; in other words, everything is in the same package. Since Zebra implements the split between the Routing Information and the FIB, the FIB only sees that the routes were updated from the zebra daemon.

This brings up the question of how to tell which routes came from which protocol within the Zebra suite. Recall that there is a telnet interface to the local daemons for the Zebra suite. To see what the various routes are from you need to connect to the various daemons and look at their individual internal routing tables. This is also where the additional information such as area for OSPF is located.

There are two ways to connect to the daemons for information. The first one is to telnet to the appropriate port for the local daemons individually. In this case zebra is on 2601 by default and ospfd is on 2604. This method requires that you connect to the ospfd for OSPF information and zebra for static and interface information. The alternative method is to use the integrated shell. This is vtysh. You can simply execute this command and have access to the various parts of the Zebra suite from one command line. Due to the integration and single point of information, you decide to just use the vtysh. It is simply executed from the command line. Note that there is the full Cisco IOS–style execution with a user-level prompt (>) and the enable or superuser prompt (#). See the Zebra documentation for details.

```
[root@paksecured /root]# /usr/local/bin/vtysh

Hello, this is zebra (version 0.89a)
Copyright 1996-2000 Kunihiro Ishiguro

zebra> en
zebra# sh ip ro
Codes: K - kernel route, C - connected, S - static, R - RIP, O - OSPF,
       B - BGP, * - FIB route.

S* 0.0.0.0/0 [1/0]          eth0 (3) 192.168.3.254
O  0.0.0.0/0 [110/11]       eth0 (3) 192.168.3.254
C* 127.0.0.0/8                 lo (1) direct
O* 128.1.1.0/24 [110/11]    eth0 (3) 192.168.3.2
O* 128.1.2.0/24 [110/11]    eth0 (3) 192.168.3.4
C* 192.168.3.0/24           eth0 (3) direct
zebra#
```

This gives you the entire routing table as it is seen from the zebra daemon's point of view. Note that there is a difference between the protocols in this routing table. You want to see what the OSPF information is from the ospfd daemon.

```
zebra# sh ip ospf
 OSPF Routing Process, Router ID: 192.168.1.1
 Supports only single TOS (TOS0) routes
```

```
This implementation conforms to RFC2328
RFC1583Compatibility flag is disabled
SPF schedule delay 5 secs, Hold time between two SPFs 10 secs
Refresh timer 10 secs
Number of external LSA 3
Number of areas attached to this router: 1


Area ID: 0.0.0.0 (Backbone)
   Number of interfaces in this area: Total: 1, Active: 1
   Number of fully adjacent neighbors in this area: 1
   Area has no authentication
   SPF algorithm executed 5 times
   Number of LSA 3

zebra#
zebra# sh ip os nei


Neighbor ID      Pri   State          Dead Time   Address   \
      Interface             RXmtL RqstL DBsmL
192.168.1.254      2   Full/DR           00:00:32   192.168.1.254  \
   eth0                    0     0     0
zebra#
```

Now you are also curious as to how the interfaces are functioning. So you look at the information for eth0:

```
zebra# sh int eth0
Interface eth0
   index 3 metric 1 mtu 1500 <UP,BROADCAST,RUNNING,MULTICAST>
   HWaddr: 00:50:56:8b:03:0d
   inet 192.168.1.1/24 broadcast 192.168.1.255
   inet6 fe80::250:56ff:fe8b:30d/10
     input packets 3297, bytes 1337231, dropped 0, multicast packets 0
     input errors 0, length 0, overrun 0, CRC 0, frame 0, fifo 0, missed 0
     output packets 1101, bytes 86436, dropped 0
     output errors 0, aborted 0, carrier 0, fifo 0, heartbeat 0, window 0
     collisions 0
zebra#
```

This interface gives you all the information you would need to manage and troubleshoot the system.

CAUTION

The vtysh interface functions by using the terminal interfaces to the various daemons. These interfaces are standard telnet connections and all data is passed in the clear. You can disable the terminal interfaces by simply remarking out or not including the password and enable password lines in the configuration files. However, you then disable the ability of vtysh as well.

From a security standpoint, you would only want to run these daemons with the terminal interfaces if you have taken other precautions to disable access to those ports.

Rules and Dynamic Structure

All of the testing you have performed to this point has shown you how to implement dynamic routing using either gated or the Zebra suite. But you do not know how these dynamic routing suites can interoperate with Policy Routing. You note that to this point all of the routes from either gated or Zebra have been installed into routing table main.

What if you could specify which table to use for the routes? Then you could use the rules to set up special implementations of dynamic routing interfaces. You could run many different versions of dynamic protocols on the same system and have different versions of the routes connecting through your network.

gated and Multiple Routing Tables

This is where Alexey's patch to gated provides needed extensions. In addition to providing for the provisioning of realms, it also adds a command-line switch that tells gated what routing table to use. As you recall, gated is monolithic and runs with all interactions providing data to a single routing structure. This command-line switch is simply -T{#}, where you would replace {#} with the number of the routing table to use.

```
[root@paksecured /root]# ip ro li tab 128
[root@paksecured /root]#
[root@paksecured /root]# /usr/local/sbin/gated -T128
[root@paksecured /root]# ip ro li tab 128
127.0.0.1 dev lo  proto gated/conn  scope host
192.168.1.0/24 dev eth0  proto gated/conn  scope link  src 192.168.1.1
128.1.1.0/24 via 192.168.1.2 dev eth0  proto gated/ospf
128.1.2.0/24 via 192.168.1.4 dev eth0  proto gated/ospfase
[root@paksecured /root]#
```

As you can see, this has placed all of the gated routes into the routing table 128. If you want you can use this fact to assign realms to these routes based solely on the routing table:

```
[root@paksecured /root]#ip ru add pref 32000 table 128 realms 2/3
```

Now you have assigned a source realm of 2 and a destination realm of 3 to all routes in table 128. Then all of the standard commands listing realms apply.

Zebra and Multiple Routing Tables

As of the release of Zebra considered herein, 0.89a, only one official usage of assigning a routing table is allowed. This is within the zebra daemon itself and refers specifically only to static routes. You can specify in the configuration file that you want all static routes to be placed within a single table.

Suppose you wanted all of your static routes to be placed into table 129. You would configure the zebra.conf file with the following:

```
! Static default routes.
! Select table 129 for static routes
table 129
ip route 0.0.0.0/0 192.168.3.254
!
```

This would place all the following static routes into table 129. But those are the only routes that would be placed into that table.

Based on several private conversations I have had with other people active on the Zebra mailing list, this type of functionality is being actively considered for both the OSPF and RIP daemons in both IPv4 and IPv6. Recent indications are that this type of command will be available through patches for all of the various daemons.

For example, as of 10/10/2000 an unofficial patch to the bgpd daemon exists that allows bgpd to use a specific route table. This specification is coded as part of an extension to the route-map command. The route-map command allows you to specify filters to be applied to the BGP protocol inputs and outputs. Using this patch you can specify specific ASPATH IDs for matching and assign them to a specific route table. This is a very powerful feature especially when you consider larger multi-connected peerings. Simply being able to separate out the AS by table is a very powerful tool when considering applying Policy Routing structures within such an environment.

gated & zebra & rules = FUN

As it stands now one of the tricks of the trade is to run gated with OSPF only or maybe RIP and OSPF and send it to a single table, such as table 128. Then run zebra to handle the static routes to a table, say 129. Finally, run the bgpd from zebra and tell it to send its information to table 130 and higher.

From there you can assign realms for tracking and use rules to determine which traffic gets routed through which set of connections. Think about modifying the Bounce Table Walking and Tag Routing examples from Chapter 6 using this new set of tables. The possibilities are limitless.

In all of this you must remember that dynamic routing is simply a means to distribute a complex routing table between systems. You need to realize that a dynamic routing protocol, such as OSPF or even BGP, effectively provides a distribution mechanism for a single routing table. Most routers today only possess a single FIB, which is derived from all of the routes presented by the various dynamic protocols. This makes mixing and matching dynamic routing protocols not very flexible because you end up discarding duplicate routes according to a predetermined formula. So you have the concept of weighting which selects the "best" route from the routes presented by the various protocols. By contrast, in the RPDB the FIB actually can be thought of as existing per routing table. You can conceive of each routing table as defining an independent FIB. And the rules then select the FIB to use for the packet. Thus none of the routes are ever filtered out except by direct specification, and all routes from all protocols are available for use.

Policy Routing's multiple routing tables enable multiple dynamic routing protocols to be treated just as you treat multiple IP addresses. You can have a different dynamic routing protocol running for different networks on the same physical connection. The ability of each protocol to have its own routing table allows you as the policy administrator to govern and control the structure of the network without having to hassle with which protocol is weightier than the other. This provides you with the best of both worlds.

Summary

What you have seen in this chapter is how to treat dynamic routing protocols as a means to automatically distribute routing table information. Through the P olicy Routing extensions you can assign independent routing tables for use on a per-protocol basis. Then all of the Policy Routing power becomes available to you.

As you saw in Chapter 6, the range and flexibility of Policy Routing can work magic. When you couple with this the ability to segregate and distribute the route Triad element through a dynamic protocol, you effectively extend the reach of a single Policy Routing structure to many devices that cannot perform Policy Routing.

You should now be comfortable setting up and running both gated and the Zebra suite on your system. When you couple this with the skills learned in Chapters 5 and 6, you start to see the massive scope of networking under Policy Routing. In the next few chapters you will see how NAT is a function of Policy Routing and then you will learn what the future holds for IPv6 and beyond.

CHAPTER 8

NAT Functions

Dealing with the vagaries of routing structures using a dynamic routing protocol is very helpful. But it is limited in usefulness when you consider the current structure of the IPv4 Internet. Within the boundaries of a corporate network, routing is defined and scoped. Many of the routing tricks such as asymmetric, or loopy, routing, and the related structures take on a whole new meaning when applied to the border and outside of a corporate network.

While the examples you saw in Chapters 5, "Simple Network Examples" and 6, "Complex Network Examples" about border area Policy Routing work well when you consider the entire scope of the addressing space, what about cases where there is address translation? These cases of Network Address Translation, or NAT, are what you will explore in this chapter.

You will start by considering the definitions of NAT both from the technical and popular viewpoints. Then you will try out some of the various uses of NAT. Finally, you will explore the interactions between the firewalling functions and the Policy Routing structures.

Standard NAT Defined

The traditional definition of NAT is contained in the very term itself. Network Address Translation is the act of changing an address from one to another within the packet. While this change is usually of the source address, there is no restriction. This address changing function is essentially a router function when you consider the mechanisms. Any router, due to its very nature as an intermediary between networks, may perform the NAT function.

The early history of IPv4 networking did not need to consider this type of routing function very often. Occasionally the subject would come up, but those discussions usually were centered within fairly convoluted reasoning. The IPv4 address space does contain over 4 billion addresses and until the explosion of the Internet in the early 1990s, there was no solid reason to play with the addressing space. Thus, while NAT existed and was used it was not what is popularly referred to today as NAT.

Think of the traditional proxy server. Considering the entire sequence of events as seen from outside the server, it is essentially performing NAT. The request is made to the inside of the proxy from some client with some source address. The proxy then turns around and sends out a packet with its own source address. When the proxy receives the response, it responds back to the client.

This transaction is NAT as it fits all aspects of the definition. An address is translated by a router that spans two disparate networks. While you may not think that this scenario is a routing scenario, it certainly is. Remember that a router is defined as a system that allows traffic to be sent between networks. Traffic exists to request and receive services. So if you can sit at a machine on an IP network, make a request for a service on another network from some device, and receive that service, then you have used a router.

This is the core of considering NAT as a legitimate function within the scope of an IP network. IP addresses define service location. Receiving a service from a disparate network to your network requires a router. Whether that service provider actually saw your real source address is irrelevant to the networking. All that matters is that a service was transacted across network boundaries.

Seen in this light, the function of a NAT firewall is fairly obvious, especially when you consider the popular IP Masquerade. IP Masquerade is merely a many-to-one NAT. In the sense in which it is used in a Masquerading firewall, you can consider the firewall to be performing a proxy service. However, the proxy service is not specific to an application or protocol, but rather to an address.

These concepts are so important because of the misconception within the networking community that NAT is somehow dirty or evil because it supposedly breaks the end-to-end model originally proposed for IP networking. The end-to-end model is the function whereby any given service transaction is performed between two, and only two, entities. But the end-to-end model is an interpretive assumption of the communication structure. For example, consider the actual communication structure of a proxy system.

The communication is initiated by a client wanting a service. The client sends a request for that service to the original service location defined by the service's IP address. This request reaches the proxy system. The proxy system intercedes into the communication. Under most protocols, the proxy system at this point would complete the initial handshake with the client on behalf of the final service. This is important because at this point the end-to-end model is satisfied from the client's point of view as the two ends, client and service, are negotiated. From the original service's point of view nothing has yet happened. So now the proxy initiates the communication with the service on behalf of the client. From the original service's point of view, the end-to-end model is complete because the client is the proxy.

Stepping back a level there are two distinct end-to-end connections that have been formed from one original request. Think of the true communication structure between two clients on either side of a router. From the layer 2 perspective, which is where the actual packet communication takes place within a local network, there are two end-to-end communications made out of one request.

Now substitute NAT for proxy. In both cases the end-to-end model is satisfied providing that the communication always includes the middle. So you must always have a bottleneck point for NAT. Or must you?

Consider the three main types of NAT: One-to-One, Many-to-One, and One-to-Many. Both Many-to-One and One-to-Many NAT are best considered as mapping types of NAT. They take a single address and spread it across many addresses. Both of these types require a single point at which to perform the mapping and through which the reverse mapping must occur. But One-to-One NAT does not require the same location to perform the mapping.

The very name One-to-One NAT implies that there is a unique correlation between two addresses. The only differentiation is direction. In one direction, address A becomes address B and in the other direction, the reverse is true. Since NAT may be considered a router function, this map function may exist in every router that crosses the boundary defining the edge over which direction changes.

Consider the network illustrated in Figure 8.1. This is a fairly typical large corporate network with three primary sites. Each of the primary sites has a Policy Routing system connecting them to the Internet. Internally, all three sites are connected either through dedicated lines or VPN structures. Now imagine that there is a Web server at each location that will provide the location unique Internet services.

Each of these Web servers, call them WebA, WebB, and WebC, are addressed with internal addresses appropriate to the location. From the Internet's perspective there are three addresses assigned in DNS to each of these Web servers. The company has a registered block of IP addresses that it uses for all of its Internet-related activities. All three ISPs allow any of these addresses to enter or leave the local connection.

Since the internal addresses are in compliance with Private IP addressing (RFC-1918), the Web servers must be NATed when they route to the Internet. But which router should perform the NAT? All of them.

Think for a minute about the routing structure as it pertains to the Internet traffic. Each local machine within a corporate sector may route to the Internet by whatever path is specified as default according to the local internal router. But Internet traffic may enter the network by the closest router in relation to the traffic's origination. That is, traffic to the corporation that originates in Japan (JP) will enter the corporate network through Router3. But what if that traffic is destined for WebA?

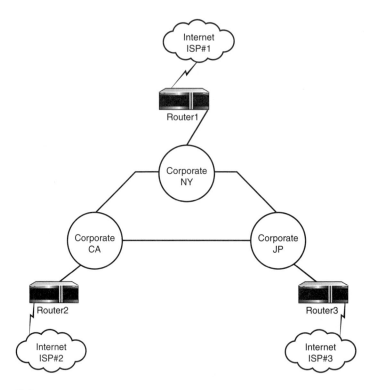

Figure 8.1

MultiRouter NAT network.

In this scenario, under traditional routing all traf fic destined for WebA is given a sin-gle connection point. So consider that under traditional routing all traffic destined for WebA must be routed through RouterA whether or not RouterA is available. But under Policy Routing the traffic may enter at any of the three routers because the NAT may be performed at any of the three routers. Remember that NAT is a router function and that this is One-to-One NAT.

In the Policy Routing scenario, all three routers will contain the NAT definitions. All three routers contain the NAT map function as each router spans the boundary defining the edge over which traffic direction changes. NAT is truly a router function and Policy Routing provides the framework for defining the entire routing function scope of appli-cation.

Policy Routing NAT

Since NAT is a routing function, you decide you want to try out some of the various uses. You decide to return to the test setup you had in Chapter 6. This scenario is shown in Figure 8.2 as a refresher.

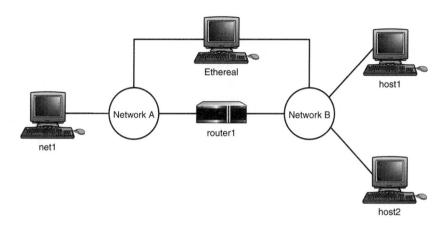

Figure 8.2

Test network schematic.

You are now going to use router1 to do some testing. To this end you set up the testing environment as follows:

```
NetworkA        192.168.1.0/24
NetworkB        10.1.1.0/24
net1     192.168.1.1/24
router1 A       192.168.1.254/24
router1 B       10.1.1.254/24
host1    10.1.1.2/24
host2    10.1.1.3/24
```

Since you have the capability of looking at the actual packet traces, you decide to try a simple NAT in which all packets from net1 to host2 are NATed by router1 to 10.1.1.253. The `ip` utility allows you to perform a one-to-one NAT mapping, which is called FastNAT in the kernel documentation. You decide to try out the FastNAT setup with `ip`. The command sequence you determine for the `ip` utility is as follows:

```
ip route add nat 10.1.1.253/32 via 192.168.1.1
ip rule add from 192.168.1.1/32 nat 10.1.1.253 prio 15000
```

Now from net1 when you ping, telnet, or use any other IP transport-based protocol to get to host2, you see on the packet dump that the source address has been changed to 10.1.1.253. Indeed, if you use net1 to go to any of the 10.1.1.x addresses you see that the source is changed.

This is a complete One-to-One NAT between these two addresses. If you use a packet generator or protocol that embeds the original address within the data section of the packet, you see that the only address changed is the header source. The embedded address does not change. This is the main reason certain protocols, such as IPSec and SNA/IP, cannot be NATed due to their embedding the original source address within the data part of the packet. Since this is an extreme security risk on the Internet because of internal address leakage, you usually will not want to route such protocols across the Internet, but rather either encapsulate them or tunnel them. In the case of IPSec and related security protocols, the best solution is to always use legal IP addresses.

Curious as to the extent of the routing NAT structure, you decide to see if you can perform an extended NAT mapping. You want to see if you can do a group One-to-One NAT from the address space 192.168.1.32/27 to 10.1.1.32/27 and see if the changes are mapped One-to-One. So you add the following rules:

```
# On net1
i=32
while [ $i -lt 64 ]; do
ip addr add 192.168.1.$i/32 dev eth0
i=$((i+=1))
done
# On router1
ip rule add from 192.168.1.32/27 nat 10.1.1.32 prio 14000
ip route add nat 10.1.1.32/27 via 192.168.1.32
```

From the packet traces on Network B you can see that the mapping is correctly One-to-One across the range. If you use the 192.168.1.37 source you get the translated address of 10.1.1.37. Just to make sure you change the 10.1.1.32/27 range to 10.1.1.96/27. You see that when you use the 192.168.1.37 address it gets translated to 10.1.1.101 just as a One-to-One mapping would demand.

This result allows you to have a ranged NAT defined on all of your border routers. Recalling Figure 8.1, you could define several sets of addresses within each of the three Corporate sites and have all three border routers contain complete range NAT maps for these subnets. As an even weirder stretch you note that with a single NIC policy router you could translate local network addresses for machines without multiple address capabilities.

If you recall the setup you implemented in Example 6.3 from Chapter 6 where you implemented asymmetric routing, you see that you can now have a distributed Policy Router set up that provides all of these services plus NAT. Consider implementing Example 6.3 on a system such as Figure 8.1. Assume for a moment that your company does not own its own address block but instead depends on addressing from each of the three ISPs. Your contracts with each of the three ISPs allow outbound traffic that is addressed from any of the three, but will not route inbound except to their own address blocks. This is a fairly standard multi-ISP setup in corporate environments. Are you then limited to one ISP address block for your external Web server?

No. Consider that you have control over your corporate DNS. You can specify multiple addresses for your Web server in the DNS, say one address from each ISP. Set up a single common Web server with three addresses. Each border router now has an inbound NAT mapping for the local ISP address that is DNS-coded for the Web server, and three outbound NAT mappings for each of the three addresses. If you track the local routing structure on your border routers, the outbound packets from the Web server can be routed by whatever border router is closest to the destination and will receive the correct outbound address that was used to query the server. In this case you get effective failover for the Web server as seen by the outside world. If any of the ISPs is down, you still have Web services available.

NOTE

The scenario mentioned above where one ISP allows you to route outwards through their network the set of IP addresses you obtained from a different ISP was a common practice in 1994–1996. With the advent of many of the IP Spoofing attacks and Denial-Of-Service (DoS) attacks, this output of addresses became a suspect activity. RFC-2267 (January 1998) urges ISPs to implement filtering to prevent IP addresses other than the ones that the ISP themselves own out from the ISP's network. This is often implemented as an ingress filter on the ISP's internal network, hence the referral to Ingress. While this mitigates some menial forms of IP Spoofing, it does not control the notorious DDoS (Distributed Denial of Service) attacks. These are DoS attacks that are launched from a collection of "zombie" machines by a single controlling administrator. Thus the recent dramatic increase in use of DDoS engines. Indeed, the increasing implementation of RFC-2267 is also driving the use of NAT as a method of maintaining a multi-ISP spanning Internet connection. Adding more extensive use of NAT to the ubiquity of DDoS slave engines being installed is a very frightening scenario. But the willingness of ISPs to at least start implementing some control mechanisms is a very promising move. Hopefully, the greater addressing space structures and formalities of routing IPv6 will help every multi-connected company obtain and manage its own legal IP address space, which will moot all of this discussion.

Of course in many of these cases there are security consequences for which you must allow. And the interactions between the security structures and the NAT structures can get very hairy. When you consider them both under the umbrella of the global routing structure, it is easier to see what points of contention will arise. Since you do run packet filtering and stateful inspection firewall systems, you turn your attention to the interactions that exist between these types of systems and your routing NAT structures.

NetFilter NAT

As you explored in Chapter 6, the packet filtering structure within the Linux 2.4 series kernel is NetFilter. Because you had used the fwmark interface (called nfmark in NetFilter) to tag packets, you noted that there were structures that existed to allow for NAT within the NetFilter architecture. To determine how these structures function within the Policy Routing arena, you perform a series of tests within your test network setup.

First you do some research into the style of the NetFilter structure as it pertains to the NAT function. In contrast to the bidirectional routing NAT style, NetFilter treats the direction of the NAT as an element of the NAT function. This granularity provides an additional construct that can provide for unidirectional NAT.

The two types of NAT as defined by NetFilter are the Source NAT (SNAT) and the Destination NAT (DNAT). SNAT maps outbound packets as they leave the system, hence the name Source NAT rightly implying that the source address changes. DNAT maps inbound packets as they enter the system, hence the name Destination NAT rightly implying that the destination address changes. These mappings may be applied using any of the NetFilter packet selection mechanisms, thus providing a level of granularity in the packet selection mechanisms.

After studying the NetFilter command structures, you first decide to try to rework your One-to-One NAT setup using the facilities provided by the NetFilter architecture. To this end you ensure that the `iptable_nat` module is loaded (see the NetFilter documentation for details), and then you set up the same One-to-One NAT using the original single address model. You end up with the following series of commands:

```
iptables -t nat -A POSTROUTING -o eth1 -s 192.168.1.1/32 \
     -j SNAT --to 10.1.1.253
iptables -t nat -A PREROUTING -i eth1 -d 10.1.1.253/32 \
     -j DNAT --to 192.168.1.1
```

Upon issuing any IP connection from address 192.168.1.1 to host2 you find no connection is completed. Inspecting the packet trace from Network B you see that the packets leave router1 with the NAT addressing correctly changed, but that host2 does not know how to respond and ARPs repeatedly for the 10.1.1.253 address. This is unlike the situation in FastNAT where router1, the default router for host2 in both cases, received the packet and applied the translation without needing to own the address. But you find that NetFilter requires router1 to own the address 10.1.1.253. Upon adding in the command **ip addr add 10.1.1.253/32 dev eth1** and running **ip route flu cache**, you see the NAT working correctly.

Now you know how to do a simple One-to-One mapping in NetFilter. You then try to set up the extended One-to-One NAT mapping such as you had done with the routing NAT function earlier. So you try the following set of commands:

```
iptables -t nat -A POSTROUTING -o eth1 -s 192.168.1.32/27 \
     -j SNAT --to 10.1.1.64-10.1.1.95
iptables -t nat -A PREROUTING -i eth1 -d 10.1.1.64/27 \
     -j DNAT --to 192.168.1.32-192.168.1.63
```

When you start testing from the 192.168.1.32 address, you notice on the packet dumps from Network B that the source addresses are incrementing upwards for every packet you send. So your first packet through from 192.168.1.32 has a source translation of 10.1.1.64, the second packet is 10.1.1.65, and so on. Not even close to the behavior of the FastNAT. Then when you look at the verbose output of the NetFilter information, using **iptables -t nat -L -n -v**, you see that the DNAT setup has no packets using the rule at all. Just out of curiosity, you delete the DNAT rule and note that the operation of the system is unchanged. You finally deduce that to do One-to-One ranged NAT with NetFilter you must specify each NAT transaction independently.

For most of the cases where you would be making use of these structures you would use fairly static defined mappings anyway. The additional setup would not be a big deal unless you were doing wholesale NAT translations of complete IP address spaces, and in that case you could use the FastNAT construct.

You note that in the case where you specify this command sequence using only a single address on the one side and a range of addresses on the other, you have a clear example of One-to-Many NAT. This type of NAT structure is not very interesting for you but you can see some simple load balancing uses for it, such as multiple internal Web servers.

One of the security structures that does interest you is the use of the Many-to-One NAT. In Linux this was traditionally called IP Masquerade, and you would like to implement it for some sequences of addresses. To this end you first try a quick test to masquerade all output to Network B as router1, 10.1.1.254. You implement the following commands:

```
iptables -t nat -A POSTROUTING -o eth1 -j SNAT --to 10.1.1.254
```

The packet traces from Network B show that all traffic from net1 to either host1 or host2 has a source address of 10.1.1.254. Now you know that the SNAT worked due to router1 owning the 10.1.1.254 address. This makes you wonder what constitutes ownership. From your solid understanding of the Address Triad element you suspect that any assignment of the appropriate address to the system would work. To prove your conviction you delete the preceding SNAT rule and try the following sequence:

```
ip addr add 172.16.13.13/32 dev dummy0
ip link set dev dummy0 up
iptables -t nat -A POSTROUTING -o eth1 -j SNAT --to 172.16.13.13
```

And, voila, the output from router1 into Network B has source address 172.16.13.13. Finally, to ensure that you are truly into twisted setups you add the following command:

```
iptables -t nat -A POSTROUTING -o eth0 -j SNAT --to 172.16.13.13
```

You can now see that the source address for packets on both Networks A and B is 172.16.13.13.

But there is a catch that makes you pause. You notice that the SNAT only takes place when the origination of the initial connection is from the affected network. In other words, you only see the source translation on packets that are not responses. To illustrate, you look at the sequence where you send packets from net1, 192.168.1.32 address, to host2, 10.1.1.3. The packet traces from Network B show the source translated to 172.16.13.13. But the packet traces from Network A do not show the responses from host2, 10.1.1.3, translated as you would expect from the dual SNAT. When testing from host2 to net1 you find the contrapositive sequence.

This is a function of the connection tracking mechanism within NetFilter. The connection tracking is what negated the DNAT in the test of One-to-One NAT and also in the testing of extended NAT. The connection tracking mechanism performs exactly as you would expect from the name. However, this is also the feature that negates the status of NetFilter NAT as a routing function and relegates it to a packet mangling function performed solely on a single system.

Consider that you have a triple connection setup as in Figure 8.1. You would like to implement an asymmetric, or loopy, routing structure. In this structure, traffic destined for the corporate Web server will enter only through the ISP#1 connection. When it enters it will be NATed to an address in CA. The response then returns to the Internet through ISP#2 with the same original destination address from ISP#1. Under NetFilter there are time-outs and connection tracking overhead associated with the SNAT and DNAT features. Each time a packet comes in through Router1 there is a connection track set up for the eventual "return" of the response. Similarly, each time a packet leaves through Router2 there is a connection track set up. These connection tracks take time to timeout. There is also a finite number of such connections that may be tracked due to memory and processing power on the system.

Interactions Between FastNAT and NetFilter

This consideration brings you to the question of the interactions between the FastNAT and the NetFilter NAT. From your studies on the packet pathing in Chapter 3, "Linux Policy Routing Structures," you assume that you could have FastNAT and NetFilter too. After all, FastNAT is implemented within the RPDB while NetFilter NAT is implemented at the PRE and POST ROUTING hook points.

Such a view does not consider the reality of the kernel packet processing functions. While ideally this would be a perfect complementary function set, the reality is that there are only a few places where the packet header may be manipulated by either system. In testing the various functions you note that so long as you do not load up the actual NetFilter NAT module, `iptable_nat`, you can do FastNAT. As soon as you load the `iptable_nat` module, FastNAT stops working even without any NetFilter NAT rules defined.

At least you understand now how each of these NAT mechanisms works and some of the uses and drawbacks of each. For granularity of NAT specification and flexibility of NAT structures you can use NetFilter. For speed, Policy Routing structures, and asymmetric routing you can use FastNAT. And you do note that by a simple addition of a Policy Routing system with FastNAT on the internal network you can perform whatever pure One-to-One NAT mechanisms you wish and pass those packets unmodified through the NetFilter box.

One other thought does strike you. When you consider the FastNAT structure you realize that in the case of only needing routing-based NAT you can use the NetFilter filter and mangle tools on the same box as a FastNAT, thus providing a way to select and filter NAT-destined packets. As a quick example you consider that by defining a packet filter on the PREROUTING hook that only allows packets destined to a certain port, you effectively allow for a FastNAT based on a single port. A whole realm of possibilities opens up for those scenarios.

Summary

You have defined NAT within the Policy Routing structure. You have seen how a pure routing NAT structure runs with both asymmetric and single point setups. Using FastNAT you have explored how to translate entire address spaces from one to another bidirectionally.

You then worked through the uses of the NetFilter NAT constructs and saw how these constructs complement the FastNAT structure. You understand how each type of NAT has a use within the overall network structure. Also, you determined that the two structures do not at this time coexist with each other.

But as you think about these uses of NAT you begin to ponder why it will be important in the long term. In IPv4 NAT has grown from an esoteric oddity to a daily necessity. But you know that IPv6 does not need or allow NAT. You decide to find out what Policy Routing is all about under IPv6.

CHAPTER 9

IPv6

You appreciate the detailed control of the routing structure that you possess under IPv4 with Policy Routing. You ponder the scope and uses of the various parts of Policy Routing itself within the definition of your current IPv4 network. But you know that IPv4 is in transition to a more powerful and comprehensive protocol, IPv6.

With your knowledge of the workings and the reasoning behind Policy Routing under IPv4 you wonder how and what IPv6 will change in Policy Routing. To this end, this chapter explores IPv6 and especially the relationships of IPv6 to the core Policy Routing structures. At the end of the chapter you will see where Policy Routing fits into this new protocol suite and what the future will hold.

Theory and History

By the late 1980s, members of the IETF (Internet Engineering Task Force) started discussing the possible future limitations and conceptual problems of IPv4. With the invention of the World Wide Web protocol by Tim Berners-Lee in the early 1990s came an explosion of interest in the Internet outside the academic and research oriented non-commercial Internet user base. Much of that explosion hastened the discussions of the successor to IPv4. The end result was the creation of the IPv6 protocol family whose RFCs began rolling out in 1995.

> **NOTE**
>
> Note that there was an IPv5 specification produced in the late 1980s. However, even within the RFCs defining IPv5 it was referred to and considered as an "experimental" protocol. It was never really intended for general public consumption. Much like the Linux development kernel series, you were free to play with it but it was not expected to work or be compatible. Some of the ideas from that protocol family ended up driving some of the designs of IPv6.

IPv6 drew upon many of the ideas and lessons learned from many protocol families, not just IPv4. The auto-addressing facilities of IPX, hierarchical routing structures from OSI and SNA, and the speed of fixed packet header structures in link-layer switching are but a few of the collective condensations of ideas. The flurry of ideas resulted in many RFCs, draft RFCs, and informational documents in 1994 as the IETF began the process of codifying the steps towards IPng (Internet Protocol Next Generation). IPng was to become IPv6 when ratified. Many of the ideas flying around in these documents were initially coalesced into the first set of IPv6 RFCs released in 1995.

RFC-1883 first specified IPv6 as a standard in December of 1995. The range of RFCs from 1883 through 1888 was the first release of the new IPv6 protocol family as proposed standards. These initial RFCs have been superseded by newer developments, but most of the newer developments are merely refinements of the structures. To understand IPv6 you should obtain and read through the current standard RFC-2460. To date there are several dozen RFCs that are standards or draft standards for many aspects of IPv6. A good reference site is at http://www.ipv6.org.

Many popular notions of IPv6 abound, especially in the various trade groups and magazines. For your purposes the core reasons are that IPv6 contains 128-bit autoconfiguring addresses, an aggregatable address space, and automatic routing configuration capabilities. The streamlined header and packet design refinements fix nagging issues with IPv4 such as network autoconfiguration, mobile IP, IP security, fragmentation, and source routing, and allow for very large packets known as jumbograms.

IPv6 Addresses

IPv6 addresses are 128 bits long. While this fact has been used to try to scare small children by various groups who had problems implementing IPv4, IPv6 addresses are actually very easy to use. You must remember that IPv4 addresses are not defined by dotted decimals. Dotted decimal notation (192.168.1.1) is merely an easy way to humanly state an IPv4 address. IPv4 addresses, as with IPv6 addresses, are more properly considered as large binary numbers. When dealing with IPv4 addresses in many cases, as you saw to some degree when you used the u32 classifier in Chapter 6, "Complex Network Examples," you specify them in hexadecimal equivalent (192.168.1.1 = 0xC0A80101). This is also the key to, and the standard definition of, IPv6 addresses.

There are three defined types of IPv6 addresses as specified in RFC-2373 and quoted as follows:

Unicast—An identifier for a single interface. A packet sent to a unicast address is delivered to the interface identified by that address.

Anycast—An identifier for a set of interfaces (typically belonging to different nodes). A packet sent to an anycast address is delivered to one of the interfaces identified by that address (the "nearest" one, according to the routing protocols' measure of distance).

Multicast—An identifier for a set of interfaces (typically belonging to different nodes). A packet sent to a multicast address is delivered to all interfaces identified by that address.

Note that the broadcast address type extensively used in IPv4 is not defined. Although it could be considered a form of the multicast address type, there is no need for broadcast addressing within IPv6 because there is no need to reach every single IPv6 device.

The convention for writing down IPv6 addresses has a specification but the universally accepted method has become the coloned hex with zeros collapsed. The best way to define this is to run through a quick example.

A fully defined IPv6 address is written in human notation as eight 16-bit segments separated by colons (coloned hex notation) as follows:

`1111:2222:3333:4444:5555:6666:7777:8888`

Most actual addresses will contain contiguous sections of zeros. These zeros may be collapsed once and only once within the address by using a pair of colons. Consider the following full address:

`1111:2222:0000:0000:5555:0000:0000:8888`

This address may be specified in either of the following two ways:

`1111:2222::5555:0:0:8888`—First set of zeros are double colons

`1111:2222:0:0:5555::8888`—Second set of zeros are double colons

But the following representation is wrong:

`1111:2222::5555::8888`—This is illegal!

In normal usage you will usually see that the specification of the address places the double colons in the network portion of the address. That is, if the address previously had a CIDR mask of /64 then you would probably write the address as

`1111:2222::5555:0:0:8888/64`

This allows for the network portion to be noted as `1111:2222::/64` while the host portion is `::5555:0:0:8888/64`.

All of this discussion of addressing also brings up the entire notion of routing scoping and aggregation. As you have just implicitly seen, an IPv6 address has the notion of netmask as defined by a CIDR specification. I would strongly recommend that you read through RFC-2373 because it covers both the addressing and the aggregation references.

IPv6 does contain a mechanism for auto-addressing. Auto addresses are assigned in one primary use with another definition covering the concept of local addresses as you had used in IPv4 from RFC-1918. In IPv6 this is the link-local and site-local address formats (see RFC-2373 for details).

A link-local address is designed for exactly what the name implies. It is a valid address within the scope of the physical link itself. The other defined prefix, site-local, takes the place roughly of the local addressing space in IPv4 as defined in RFC-1918. A link-local address is automatically formed from a defined prefix, `fe80:`, and the MAC address or alternate globally defined unique number of the interface. So, for example, if you had an ethernet card with MAC address `11:22:33:44:55:66`, you would calculate your link-local address as

`fe80::1122:33ff:fe44:5566`

Note that this can be boiled down to the following set of steps:

1. Place the link-local ID first with a pair of colons:
   `fe80::`
2. Place the first three octets of your MAC address next:
   `fe80::1122:33`
3. Add on `fffe`
   `fe80::1122:33ff:fe`
4. Finish off with the last three octets of your MAC:
   `fe80::1122:33ff:fe44:5566`

Note that if your MAC address contains leading zeros, it is usually up to the particular IPv6 implementation as to how it handles the creation. In Linux, a 2 is added as a placeholder so that you have:

MAC = `00:11:22:33:44:55`
Link-Local = `fe80::211:22ff:fe33:4455`

Note that when you consider most of the automatic routing structures under IPv6, the last 64 bits of the address are also automatically computed according to the preceding steps.

IPv6 Routing and Neighbors

One of the more interesting parts of IPv6 lies in the extension of the auto-address configuration to the routing structure. In RFC-2461 much of the actual terminology and structure of IPv6 Neighbor Discovery is covered and is well worth reading through if only to better understand some of the conversations on IPv6.

Essentially, IPv6 provides a mechanism for hosts and routers to discover each other. You may think of ARP on IPv4, which is the link-local address mapping mechanism. If you then consider what integrating ARP with RIP would do then you have an inkling of what IPv6 Neighbor Discovery covers.

As you just saw in IPv6 addressing there are addresses that are automatically defined on your system using the MAC address of your NIC card. These link-local addresses function to ensure that there is no need for an ARP protocol in IPv6. But they also provide a means for all IPv6 devices on a local network to communicate without any further setup. The logical next step in convenience would be to have your system automatically find the routers on the network.

This next step is provided as part of the Neighbor Discovery mechanism. A router in IPv6 may be configured to send out periodic router advertisements. These advertisements are sent and received using a designated set of prefixes for routers and provide autoconfiguration of the local network for the designated advertised network prefixes. A router does not have to advertise to perform routing. Think of it more in the style of a services advertising network such as NetWare SAP on IPX or the SLP (Service Location Protocol) on IPv4.

When an IPv6 host is enabled on a network, it first sends out a Neighbor solicitation, which is a query to determine what types of neighbors it has on that link. It will send out this type of query every time an address is added. It will follow this query up with a Router Solicitation query. If a router is configured to advertise on this network, the router will respond to the Router Solicitation with a Router Advertisement. If the host hears a Router Advertisement, it will create a route to that prefix on the interface it received the advertisement on.

The actual processes of this interchange and the results are determined by the configuration of the host. You can configure a host to not listen to router advertisements on certain interfaces. But for most networking where you have a single interface host and a router connecting the local network to the rest of the world, this system works very well.

Now that you have some understanding of the basics of IPv6 addressing and have read through some of the RFCs, you decide to revisit your test network and try to set up a simple IPv6 network.

First you just want to test out the link-local autoconfiguration of the various machines on the network. Recalling your test network from Chapter 6 (see Figure 9.1), you ensure that each of the machines has a kernel with the IPv6 support compiled in. You watch the network traces while you reboot the machines. When you reboot each machine, you see that it first sends an ICMPv6 Neighbor Solicitation followed by a Router Solicitation. In all cases you then see that the systems have configured link-local addresses on their interfaces.

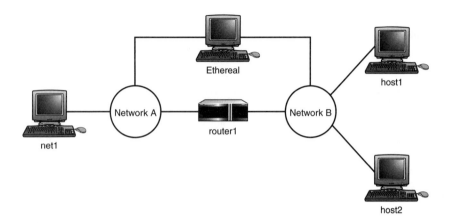

Figure 9.1

Policy Routing testing network.

You then use the ping6 utility to ping from one machine to the others on the local networks. This is a real pain because you have to type out the entire address. You place the link-local addresses into the hosts file and this allows you to ping by name to make it easier.

You try to ping across router1 but, as expected, that does not work. So now you decide to try router autoconfiguration on router1 and see how it works.

RADVD—Router Advertisement Daemon

In Linux, radvd provides the router advertisement function under IPv6. radvd only runs under the 2.2 series kernels. There is ongoing work to make sure that it will run under the 2.4 series kernels as well as an attempt to enable the router advertisement function within the IPv6 kernel code. In order to test radvd you ensure that the kernel on router1 is 2.2.12 and you obtain the radvd-0.5 source and compile it.

Once you have the daemon compiled you go about setting up a configuration file. The options for configuring radvd are numerous but there are only three options, AdvSendAdvert, AdvOnLink, and AdvAutonomous, that must be present in the configuration file. After studying the man page and the sample configuration file, you come up with the following simple configuration located in /usr/local/etc/:

```
interface eth0
{
    AdvSendAdvert on;
    prefix dead:1::0/64
    {
        AdvOnLink on;
        AdvAutonomous on;
    };
```

```
};
interface eth1
{
     AdvSendAdvert on;        prefix dead:2::0/64
     {
          AdvOnLink on;
          AdvAutonomous on;
     };
};
```

This will advertise the `dead:1::/64` prefix on interface `eth0` and prefix `dead:2::/64` on interface `eth1`. Now that you have this setup you start `radvd` while watching the traces on the networks.

As soon as you start up the daemon, you note that both interfaces send out router advertisements. These advertisements contain the prefix and the source MAC address of router1's appropriate interface.

Now you look at the routing tables on net1. You had saved the IPv6 routing tables to a file before starting the `radvd` daemon. This pre-`radvd` routing table looked like the following:

```
fe80::/10 dev eth0  proto kernel  metric 256  mtu 1500 rtt 375ms
ff00::/8 dev eth0  proto kernel  metric 256  mtu 1500 rtt 375ms
```

Now, after you have started the `radvd` daemon on router1 you look at the table again and see the following:

```
dead:1::/64 dev eth0  proto kernel  metric 256  mtu 1500 advmss 1440
fe80::/10 dev eth0  proto kernel  metric 256  mtu 1500 advmss 1440
ff00::/8 dev eth0  proto kernel  metric 256  mtu 1500 advmss 1440
default via fe80::2a0:ccff:fe21:eed0 dev eth0  proto kernel  metric 1024  \
          expires -1095sec mtu 1500 advmss 1440
```

You note that there is now a default route via the link-local address of router1's `eth0` interface. Also, there is a route to the prefix `dead:1::/64` via `eth0`. This is exactly what router1 was advertising. Because you know the MAC address of host2 you decide to try to ping it. You know that the prefix you told router1 to advertise on that side was `dead:2::/64`, so you try to ping as follows:

```
[root@net1 /root]# ping6 dead:2:2a0:5aff:fe05:e828
PING dead:2::2a0:5aff:fe05:e828 from fe80::210:5aff:fe05:e828 : 56 data bytes
64 bytes from dead:2::2a0:5aff:fe05:e828: icmp_seq=0 hops=64 time=1.124 msec
64 bytes from dead:2::2a0:5aff:fe05:e828: icmp_seq=1 hops=64 time=430 usec
64 bytes from dead:2::2a0:5aff:fe05:e828: icmp_seq=2 hops=64 time=416 usec
64 bytes from dead:2::2a0:5aff:fe05:e828: icmp_seq=3 hops=64 time=416 usec

--- dead:2::2a0:5aff:fe05:e828 ping statistics ---
4 packets transmitted, 4 packets received, 0% packet loss
round-trip min/avg/max/mdev = 0.416/0.596/1.124/0.305 ms
```

Just to make sure, you try once more to ping the link-local address of host2 and you get no response. Now you know you have not even been logged in to host2 since you rebooted it with the new kernel back in Chapter 6. So the IPv6 routing is now fully functional just by having router1 advertising. Quite an impressive feat if you have only dealt with IPv4 networks in the past.

But the entire trial has also left you with an uneasy feeling. You know on the networks you have dealt with that you could always figure out the addresses of systems. If necessary, you could always ping the broadcast address for the local IPv4 network and see who answered. Under IPv6 you would ping the link-local all hosts address ff02::1, which is the rough equivalent to IPv4 broadcast. However, for individual system location your testing implies that you will need to remember the MAC addresses for all of your machines as well as know which prefix is valid for that network.

This brings up the question of defined addressing. You wonder how the routing structure would be done manually and whether under such a routing structure you could assign addresses that are easier to use. To this end you decide to recode the test network using manual addressing and routing.

You first reboot router1 back into the 2.4.0 kernel. You then decide to use the same prefixes as you had just used in the radvd testing. So you set up the following logical implementation:

```
# net1
        eth0: dead:1::1/64
        route added to dead:2::/64 through router1
# router1
        eth0: dead:1::e0/64
        eth1: dead:2::e1/64
# host1
        eth0 dead:2::1/64
        route added to dead:1::/64 through router1
# host2
        eth0: dead:2::2/64
        route added to dead:1::/64 through router1
```

This setup is easily implemented using the ip utility as follows for each system:

```
# net1
ip -6 addr add dead:1::1/64 dev eth0
ip -6 route add dead:2::/64 via dead:1::e0
# router1
ip -6 addr add dead:1::e0/64 dev eth0
ip -6 addr add dead:2::e1/64 dev eth1
# host1
ip -6 addr add dead:2::1/64 dev eth0
ip -6 route add dead:1::/64 via dead:2::e1
# host2
ip -6 addr add dead:2::2/64 dev eth0
ip -6 route add dead:1::/64 via dead:2::e1
```

Now you get onto net1 and try your `ping6` command to host1:

```
[root@net1/root]# ping6 dead:2::1
PING dead:2::1(dead:2::1) from dead:1::1 : 56 data bytes
64 bytes from dead:2::1: icmp_seq=0 hops=63 time=1.627 msec
64 bytes from dead:2::1: icmp_seq=1 hops=63 time=517 usec
64 bytes from dead:2::1: icmp_seq=2 hops=63 time=507 usec

--- dead:2::1 ping statistics ---
3 packets transmitted, 3 packets received, 0% packet loss
round-trip min/avg/max/mdev = 0.507/0.883/1.627/0.526 ms
```

Now you are getting somewhere. This is much easier both in the command lines and in the addresses. So you now set up the hosts file on net1 to contain the addresses of both host1 and host2 using these new addresses, and you can simply issue a **ping6 host2** command and get results.

The more you now consider the impact of IPv6 in your networks, the more you realize that there are several evil residues of IPv4 that will probably come back into play. Specifically the DHCP (Dynamic Host Configuration Protocol) and the DDNS (Dynamic DNS) protocols. DHCP was invented to save the hassle of running around to all the various computers on a network and coding in the IPv4 address and related information. DDNS was invented to keep current DNS mappings for all of those addresses assigned by DHCP.

You must remember that IPv6 has provided a simple and easy-to-use automatic addressing and routing structure for you if you want to just have everything plug in, turn on, and network. As with IPX, in such an environment you can assign addresses to the core servers and set them up in a DNS server and have everybody work without any need for extra configuration.

And as with IPX, you have no real control over the actual addressing that the hosts end up with although you do control the routing. This last point is most important. You do control the routing through the assignment of prefixes in the advertising routers. You can also control the actual advertising of the various prefixes to each other and to the hosts. So your extensive experience in IPX networks is a great boon to using IPv6.

On the other hand, if you want the control and need to make sure that hosts are assigned only the addresses that you would like them to have, you can. So your extensive use of DHCP in your current IPv4 networks can carry right over into the new IPv6 as well. Thus, IPv6 allows you to do whatever you want to do on the network and with the infrastructure.

This level of flexibility also allows you to have both types of configurations running side by side. You can allow most of the hosts to autoconfigure and manage the routing structure for controlling their access. And you can have select groups of hosts that obtain addresses and configuration information from DHCP. This dual personality becomes important when you start to consider the usage and interconnection of IPv6 onto the Internet.

Internet IPv6 routing does not allow for NAT and thus requires that communicating hosts have assigned legal prefixes. Under this type of configuration you can limit full Internet access on the basis of assigned prefixes and addressing. The rest of the access can be via proxy servers, thus allowing those auto-addressed hosts access to the Internet services as mediated by the routing and the proxy system.

All of this is possible because IPv6 from the beginning has allowed for, and even to some extent demanded, multiple addressing on the host. You saw some of this when you added in the static addresses and noted that the link-local addresses were still present and usable. This entire subject of multiple addressing should be old hat to you by now because it derives from the Address element of the Triad. It is also the hottest topic of discussion in the implementation mailing lists due to the source address selection mechanisms (RFCs 2460, 2461, 2462) for routing and hosts.

As one final test of your IPv6 network, you remember that Zebra (see Chapter 7, "Dynamic Routing Interactions") had a module for both RIPng and OSPFv3 (OSPF for IPv6). You dig the source code out on router1 and compile the ospf6d, OSPFv3 for IPv6, module. Then you give it the basic configuration used in radvd and note that the packet traces show the OSPF IPv6 packets being issued from router1. Since you do not yet have any other routers that speak OSPF6, you decide to try again when you do.

Policy Routing Usage

All of your testing with IPv6 to this point has concentrated on the basics of standard IPv6 networking. As you went through the various tests you wondered whether additional structures were available under Policy Routing. The true answer to that question at this point in time is a definite maybe.

The current IPv6 implementation within the Linux kernel, and those of other IPv6 implementations, concentrate on providing a usable networking base for core IPv6 networking functions. While the theory and practice of Policy Routing provides many instances within IPv4 networking that are easily extensible to IPv6, IPv6 still exists mostly in a beta test period.

As you read through the RFCs defining IPv6, IPSec, and the related structures of the future Internet, you will see that the fundamentals of these protocols contain many practices grown within Policy Routing. The notion of addressing as providing a multiple source for service location provides one of the concrete examples of the integration of Policy Routing structures into IPv6.

IPv6 provides a shining example of integration and growth through cross-pollination. As time passes and the entire spectra of protocols comprising the new Internet solidify through practical use you will see more of the core routing structures and extensions as evidenced by Policy Routing under IPv4 appear in IPv6. After all, you must remember that IPv4 was initiated in the early 1980s and only in the mid 1990s did Policy Routing structures begin to change the face of the Internet. The IPv6 Internet is not even a full reality yet.

Indeed, at the time of this writing in late 2000, a commercial IPv6 offering is available in Japan. Parts of Europe and North America are rumored to perhaps have IPv6 commercial availability as soon as January 2001. And this does not even take into consideration the 6bone (www.6bone.org) or 6ren networks, which are available today to interested parties. There is even an IPv6 implementation of the NetFilter packet filtering available in the Linux 2.4 kernel. It even includes a fwmark facility, although the RPDB cannot currently support IPv6.

This brings up the core reason why there is not an IPv6 Policy Routing structure within Linux today. Essentially, the RPDB replaced the IPv4 routing and addressing structure within the Linux kernel (see Chapter 3, "Linux Policy Routing Structures"). The IPv6 structure within Linux was implemented outside of that core structure. Although they do share some facilities, the essential RPDB structure does not participate in or with the IPv6 addressing and routing structures. This will change, although it probably will not be until the 2.5 development kernel series slated to fork in early 2001.

Until then you have much to play with in your Policy Routing structures. The current IPv4 Internet will exist for at least another five years. And because the two network structures are coexistent, there will be use for many of the structures for some time to come.

Summary

You have seen how to implement and use a simple IPv6 routed network. There are many utilities that are IPv6 specific, such as those listed in the Linux IPv6 status pages (www.bieringer.de/linux/IPv6/status/IPv6+Linux-status.html) that you can compile and use on your IPv6 network. Both types of networking coexist so you can play with both your IPv4 and your IPv6.

From here you go on to the full scope of network routing. You have your Policy Routing knowledge and an inkling of the future to come.

CHAPTER 10

Future Musings

You have seen the theory and a practical implementation of the theory of Policy Routing. Many of the concepts have been part of the routing structures for IPv4 and other protocols for years. The explosion of interest in the Internet has led to a wide-scale need for and adoption of Policy Routing structures.

This chapter covers some of the thoughts and projections of direction for Policy Routing. Some of these concepts are extensions of logic, others are merely wishful thinking at this stage. I hope that you will have your own thoughts and inferences to add to this list.

Policy Routing Triad

Back in Chapter 2, "Policy Routing Theory," you were introduced to the concept of the Triad of Policy Routing. This concept was developed through theory and implementation within the context of the IPv4 networking structure. The core provisions for this concept consist of the definition and scope of action for the three main elements of Policy Routing structures. In review, the three elements are

- **Address**—Provides the mechanism of service location.
- **Route**—Provides the guide to reaching the address.
- **Rule**—Provides the logic structure for selecting route.

As you have seen and explored, each of these elements contains a wealth of detail in use and construct. The interactions between these multi-faceted elements defines the range of actions possible under Policy Routing.

What you saw in Chapter 9, "IPv6," was how the nascent format of IPv6 has made use of some of these constructs and yet seems not to have implemented the core. This will change. As discussed in that chapter, IPv6 is still a very young and sparsely used protocol. Even IPv4 did not need to use Policy Routing in the first few decades.

IPv6 will become the new Internet protocol suite. Many of the uses of the Internet are, as with everything Internet, changing at a rapid pace. Think back merely five years, to the release of the first IPv6 RFC in December of 1995, to see the difference. In 1995, not having a Web address was normal and having one was "cutting edge." Cutting edge is a polite way of saying "too risky" and "fit only for the severely bored." Microsoft was busy dismissing the Internet as a fad and trying to release Windows 95. Novell's NetWare still pretty much ruled the corporate network with IPX. Ethernet was just overtaking TokenRing as the corporate LAN topology.

Now think of today. Not having a Web site or at least an email address indicates you are a nobody. Even if that address is on AOL or MSN or Hotmail, at least you "get it" (whatever "it" is). And that's what makes this entire sequence so downright funny to those of us who remember ARPAnet, BITnet, Vaxen, that newfangled Usenet (remember the old uselessnet jokes...), and specifying email addresses in terms of gateways and uucp paths. Back then many of us looked down on those poor local users (lusers in the trade...) who did not grok the wonders of communicating the computer way.

What will you think when the next generation, or even the one beyond that, walk up to you and tell you about how wonderful this Policy networking stuff is, and how you old fogeys don't get "it"? It will happen. You stand today on the shoulders of shoulders of giants. Much of what is so gee-whiz today has been around for eons as translated into Internet time, and you see that nothing really has changed in computing terms. However, in human terms the change is fundamental.

So it will be when IPv6 finally becomes the only reality in the Internet. The fundamental definitions of the Triad will probably be reworded, but they will exist. And the decisions that drove Policy Routing to what it is today will re-emerge. Networking defines a continuous, multiconnected structure.

Consider the evolution of networks themselves. Think of the early point-to-point structures, such as a mainframe with terminals. Note the evolution into multiconnected structures such as LANs. A LAN defines a group of points that each connect at one location, with the allowance that any particular point may talk to any other point. Now consider that a LAN can be thought of as a single point on a network. Initially, you may have connected your LAN points with a WAN. Traditionally you had a point-to-point WAN, then you evolved into a multipoint FrameRelay, where any point in your corporate network can talk to any other point. Step back once more and look at your entire corporate network as a point, and the Internet as the WAN to all the other points. And for the final consideration, think of your point as having more than one connection into this WAN.

At this stage you see how Policy Routing has entered the game. But that could have happened at any of the transitions between single to multiple connections. Today, IPv6 usage on the current Internet is at the point-to-point LAN stage. When we grow into the full multiconnected WAN, Policy Routing will be implemented yet again to suit the new structures.

In this manner, the basics of the Triad have not and will not change. The implementation and the actual uses will probably differ, in some cases substantially. And new uses not yet dreamed of will burst into life much as the Web transformed the use of the Internet in 1993. The ride will be fun, so long as you want the thrill.

The Protocols: IPv4, IPv6, and IPSec

Thinking about how the evolution of networking has driven the fundamental features of Policy Routing brings up the subject of the other foundations of networking: the protocols. As with many of the facets of modern life, you seldom stop to consider the fundamental building blocks. And yet these fundamentals funnel your actions in many ways.

Consider the way in which an actual information exchange takes place under IPv4. "Ah-hah," you shout, "Are you using TCP or UDP?" "Neither," I will reply, but thanks for asking. The point not so subtly made is that the mere definition of the protocol in question defines the mechanism of communications. As you well know, TCP shakes hands whereas UDP could care less.

But what about telnet? Oh—that is TCP. Or is it? Can you do telnet over UDP? Sure you can, but that is not the definition according to the RFCs. So you need to have an RFC to communicate? No, it just ensures that the communication is standard. And that is the root reason for all the usefulness and all of the problems with any of the protocol suites. The standard definition of the protocol as ratified and encoded in a document defines the methodology for using said protocol across a network. Why would you care? Think of the following sequence.

You are reading through one of the IPv6 RFCs. It talks about how a router treats the packets. You come across the statement that the router must not perform a certain action. Are you on the level or are you curious? On the level, you decide to ensure that your routing code will never perform that action. As a curiosity, you work up some routing code to perform that action and see how it affects the rest of the network.

This thought sequence plays out all over networking. But the black-and-white definition rarely is true. Shades of gray dominate the Internet. Many examples exist of incorrect implementations of standard protocols. Look through many of the core attack formats for networks. Many of these attacks make use of a particular implementation type. Arguments rage constantly on how to interpret statements within the RFCs and in some cases on how to even implement an agreed upon definition.

Indeed the mere concept of host fingerprinting exists due to variations in implementation. Host fingerprinting refers to the process of determining an OS type by looking at the sequence of responses to types of communication. And much of this difference in communication actually refers to responses to very defined and structured packet sequences. But if you have ever written code, especially for something as complicated as a network communication protocol, you know that more than one method is usually feasible.

From this viewpoint of the vagaries present, even in defined and well accepted actions, you see that the vague specification and tricky definitions of other actions leaves a wide open gap. Much as Policy Routing seems now a foregone conclusion, many of the structures in networking in general only solidify over time. The usual consideration provides that all matters will eventually either solidify through consensus or be discarded by friction.

While this viewpoint implies that the best course of action may be to ride out the storm, the best course of action bails the boat. Wisdom is the application of intelligence to experience. You must have both prerequisites. Thus while waiting around to gather experience, you should study the definitions. One overriding truism in networking, as in many other endeavors, notes that the larger-scale phenomena recur. By positioning yourself in the thick of the struggles that define and shape the Internet, you will understand and manipulate the result in ways you cannot even now imagine.

The fundamental concerns of this outlook define an inquisitive course of action. As you study the RFCs and the code that implements the action studied, try to think of the action from both sides—what would happen if the action is correct and also what would happen if the action is incorrect. Just as with the asymmetric NAT routing, you need to see the entire scope of the problem along with noting the details. Policy Routing is extraordinarily powerful, but if you only have one IP address on one computer with one Internet connection, what does it matter? Conversely, why implement ten traditional routers when one policy router would suffice?

This spectrum will come to a particularly crucial point when IPSec becomes as widely implemented as the original specifications imagined. IPSec was and still is designed as an integral part of a comprehensive IPv6 Internet. The idea is that all parties within the Internet can be assured of each others' identity and may securely converse. This authenticated, non-repudiated, and encrypted structure will be provided transparently. Ignoring for the moment the practical problems with key exchange, DNSSec, and so on, consider the mere definition of a multiply-connected gear meshed system that this provides.

In a gear meshed system, all points of multiple connection are conceived of as three dimensionally connected points, kind of Escherian in scope. Think of a traditional star network. Now consider that all of the remote points of that star are stars themselves. Consider that some of those stars connect to stars that then eventually connect back to the original star. Visualizing that web of connections in two dimensions is hard enough. But now think of each star as drawn in two dimensions as a gear. And where those gears mesh together is the mutually shared point of contact. Now extend down from each gear a shaft on which other gears are located. That is a fully gear meshed network. And designing one of those buggers really illustrates Policy Routing.

Conceiving that a fully IPSec-enabled Internet defines a gear meshed network, you realize the full future and potential of Policy Routing structures. While ideally you would never worry about the integrity and security provided in such a system, in practicality you would be scared stiff. Consider that you are connected to a pure embodiment of network evil, which according to the media would equate to a normal 14-year-old online male. You have an authenticated, non-repudiated, encrypted connection to said person.

So when he wreaks havoc on your systems, you have no problem because you know who, what, and where. Of course your systems are destroyed, your business fails, and you are now homeless. But at least you had an authenticated, non-repudiated, encrypted connection to that person. Oh, but he was located physically in some small island within the Indonesian archipelago where you have no extradition rights and where what he did was not considered a crime. In hindsight you would have rather had a Policy Routing structure where you control access and availability to your systems.

And therein lies the long-term viewpoint. If you peruse history as it was actually recorded rather than as the predistilled pap you may have memorized in school, you see that the overall driving factor of any technology is human. The invention of the highway system meant serial killers now had larger scopes of action. Oh, and it also allowed you to live in the suburbs and move several hundred miles away from your parents and still be close to home. The point is that the technology itself did not change fundamental human behaviors so much as it provided new avenues to pursue the same interrelations as had always been pursued.

So it will be in the Internet. The real explosion of growth has not been fueled by the technocratic elite but by common humanity. To connect with each other and feel ourselves connected to by others drives the fundamental impetus of this technology. People do not consider or even care how the connections are made and what drives the actions, they merely want to connect. On the other hand, you will be ensuring that they do connect and that such a connection is made with the provisions of security, stability, and ease.

Security and Commerce

Security, stability, and ease are a holy grail to current e-commerce vendors. The usual disclaimers and arguments prevail about the scope of the supposed problems. These are all very technically interesting, but from the point of view of the end user, all very irrelevant. The original demographics that drove the interest in e-commerce are simple.

Remember back to some of the original surveys of Internet denizens in 1993/94, especially some of the "average Web user" results. Most of these surveys showed that the average Web surfer was highly educated, upper middle class income, with rather large discretionary spending habits. And at that time that was mostly true because outside of the University settings, only the somewhat technocratic elite even had an inkling of the Web thingie.

Show those demographics to a marketing manager and he or she practically starts panting and drooling. Thus the Internet Gold Rush was born. As with the real gold rushes of the past few centuries, most of the real, hard cash was made by providing the miners with supplies. ISPs, Web site creators, network and computing hardware vendors, and related infrastructure providers grew and prospered.

The last thing on the suppliers minds in most cases was security. Next to last was long-term planning. While the early Internet had security problems, the stresses were moderate and fairly convoluted in use. Breaches tended to be few in number but complex and convoluted in execution due to the preponderance of large time-shared systems with accounting structures.

Security was a subject that was researched and catalogued, a la CERT, CERIAS, and similar organizations. There were alerts and processes for patching and mitigating the breaches. The process was almost leisurely in contrast even to the long-term development of the protocols. The actual connection density of the Internet was only beginning to expand. And as with the superhighway system, the greater connection density and mobility of the Internet would fracture the security model and force a whole new structure.

As with the automobile and the telephone, the emergence of the Internet started over a period of time with fractional parties fighting to promote their service and vision. With standardization and eventually serious commercial reasons, a la the Web, the use of the product surged. The masses had arrived. What goes around comes around, especially when considering a redefining technological invention.

Consider that before the advent of direct dial you would have a difficult time making a crank call. Noting that direct dial was the direct result of a perceived commercial problem, you can easily see the parallels to the Internet of the early 1990s. Once the masses were ensconced, the rules of the game changed.

Consider today the reference to the "Slashdot Effect," usually e-coded as "/. effect". This effect refers to what happens when you are mentioned on a widely read Internet news source and suddenly millions of people are trying to reach your Web site. Many sites have crashed or at least slowed to a crawl due to the massive surge in volume. Indeed, there is at least one instance where a suspicion exists that the site was purposely promoted to an Internet news site in order to slam the referenced site into the ground.

Such actions are only the tip of the iceberg. Just as crank calling evolved into phreaking and other attacks using the telephone systems, so too with the security structures of the Internet. As with most phenomena it was predictable yet unknown. The supposed power brokers tried to pan it off as rogue adolescence that would fade as new, more powerful and well-designed computers and operating systems were released onto the market. So here we are with all of these more powerful operating systems and computers fighting a battle for control against the dark side.

What exactly is being fought? Is it a ruthless, intellectual elite bent on wreaking world havoc? A global conspiracy to silence the oh so wonderfully innovative companies whose dazzling products are the salvation of computing kind? Or just a bunch of inquisitive people? Sadly, the answer lies more toward the last group.

As with the commercial interest that produced the automatic dialing systems, most computing products, especially operating systems, are designed for the benefit of the manufacturer. Security is a cost center, just as Information Technology is a cost center.

To paraphrase the IBM commercial, realizing that your business is based on your Web site—that is an epiphany. And that epiphany has not yet taken hold.

Rather than promote security to a profit center by blending it into the design and development of a product, it is easier to blame the evil forces that surround each and every one of us. And as with the computer virus problem, why design to remove the problem when you can make a profit tending it instead? Just think of the financial losses that would be incurred if any of the secure computing structures designed several decades ago were to be enforced. Most of the anti-virus, firewall, and security consulting firms would crash and burn.

No, those structures are not hard to use. Just ask anyone who has a higher level security clearance who has been a user on a trusted computer system. The vast majority of the time you do not notice that the system prevents you from doing harm. It is only if you try to do something that is not permitted for your level that you see the results of the security structure. Now the old draconian lockstep argument arises. We would all be slaves to the machines is the battle cry.

The point is that if you consider the vast majority of supposedly horrific attacks, especially in terms of costs, on the Internet in the last half of the 1990s, over 85% of them would not have occurred with just a modicum of security structures within the computing platforms and networks in use. Some of the simple steps are being taken but often are both seen and advertised as amazing and difficult work.

In such an environment, can you imagine the carnage of the implementation of IPSec or IPv6? It's bad enough that in many cases IPv4 is still not implemented correctly. And consider too the current status of Policy Routing.

From this perspective the current statements about e-commerce and security are inherently ludicrous. For every single credit card number stolen on the Internet in 2000, dozens or hundreds of people were mislead by telesales, swindles, and other direct interface security breaches. That pendulum is starting to swing. The necessary technical systems and structures do exist to prevent that swing. But it remains to be seen whether the commercial incentive will be seen in time.

And that brings up the other problem of the Internet Gold Rush: long-term planning. The security problems faced on the Internet are much the same in concept as the security problems of the telephone and the automobile. You can break into a site and make your getaway with the goods. You can impersonate or internally compromise a site. And you can coerce others into giving you the goods in good faith.

Today if you were to start a physically located business, say in a strip mall, you would leave the doors unlocked at all times. Especially when you were not there. And you would not bother using a cash register that locks or even closes the cash drawer. And most assuredly you would not know what you had in stock at any given point in time because you were only interested in this minute right now.

Ok, you can tone down the laughter. All of these steps are essentially what you would obtain today with the vast majority of Internet commerce proposals. And this includes just being a participant, let alone the proprietor. This is largely due to a lack of fore-sight, also called long-range planning.

If you go into a bank, or to the Venture Capitalists, or other sources of business fund-ing today for your strip mall store, you will find that what they really want to see is whether you have planned out the long-term and short-range goals. This is often referred to as a business plan. If in the details of your business plan you have not allowed for some basic security structures, you will be denied immediately. Unfortunately, that is only now starting to be implemented for Internet commerce.

The long-term planning of most e-commerce sites even now consists of: Grow big by losing money, IPO and sell out. Usually the entire sequence is considered to be com-plete within two years. The long-term planning that is starting to be seen, especially in the details, is more along the lines of: Protect the assets, and nurture the position into recurring revenue. And you can bet that those details now contain the locks, keys, and provisions for counting the merchandise before and after the sale.

So the security, stability, and ease factors are starting to return. Ease was first and often at the complete detriment of stability and security. Now a balance is being found as the hollow tones of "you cannot have your cake and eat it too" are being shown as simple lack of foresight coupled with a sales incentive to care less about the actual consumer. The security and stability of systems are ever increasing with the same ease still pre-sent. And this is mainly due to the leap of the competing interests and proprietary sys-tems into the acceptance and implementation of standards.

As with the early telephone systems standards and the issuance of rules of the road, the standards of the Internet are evolving to promote cooperation and foster a secure, sta-ble, and easy path to interconnection. Progress can be seen in the mere acceptance of many of the system design security standards laid down in the seminal 1975 article of Jerome Saltzer and Michael Schroeder from Proceedings of the IEEE 63(9) pp 1278-1308. As time marches on in the Internet, the standards change. Perhaps the best point about the change structure of the Internet is that it is not driven by any one or any group of corporate interests. Thus the eventual apogee will provide security, stability, and ease of use for all.

Summary

I hope you have enjoyed your ride through the theory and practice of Policy Routing structures. As with most network concepts, the principles may be timeless but the implementations change and flow. The future of IPv6 and beyond slowly coalesces. In general, the direction is pretty much the same. In detail lies the excitement and won-der. I hope you have seen the wonder and excitement and are itching to go change the world.

PART III

Appendixes

APPENDIX A

Glossary of Terms

ACL   Access Control List. This is a list of commands or filter specifications that define the allowed accesses or uses of a device or other object.

ARPAnet   The original "Internet." The ARPAnet was the creation of the United States Advanced Research Projects Agency. ARPA evolved into the Department of Defense ARPA (DARPA). The original project that became the "Internet" we know today was an attempt to create a computer communications network that could survive a nuclear war. Luckily those parts of the design were never tested.

ASE   Autonomous System External. See OSPF or BGP RFCs for details.

BGP   Border Gateway Protocol. See also RFC-1771 and for IPv6 references see RFC-2545.

CIDR   Classless InterDomain Routing. RFC-1519. Removes the original definition of class in IPv4 addressing structures.

Cisco IOS   Cisco Internetwork Operating System. The software that runs Cisco routers. See `http://www.cisco.com` for details.

DiffServ   Differentiated Services. RFC-2474 among others. This is one of the two main contenders resulting from the development of QoS in the Internet IPv4 structure.

DMZ   DeMilitarized Zone. Taken from the military usage this refers to the network between the Internet router and the firewall system. The best reference is found in *Building Internet Firewalls* by Chapman and Zwicky.

FIB   Forwarding Information Base. Refers to the actual memory hash kept by an IP network stack for actually sending the routed packet on it's way.

ICMP   Internet Control Message Protocol. RFC-792/950 for IPv4. Part of the Internet Protocol Suites.

IntServ   Integrated Services. This is the other half of the QoS growth curve. See also DiffServ.

IPROUTE2   Alexey N. Kuznetsov's powerful utility suite implementing Policy Routing in Linux. Refer to Chapter 4 for details.

IPSec   The IP Security protocol suite. Originally conceived as a security methodology for all IP packets (RFC-1825). Current standard is RFC-2401 and related RFCs. RFC-2401 is a very good read for anyone interested in network security in general.

IPv4   Internet Protocol Version 4. RFC-791. Get it, read it. This is the networking structure of the Internet as of 2000.

IPv6   Internet Protocol Version 6. RFC-2460. Ditto. This is the future of the Internet. Currently available in certain parts of the world and through tunnelling mechanisms.

LSA   Link State Advertisement. See OSPF.

MAC   Media Access Control. The address defined by the IEEE that must be present in order for your network card to talk on the network. See any good basic networking primer for details.

MTU   Maximum Transmission Unit. The maximum size packet that can be transmitted through a network interface. Defined usually by the actual interface parameters.

NAT   Network Address Translation. The art of changing a packet's IP source or destination address from that which was originally used without notifying the original inserting system.

NOC   Network Operations Center. Informally sometimes referred to as the glass house. This is where the rare and costly specimens of technical talent are often ensconced. Usually full of computers.

OSPF   Open Shortest Path First. RFC-2328 latest (original RFC-1131) A link-state routing algorithm for dynamic routing.

QoS   Quality of Service. A catchall phrase that refers to providing different routing structures, traffic shaping, and packet paths depending on the needs and uses of the packet. (RFC-2386 and IEEE Transactions on Networking.) See also DiffServ and IntServ and Cisco IOS Quality of Service Solutions Configuration Guide, Release 12.1 (`http://www.cisco.com/univercd/cc/td/doc/product/software/ios121/121cgcr/qos_c/index.htm`).

RIB   Routing Information Base. This is the concept of the "rest" of the routing information that specifies a route. The FIB is that actual forwarding mechanism part.

RIP   Routing Information Protocol. The original dynamic routing distribution mechanism. RFC-1058 is the original with RFC-2453 the current specification.

RPDB   Routing Policy DataBase. See Chapters 3 and 4 for details. This is the implementation of Policy Routing in Linux.

RSVP   Resource Reservation Protocol. Part of the IntServ/QoS structures. See RFC-2205/2750 for details.

TBF   Token Bucket Filter. A type of scheduling structure available under QoS. See the Linux kernel source for schedulers for details.

Token Ring   A LAN topology made popular by IBM.

TOS   Type Of Service. A data field within the packet header of IPv4 and IPv6. Standard values are defined by the Internet Naming Authority. Details can be found at `http://www.iana.org`.

UDP   User Datagram Protocol. Part of the IPv4 networking protocol suite. See IPv4 for details.

APPENDIX B

Source Code Listings and Locations

This appendix covers what you need to perform the examples and actions in this book. First you will see which Linux kernels from the 2.2 and 2.4 series were used. The kernel configurations and patches will be shown. Next you will see the various patches used for NetFilter and the related utilities. And then you'll see a listing of most of the software versions and dates for the software used.

This leads into the installation and configuration guide for the PakSecured distribution on the CD. This distribution was used to test and run all of the examples and compile all of the software referred to throughout the book.

Kernel Configuration and Patches

The examples and concepts of this book were drawn from two distinct kernel lines. The stable kernel series as of the initiation of this book was the Linux 2.2 kernel series. All of the references to the 2.2 kernel series in this book refer to this series and most specifically to kernel 2.2.12. I do not use any kernels in the 2.2 series after 2.2.12 in any of my 2.2 systems. The current stable kernel series is the 2.4 kernel. The 2.4 series kernel used to check and generate most of the examples and concepts in this book was 2.4.0. All of the patches and changes to the kernel as described in the following section are applicable to any of the 2.3/2.4 pre development kernels and apply cleanly to the 2.4.0 stable kernel release.

Kernel 2.2.12

The 2.2.12 series kernel was used for all references to the 2.2 series kernel in the book. The patch listing for this kernel is rather minimal. It consists only of the DiffServ patch, ds-8. This patch is available on the CD as well as on the Web site at `http://www.policyrouting.org/PolicyRoutingBook/`.

Within the ds-8 patch is the 2.2 kernel patch as well as a patch for the IPROUTE2 utility suite. You can safely ignore the patch for the IPROUTE2 suite because all it does is change a configuration entry in the Config file. This is noted in the Config file for IPROUTE2 itself.

To install the kernel patch you must have a clean 2.2.12 kernel source tree. Change to the source directory (`/usr/src`) and untar the patch file into that directory. Then simply make sure you are in the root of the source tree (`/usr/src/linux`) and apply the patch with `patch -p1 < /usr/src/ds/patches/kernel.patch` and you will be able to configure and make the kernel. If you are not comfortable with this procedure, note that a prepatched kernel is available on the CD and the Web site.

Kernel 2.4

This section of this appendix uses the 2.4.0 kernel as the reference platform. For this kernel you will need to have applied the PakSecured IA32 kernel patch as available on the CD and Web site. A prepatched version of the latest 2.4 series kernel is also available on the Web site. Note that general PakSecured patches are versioned for different processor platforms. Be sure that you use the relevant patch. The version of PakSecured on the CD is for Intel 32-bit platforms only. If you would like the other architecture versions, please visit the PakSecured Web site at `http://www.paksecured.com`. PakSecured is under full GPL.

Once your 2.2.12 or 2.4.0 kernel is patched you can then configure and compile the kernel. The configuration listing for the kernel is quite long. A premade config file that covers all of the networking protocol configurations that you will need is available in the prepatched kernel, on the CD, and on the Web site. It does not have any network cards or other hardware defined that you may need for your system. For configuring these items and for kernel configuration and compilation in general, please read the Kernel HOWTO. It is available through the Linux Documentation Project, a mirror of which may be found at `http://ldp.pakuni.net`. The complete archive of the LDP as of January 1, 2001 is also included on the CD.

IPROUTE2

Once you have compiled and installed your kernel, you then need to compile the IPROUTE2 utility for use with the DiffServ extensions. First obtain the latest source code for IPROUTE2. As of this writing the latest release was `iproute2-2.2.4-now-ss001007.tar.gz`. To compile the utility for use with the DiffServ extensions, you need to change a line in the Config file located at the root of the source directory. Open the `/usr/src/iproute2/Config` file and change `TC_CONFIG_DIFFSERV=n` to

TC_CONFIG_DIFFSERV=y. Then compile the utility suite with make. Note that IPROUTE2 does not have an install routine. You must manually place the binaries in the appropriate locations. Also note that RPMs such as from Red Hat or SuSE do not have the utility compiled appropriately for many of the advanced uses. You are better off either compiling your own or using the binaries provided in PakSecured. The PakSecured binaries are in the /sbin directory.

You now have a patched kernel and the necessary ip utility for running through all of the examples in the book. For the NAT and tagging examples you will need the patched NetFilter utility for Kernel 2.4. The ipchains utility for Kernel 2.2 is standard and you can either compile it or use an RPM.

NetFilter Patches

The NetFilter version used in this book was the CVS version. The latest one used with all PakSecured patches applied is available as a source tarball on the Web site and CD. Also available is the PakSecured NetFilter patches to apply to a NetFilter CVS source code tree. Both the patches and the fully prepatched tarball are maintained. You can obtain the latest version through the book Web site and also from the PakSecured Web site.

NOTE

The latest version of NetFilter 1.2 released January 8, 2001, contains the PakSecured patches. You do not need to apply the following patch if you are using NetFilter 1.2 or later.

If you downloaded the patch you can apply it to NetFilter CVS using the following steps:

1. Change into the root source directory for NetFilter (/usr/src/netfilter).
2. Untar the patch file (FTOS.cvs.tar.gz) in that directory. If you do not have the CVS source there is a version of the patch that will apply to the released iptables utility package. Note that you must compile NetFilter from source for these patches to work.
3. If you have used one of the 2.4 patched kernels from the CD, you can simply compile and install NetFilter at this point. If not, you need to compile and run one of the patched kernels in order for the NetFilter compile to work.

The patches install the FTOS extension as used in Chapter 6, "Complex Network Examples," and also the IPv6 marking facilities. The IPv6 assumes that the IPv6 NetFilter parts of the kernel have been patched. The FTOS extension assumes that you have either applied the PakSecured patch to the kernel or you have run patch-o-matic from the NetFilter distribution and selected FTOS.

The binaries for the NetFilter that correspond with the PakSecured kernel source is available as well through the Web site and on the CD.

Software Versions

The versions and patch levels of the software in PakSecured are located on the CD in the PakSecured source directory (`/src/PakSecured`). This is the software that was used to create and test the examples and concepts in this book. Some of this software is not relevant to actually running Policy Routing, but it is included in case you have difficulties making the examples work with your Linux system. These are the actual software release versions and in some cases the CVS download date.

Also located in the `/src` directory is the Patches directory, which contains the Kernel, NetFilter, and other utility patches that were mentioned in the previous sections. The install file in HTML format is in the `/doc` directory.

PakSecured Installation and Configuration

Minimum System Requirements

- Pentium Processor
- 16MB RAM
- 500MB IDE Hard drive
- Network Interface Card
- Bootable CD-ROM or 3.5" floppy drive

Phase I—Initial Files Install

The installation of PakSecured Linux will *destroy* any data you have on your hard drive. Make sure that you have a new hard drive or that you have backed up all critical data from your existing hard drive. Once you are ready to proceed, collect the following information, which will be necessary for the installation:

IP address in CIDR notation for your server
Example: 192.168.1.1/24

IP address of your default router
Example: 192.168.1.254
Note that this can be set to the interface address if you do not have a default router

IP address of your nameserver
Example: 192.168.1.128
As with the router this can be set to the interface address

FQDN (Fully Qualified Domain Name) for this server
Example: paksecured.mynet.com

Root user password

You must supply all of this information on the appropriate screen. The way the install is designed, if you do not provide any single part of this information the install routine will assume that you do not want to continue and will stop the installation process. However, your hard disk will have already been partitioned.

CD-ROM Install Process

1. Boot from the CD.
2. Press enter at the LILO prompt to start.
3. When prompted for "Select Installation Media," select CDROM.
   At this point in the installation process, the CD-ROM is mounted, and the hard drive is partitioned as follows:
   hda1 is 64MB swap
   hda2 is 400MB for /
   hda3 is the rest of the hard drive for /var
4. You will then be prompted to enter your networking information.
   Enter all of the information you collected above.
5. PakSecured Linux is installed on the drive.
6. When the installation is finished, supply the root password.

After providing the root user password, `lilo` will be installed and the CD-ROM will be ejected. At this point the system will ask you to reboot. Press Enter and then continue on to the next phase.

HTTP/FTP Install Process

1. Boot install floppy (`disk1-boot.img`).
2. Press Enter at the LILO prompt to start.
3. When prompted for "Select Installation Media," select http/ftp.
   You will then be prompted to enter the driver floppy disk (`disk2-drivers.img`).
4. Enter your networking information.
   If you do not have a default router, enter your local interface. You will need to have already set up a Web server on that local network.
5. Select the location of the PakSecured image file:
   Example: `http://205.138.121.147/software/paksecured.tar.bz2`
   If you have set up your own server, note that you MUST use the IP address of that server and the server needs to respond on that address. There is no DNS capability at this point in the install.
6. PakSecured Linux is installed on the drive.
7. When the installation is finished, supply the root password.

After providing the root user password, lilo will be installed and you need to remove all floppy disks from the drives. The system will request confirmation of reboot and continue into the next phase of the install.

Phase II—Kernel Configuration

Once the initial files install is completed, you will be prompted to reboot the PC. Remove all disks and CDs from the drives and press Enter to reboot. The system will come up automatically into the menuconfig kernel configuration screen. Select all the relevant network card drivers and other devices needed for your system. At a minimum you will only need to select your network card driver. All other options needed for running PakSecured are already selected.

> ## WARNING
>
> *Do Not Change* any of the already selected options, especially in the networking sections, unless you REALLY KNOW what you are doing. Deselecting some of the options in the kernel configuration could cause your system to be completely useless.

Minimum Kernel Configuration

The system will boot straight into Make Menuconfig so that you may select the appropriate network drivers for your kernel.

Select Network Device Support from the menu.
Select Ethernet (10 or 100Mbit) (or TokenRing or ...).
Now select the drivers for all your network interface cards.
Select Exit twice.
When prompted to save your configuration select Yes.
Your kernel will be compiled and installed automatically.

The system will automatically compile and install the kernel and all modules needed for operation. After this is done, the system will reboot to use the newly compiled kernel.

Final Phase—PakSecured Configuration

Once the system has rebooted with your new kernel image, you will be given a standard login prompt. You may now login as `root` to the system. Note that as part of the previous installation phases several parts of the system were configured. These are as follows:

A user called "tech" was created during install
The password for "tech" is what you typed in during install
tech's ssh keys were generated
System SSH keys were generated
The basic networking as entered in the install process was configured.

You will now want to perform any advanced configuration of the system. The initial networking values you entered during the install process have already been saved, so you should have device `eth0` already functional. You can check this by entering the following commands:

`ip addr` (will show the address you entered for `eth0`)
`ip route` (will show the route for the gateway you entered)

Note that this system does not have `ifconfig` or `route` installed. The only networking utilities are `ip`, `tc`, and the set from Alexey's iputils package.

PakSecured is designed to allow for simple operation through a global firewall system configuration file. All standard networking is performed through standard independent configuration files such as listed below. Within the global configuration file is allowance for calling scripts to perform advanced Policy Routing structures. The following listing provides some of the relevant files for configuring and maintaining the system.

- Networking configuration files and the advanced policy scripts are located in `/etc/sysconfig/network-scripts/`.
- Within this directory are the `ip4cfg-{network}` configuration files for the network interface cards. You should already have an `ip4cfg-eth0` in this directory from the install.
- There is a `sample-ip4cfg` provided as a template to configure any other interfaces you may need (`ip4cfg-eth1`, `ip4cfg-tr0`, and so on). Note that you cannot use the `ip4cfg-*` files from any other distribution because they do not use Policy Routing.
- The routes needed for the system on startup are contained within the `ip4cfg-routes` file in this directory as well. Look inside that file for the current routing setup and some samples for additional routes.
- Also within this directory are some sample files for performing advanced Policy Routing structures. The `mail.fw` file is a simple single machine policy for allowing a unique route for a single machine. Note that this file also contains the commands for setting up the firewalling functions that are associated with the policy.
- You can find some advanced configuration files on the Web site that implement parts of the book examples. These files would be placed into this directory for use.

pakfw.config

The global configuration file for the firewall part of the system is the `pakfw.config` file located in `/etc/sysconfig`. The file is commented. Note that many of the sections in the file contain loop structures. This is one of the more powerful uses of the configuration structures. To best illustrate how it works consider the final section, MISC:

```
MISC_HIGH=0
MISC0="mail.fw"
MISC1=" "
MISC2=" "
```

As you can see, there are variables that are numbered consecutively. These are the actual run variables. In this case the `MISC0` variable contains the name `mail.fw`. The loop variable is the `MISC_HIGH` variable.

When the loop variable is set to 0 as it is here, this section is deactivated even if the global logic variable `MISC` (located at the top of `pakfw.config`) is set. This loop variable controls the number f procedures that would be run. So if you want to run the `mail.fw` script you can set the `MISC_HIGH` variable to 1. Note that this is one greater than the number of the variable. This is where the looping comes in. Say you wanted to code up all 8 examples from Chapter 5, "Simple Network Examples," to run as MISC additions. You would set the loop variable `MISC_HIGH` to 9 and place the names of the files you created to run the examples in the appropriate lines. You may end up with a MISC section that looks like this:

```
MISC_HIGH=9
MISC0="example5.1"
MISC1="example5.2"
MISC2="example5.3"
MISC3="example5.4"
MISC4="example5.5"
MISC5="example5.6"
MISC6="example5.7"
MISC7="example5.8"
```

Now the fun part is that you can also set the loop variable to 3, in which case you would only run examples 5.1–5.3.

These variables control the information needed to run the system. If you want to see how these variables are used, look in the function definitions. These are located in `/etc/rc.d/init.d` and are the `pakfw.functions` and `pakvpn.functions` files. There are other function definitions located in `/etc/sysconfig/network-scripts`.

Enjoy your PakSecured system.

INDEX

Symbols

E-F

N

What's on the CD-ROM

The companion CD-ROM contains the PakSecured™ Linux v2.4.0 distribution; a complete snapshot of the Linux Documentation Project as of January 1, 2001; patches to the 2.2 and 2.4 series kernels; and example scripts used in the book.

Linux Installation Instructions

Everything you need to know to install or set up Policy Routing using Linux can be found in Appendix B, "Source Code Listings and Locations."

Read This Before Opening Software